CW01632596

The Villanova Track Story 1966–1981

Touching Greatness, Forever Together

Jerry Bouma

Three Rascals Press

Published by
Three Rascals Press, Edmonton, Alberta
3rascalspress@gmail.com

First Edition, February 2022

Publishing Management: Kathleen A. Knowles
Editorial: Nancy Mackenzie
Design: Jaclyn Draker

Photo Credits and Permissions

Jerry Bouma Collection: 7, 9, 11, 15, 17, 18, 108, 140, 183, 184, 199

Jeff Johnson Collection courtesy of Walt Chadwick and Dr. William Clark: 63, 79, 81, 137

Dave Patrick/Tom Papageorge Collection: front cover, 8, 21, 37, 42, 51, 57, 152, 164, 167, 177, 194, 196

Villanova University Track Office Collection: 4, 45, 59, 64, 66, 83, 88, 91, 94, 95, 98, 121, 126, 134, 136, 138, 141, 153, 156, 161, 172, 197

Chris Mason: 111. Eamonn Coghlan: 116. Nick Lees: 119. Marcus O'Sullivan: 185, 186

Cover caption: Dave Patrick wins IC4A Mile: 1968

Library and Archives Canada Cataloguing in Publication

Title: The Villanova Track Story 1966-1981: touching greatness, forever together / Jerry Bouma.
Names: Bouma, Jerry, author.
Identifiers: Canadiana (print) 20210388412 | Canadiana (ebook) 20210388447 | ISBN 9780993670251 (hardcover) | ISBN 9780993670268 (softcover) | ISBN 9780993670244 (ebook)
Subjects: LCSH: Villanova Wildcats (Track and field team)—History. | LCSH: Penn Relay Carnival—History. | LCSH: Track and field athletes—Pennsylvania—Villanova—History. | LCSH: Track and field—Pennsylvania—Villanova—History. | LCSH: Track and field clubs—Pennsylvania—Villanova—History. | LCSH: College sports—Pennsylvania—Villanova—History.
Classification: LCC GV1060.62.P4 B68 2022 | DDC 796.42/0974811—dc23

Printed in the USA

The Villanova Track Story 1966–1981

Touching Greatness, Forever Together

*"To win one Penn Relays Championship race is a triumph.
To win four years in a row is a dynasty.
To win 16 consecutive years is out of this world!"*

Dave Patrick

"To be at the best place at the right time is a dream come true. Villanova was that place and this is the story of that time."

Marty Liquori

"When I arrived at Villanova, I knew the program had a tremendous winning tradition from the fifties and sixties. It was incumbent on those of us who came in the early seventies to continue. It was very motivating to be in a position to honor that legacy."

John Hartnett

"This remarkable book stirred great memories of my Villanova years racing at Penn Relays. The team members before me and after me were truly amazing. Sixteen DMRs in a row will never happen again."

Ken Schappert

"I was lucky for the opportunity to be part of the Villanova track history. Jerry's book gives a first-hand insight into that incredible experience, the team, and how the legendary coach Jumbo Elliott moulded and instilled a winning belief in all of us, both on and off the track."

Eamonn Coghlan

"Success doesn't happen without coaches who know how to recruit, and training partners who make you strong. But in the end, it's the competition like Penn Relays that brings out your best. Reading The Villanova Track Story *tells how this happened to many of us."*

Mark Belger

Contents

Preface

This is a story about a group of exceptional young men, who at a certain time and place, became the best track team in the world. That group was the Villanova Track Team; the time was from 1966 to 1982; the place was Villanova University, located 12 miles west of the center of Philadelphia; and the featured performance stage—University of Pennsylvania Relays, better known as the Penn Relays—the oldest and largest continuous track and field meet in the world.

It is the story of enormous triumph peppered with a continuous array of challenges and personal trials. For 15 years, the Villanova Track Team dominated the Penn Relays like no team before or after. During that entire period, the team won the Championship of America distance medley relay (often referred to as the DMR) every year, leaving a winning streak that exceeds the longest streaks in professional or amateur sport by a factor of two. What makes this streak so remarkable is that no individual athlete was a member of any winning team for more than three years. Thus, the excellence extended through five complete turnovers of student-athletes.

It is a story about coaches, conditions, and characters—those unique individuals—many who rose from relative obscurity as high school athletes to become national and world champions. Indeed, it is a story about what can happen when a group of talented athletes are brought together under strong leadership and vision to achieve a greater purpose.

The focus of this story is largely on that special group of middle-distance runners—those who ran the half mile (or 800 meters); the ¾ mile (or 1200 meters) and the mile (or 1500 meters). There were also athletes on these teams who were sprinters (200 meters, 220 yards, 400 meters, and 440 yards), and the attention that is due them will need to be pursued by another writer.

It should also be noted that the Villanova Track and Field Women's program took root just as this story ends. That program has also produced an incredible array of world-class athletes and relay teams—another story that awaits a detailed telling by someone more qualified and knowledgeable than me.

Jerry Bouma
February 2022

Acronyms

AAU	Amateur Athletic Union
DMR	Distance Medley Relay
GOAT	Greatest of All Time
IAAF	International Association of Athletics Federations
ICAAAA (IC4As)	Intercollegiate Association of Amateur Athletes of America
IOC	International Olympic Committee
NBA	National Basketball Association
NCAA	National Collegiate Athletic Association
NYAC	New York Athletic Club
UCLA	University of California, Los Angeles
USC	University of Southern California
USOC	United States Olympic Committee
UTEP	University of Texas El Paso

Prologue

Penn Relays, April 23, 1971

Friday afternoon, 3:15 p.m. There I stood as a Villanova freshman in the northwest corner of Franklin Field for the very first time. I was dwarfed by the vast, aging, brick double-decked stadium that had all the trappings of the ancient Roman Coliseum. With a capacity for 50,000 spectators, it wrapped around on three sides like a giant horseshoe. But the fourth or west side, where all the athletes were gathering, stood in sharp contrast—a stately three-story academic-looking structure covered with ivy that would fit in nicely at Harvard, Oxford, or Cambridge. After all, this was the Ivy League and the University of Pennsylvania, founded nearly 200 years ago by none other than Benjamin Franklin, one of America's most venerated Founding Fathers of Independence, and the reason why the stadium bore his name.

Noise and people were everywhere! The place was a veritable ensemble of motion and sound—track uniforms with every imaginable color combination swirled in all directions. The area around the west end of the track was like a swarm of scrambling locusts. Amidst that swarm, just meters from the start line, stood a fenced-off area known as the paddock. Packed with runners, stripped of their sweats, ready to go, huddled some 20 teams (80 runners in total) nervously awaiting the call for the next race in an area not much larger than an average-sized living room.

"Ladies and Gentlemen. The next event on the track: The Championship of America Collegiate Distance Medley Relay! Are you ready?" Penetrating the many layers of noise, came the clear, smooth voice of the classiest announcer in America: Jack O'Reilly, synonymous with the sound of the Penn Relays. It reverberated as if from heaven … the call for one of the most prestigious races to be held each year had come.

I peered through the crowd and there stood my teammates, pensive, nervous, just itching to get going: Wilson Smith—the affable half-miler from West Virginia; Greg Govan—our smooth striding quarter miler from New York City; Chris Mason—the gritty, hardworking sub-four-minute miler from Sheffield, the heart of industrial England; and Marty Liquori—our superstar, the number one ranked miler in the world in his usual cool, aloof, sublime manner. Everyone knew the favorite. This should be an easy win.

The buzz of the crowd continued to rise, and all eyes focused on the start area. John Hartnett my teammate from County Cork, Ireland standing to my left looked at me but said nothing. Silently, we both were beginning to realize how big of a deal these Penn Relays really were! Neither one of us knew anything about them before coming to Villanova. But when we arrived in September 1970, we started to hear the stories: the string of Villanova victories that was unbroken since Ron Delany and Charlie Jenkins's win in 1955; the winning of five major Championships of America races in 1968 led by Dave Patrick; the incredible and perhaps the fastest quarter mile ever run, to win that fifth race—the mile relay by Larry James now better known as the Mighty Burner. And the streak of five consecutive distance medley relay wins since 1966 that was now on the line for Villanova.

As the first leg of runners came to the starting line, my nerves were really starting to tingle. John was injured but relaxed and taking it all in. But me? Earlier in the week, I had been picked by our legendary coach Jumbo Elliott, to lead off the 4 x Mile relay scheduled for the next day. This would be the first time freshmen were eligible to compete in the Penn Relays. And me—the very first freshman to run for Villanova—and to lead off, at that. The full weight of responsibility started to take hold of me. I studied the paddock and asked myself—will I be up for that in just under 24 hours? And one more thing. My back had been bothering me since Monday. I hadn't told anyone. Some easy jogging and a late class on Tuesday and Wednesday had set off no alarm bells with my teammates and Mr. Elliott. No one knew. But I knew because I tried to do some strides. And my back was not liking it.

The half-milers were now on the line. Once the starters made sure that all the runners were in proper position, it was a crouch, the gun, and off they went. The usual jostling around the first turn unfolded and things quickly settled down. Wilson Smith looked comfortable—he could run a 1:50 for the half mile any day of the week; twice if he had to. All he had to do was stay out of trouble and hand off in the top three. For that matter, all the first three runners had to do was get the stick to Liquori. And he would do the rest. We all knew that.

But suddenly Wilson was struggling. On the second lap, runners started to pass. You could see on his face that he was in distress as his stride became markedly clipped. He had clearly pulled something. But he kept going. Now he was close to the back of the pack. You could hear the shift in the noise of the crowd—it altered from the sounds of a carefree cheer to the tense expression of yells and urging on. Even the running commentary delivered by the velvety-voiced Jack O'Reilly showed signs of strain as he tried to hide his concern and partiality to the school he openly admired. Meanwhile, the waiting Greg Govan, our quarter miler, kept shifting further to the outside lanes on the starting line. He had been in second position after the pack passed the finish with one lap to go; then fifth; now he was being guided to 10th ....11th ....14th. Chris Mason, who would be up next, appeared uncharacteristically anxious with a look that none of us had seen before.

A sea of questions flooded the minds of everyone who watched what was unfolding, myself included. John and I looked at each other again. Nothing needed to be said. We knew exactly what the other was thinking. Would Wilson Smith make it to the finish? Was the five-year DMR-streak over? Had Villanova finally met its match? Had Lady Luck left Villanova and chose to shine her fortune on another team? At the same time, my own personal concerns rose to another level. With my sore back, could I possibly be the next leadoff victim tomorrow? Did this have all the makings of a Penn Relays carnage for the fabled Villanova University Track Team? Welcome to the Penn Relays and the incredible history of Villanova Track. My head was swimming and my nerves tingling. For the full telling of the outcome, see Penn Relays 1971 in Chapter 5.

Acknowledgements

This story is possible only because of the extended list of remarkable individuals who made it happen. I will start with Dave Patrick, who effectively set the stage by anchoring the first three wins of this remarkable winning streak of 16 consecutive distance medley relays at the Penn Relays. Dave supported me every step of my journey as I wrote this book. Dave was also my host when I first visited Villanova University as a high school recruit in June 1970.

In order of their first appearance from 1966 to1981, those distance medley relay teams included the following athletes: Alan McCafferty, Bill Heidleberger, Ian Hamilton, Dave Patrick, Frank Murphy, Charlie Messenger, Bob Whitehead, Chris Mason, Lamotte Hyman, Marty Liquori, Wilson Smith, Greg Govan, Ken Schappert, Tom Gregan, John Hartnett, Brian McElroy, Jack Garniewski, Greg Eckman, Eamonn Coghlan, Mark Belger, Phil Kane, Ed Takacs, Glen Bogue, Anthony Tufariello, Don Paige, Mike England, Al Graves, Sydney Maree, John Hunter, Carlton Young, and Marcus O'Sullivan. I would like to note that many of these athletes made multiple appearances during their Villanova careers. I extend my deep thanks to those many athletes and former teammates who took the time to be personally interviewed for this book.

Special thanks to John Burns, Jay Cook, Russ Ebbets, Kevin Leonard, Mike McDonnell III, Gerry O'Reilly, Jim Sansevero, and Jay Woods, who provided "trackside" perspectives on the stories and characters who made this story possible. Also, special mention to Frank Watkins, who diligently researched the many newspaper articles specific to the Penn Relays during the entire 1966 to 1982 period.

Finally, a sincere thanks to my two close track aficionados and dear friends, who live in Edmonton, Alberta, Canada and share my continued interest in the sport: Ross Munro, a fellow Canadian who attended Western Kentucky University on a track scholarship when I was at Villanova University, and Dr. Jim Denison, a track athlete, now professor at the University of Alberta, who attended Fordham University, competed at the Penn Relays, and also an author[1], who provided both guidance and inspiration.

1

Sport Streaks

"The difference between the impossible and the possible lies in one's determination."

Tommy Lasorda

Sports buffs love to talk about the best. About winners. About the Greatest of All Time (GOAT). About moments, streaks, and memories that stand above all others—the best teams, best players, superstars, greatest legends, and feats and accomplishments that have no equal—citing the unparalleled performances of athletes like Joe DiMaggio, Bill Russell, Maurice Richard, Wayne Gretzky, or more recently, Tom Brady.

And when it comes to teams, hard-core sports fans in North America move quickly to such legendary institutions as the Boston Celtics, New York Yankees, Montréal Canadiens, New York Islanders, Edmonton Oilers, the Pittsburgh Steelers, and the New England Patriots. Then comes the topic of streaks: wins in a row, wins per season, but most importantly, the number of winning championships—specifically, the number of consecutive championships, winning year-in, year-out no matter what the challenges might have been. Yes, the streak—the ultimate measure of the great teams.

When it comes to streaks, the history of professional sports illustrates that the Boston Celtics lead the way—eight consecutive NBA championships from 1959 to 1966. Or the "Bill Russell Era" as it is aptly referred to. Russell changed the game and is known as one of the first true big men to dominate the court in a way that had never been done.

During that very same time (1956 to 1960), the Montréal Canadiens led by the great Maurice "Rocket" Richard, won five consecutive Stanley Cups, a feat that has never been repeated. The Province of Quebec, through hockey, experienced an era of pride and accomplishment like never before. Not satisfied with five, the Canadiens were just barely beaten for their sixth cup by the Chicago Black Hawks in 1961. Some 20 years later, Les Habitants, as the locals would call them, embarked on another four-cup streak, from 1976 to 1979, led by the flashy and colorful Guy Lafleur.

Similarly, in the world of baseball, the best that the legendary Yankees accomplished was five World Series in a row—1949 to 1953, which followed an earlier four-series streak from 1936 to 1939. The NFL has seen several two-consecutive Super Bowl winners, but no team has won three in a row, which illustrates how difficult the three-peat really is.

In the world of amateur, including college, sports, John Wooden's UCLA Bruins top the list with seven consecutive NCAA basketball titles—1967 to 1973. Led by the incomparable Lew Alcindor (thereafter known as Kareem Abdul-Jabbar), Sydney Wicks, and finally Bill Walton, the Bruins dominated the backboards like no other college team before or after. But that came to an end in 1974 and UCLA has one won just one championship since.

One winning streak in amateur men's sports stands above all. A streak that astonishingly is not particularly well-known and perhaps not known at all. This streak not only beats out the Boston Celtics as professionals or the UCLA Bruins as amateurs, but it also beats all sports teams whether professional or amateur, by a factor of two. A streak of 16 consecutive wins. And it happened in the world of track and field.

From 1966 to 1982, the Villanova University Track Team dominated the Championship of America Collegiate Distance Medley Relay (DMR) at the Pennsylvania Relays like no school before or after. For 16 years, the best schools in America attempted to unseat the Villanova Wildcats. And every year, the next best team in America had to settle for second place.

The DMR is unlike any other relay. Arguably, it is the quintessential middle distance running event. It is comprised of four unique distances—the 400 meters; the 800 meters; the 1200 meters, and the 1600 meters, (formerly the 440 yards; the 880 yards, the ¾ mile, and the 1 mile). Some track experts say it is the most demanding of all the relays. A school might have a great sprint program with strong sprinters or 400-meter runners and perhaps a great 800-meter runner but lack a noteworthy miler. Other schools might have a strong distance running team, a good cross-country team, and bring forward four strong milers but no one to carry the team through a blazing fast 800 meters or a competitive 400 meters. Simply put, to be successful, you need strength at every position.

Most importantly, the DMR requires speed, speed endurance, and without equivocation—the ability to finish. The ability to win no matter what was being thrown at you. No matter the competition, the weather, the injuries, the lack of fitness because of injury, whatever reason or excuse you can find or malady that might come your way. To win no matter what. Track aficionados know full well that many relay races come down to the last lap or even the last 100 meters. Whoever can pull through, fight, and "wants to win the most" will be the champion. For 16 consecutive years the Villanova University Wildcats did just that, again, again, and again.

And if the DMR wins were all the Villanova Track Team accomplished, that would be a remarkable achievement in and of itself. But the DMR streak was only the icing on a much bigger cake. There was so much more. The accomplishments that occurred during this same period are simply astonishing. Not only did Villanova track teams win the 16 DMRs in succession, but the team also won a total of 52 Championships of America Relays at the Penn Relays during that same time year period. And in many cases, those wins were the result of a small core group of runners—often two, three or four athletes who would run at least three if not four races within a 24-hour period. Against teams who were fresh and at the Penn Relays for one reason: to beat Villanova.

During this time, the legendary coach James Francis "Jumbo" Elliott compiled this record:

- 7 National Collegiate Athletic Association (NCAA) Team Championships.
- 24 Inter-Collegiate Amateur Athletic Association of America (IC4A) Team Championships.
- 82 individual NCAA champions.
- 316 individual IC4A Champions.
- 22 Olympians.
- 22 Outdoor World Records.
- 44 American and World Indoor Records.

The 16-year streak of consecutive wins takes on even greater significance when you consider the context of collegiate sports. Unlike professional sports, college athletes are limited to a four-year career—in fact until 1971—the US college athlete was limited to a three-year career since only varsity athletes were allowed to carry the college colors at major competitions. By comparison, professional sports teams typically would have carried a core group of star athletes for five, eight, or even 10 years. But the Villanova track program achieved this astounding result with essentially five completely new rosters or a complete turnover of runners every three years.

The streak begs the simple question: How does one school, one track program, over such an extended period, year-in, year-out, with runners constantly coming and going, win this quintessential middle-distance extravaganza, namely the DMR, for so many years? More importantly, how did this stream of athletes achieve such greatness over this 16-year period?

Ron Delany anchors the winning relay

How did this happen? What was the magic? What was the formula? What was special or different about these groups of runners? What was the "special sauce" that in some mysterious way was being applied again and again? How was the success of the one group or cohort passed on to the next generation—not once or twice, but through five complete cycles?

Was Villanova University simply able to consistently attract superior talent? Or was there something in the program that developed and drew out the talent unlike anywhere else? And consider the talent during this period. Villanova track history reads like a who's who of middle-distance superstars, including Dave Patrick, Charlie Messenger, Frank Murphy, Tom Donnelly, Dick Buerkle, Marty Liquori, Andy O'Reilly, Chris Mason, John Hartnett, Ken Schappert, Tom Gregan, Brian McElroy, Eamonn Coghlan, Phil Kane, Ed Takacs, George MacKay, Don Paige, Mark Belger, John Burns, Tony Tufariello, Dean Childs, Mike England, Sydney Maree, Amos Korir, John Hunter, Ross Donoghue, and Marcus O'Sullivan.

The streak beyond all streaks began in 1966. But the real beginnings of that DMR streak started two years earlier in September of 1964. To be sure, the reputation of the Villanova Track Team was already firmly established. The 1950s saw the unparalleled rise of the Villanova track program with the likes of Browning Ross, Ron Delany, Charlie Jenkins, Phil Reavis, Don Bragg, and Noel Carroll. In 1957, a seven-man Villanova team won the NCAA Outdoor Championships held in Austin, Texas. This was unheard of—such a small roster beating much larger teams with a full complement of both track and field athletes. That year,

Track & Field News named Coach James Frances (Jumbo) Elliott Coach of the Century. And by 1961, few countries worldwide could boast as many Olympic gold medals (four) in track and field as Villanova University could.

Nor was winning Championship of America relays at the University of Pennsylvania an anomaly for Villanova. The first wins came in 1955 with victories in the One Mile Relay and the Sprint Medley. Both teams were anchored by Charlie Jenkins. Ron Delany made his Penn Relays anchor winning debut in 1956 with two wins, the Sprint Medley and the DMR, while Jenkins anchored the winning One Mile Relay. That same year, Charlie and Ron went on to win gold medals for their respective countries at the 1956 Melbourne Olympics—Charlie winning the 400 meters and as part of Team USA that also won the 4 x 400-meter relay; Ron took the gold in the 1500 meters for Ireland—a win that electrified that small oft-forgotten European country—making him the second most popular man after the Pope himself. To this day Ron Delany is venerated for that win and continues to be regarded as a national hero. And every year Villanova won at least one relay at Penn Relays and some years as many as three (1956, 1957, 1958, 1961, 1964).

But in September of 1964, unbeknownst to all, a "unique package" arrived on campus. That package was most unassuming. It was comprised of two athletes from the same high school, both highly competitive, but with a bond and a spirit of fraternity that would further impact the mystique and future history of the Villanova Track Team. And it would never be the same. The winning spirit that already defined Villanova Track Team was about to move to a deeper level, cementing a new foundation of excellence.

2

The Place

"The drab and the dull may give cause to endure, but a place of beauty will surely inspire."

Jerry Bouma

Sociologists and historians may ask the question: Do the physical characteristics of a place define a people or do the people living in a specific area define the place? One might ask is this a rhetorical question or are both conditions true?

It is generally known that certain peoples have distinct characteristics. For example, Germans are considered industrious and disciplined—the result of a long-standing feudal system followed by very rapid industrialization in the mid-1800s; the Dutch combine a unique blend of cooperation with fierce independence—a reflection of their persistent "fight" against the sea as they sought both to protect and reclaim land; the British are internationalists and have a world view that extends far beyond their island due to their naval prowess and success as an empire; and Americans have an unmatched sense of destiny above all as the "New Jerusalem" devoted to freedom, self-expression, and economic success. Just as each country has its own unique geographical characteristics and location so too can each characteristic be linked to a unique set of physical features that either enhances or constrains ambition.

So, what about Villanova University, its location and ambience? What was it about this place that influenced the character and drive of so many great track athletes and teams that emerged to produce such a legend of excellence?

Or should we pose an even deeper question: Would the very same group of athletes have produced the same results in a different place or setting?

Righter's Mill Road, four miles from Villanova University

Villanova University is situated in a suburb of Philadelphia, Pennsylvania known as the Main Line. Situated approximately 12 miles west of Philadelphia Center City, it lies in one of the oldest and most prestigious neighborhoods to be found anywhere in the United States. Indeed, the area is replete with prestige—the place where the first beneficiaries of the Industrial Revolution, with their newly-earned wealth, established sprawling and in some cases, opulent estates. "Over the decades the 'Main Line' became a bastion of old money," including such families as the Rockefellers, the DuPonts, and the Hires, to name just three. The area provided a set of "benefits ... touted as 'healthy yet cultivated country living' [that in turn] attracted Philadelphia's social elite, many of whom had one house in the city and another larger 'country home'" in this exclusive area.[1]

The local topography abounds with steep hills, ravines, streams, and dense forests[2]—an ensemble of natural features that emote a sense of being apart, of exclusivity, yet only minutes by train from the city center. And over time, it served as the location of some of the best schools in the country including Bryn Mawr College, Haverford College, Rosemont College, and of course Villanova University, which grew in academic reputation under the careful guardianship of its founders, the Augustinians.

Narrow winding roads shrouded by immense oak and maple trees blanket the area with greenery and shade, radiating from campus in all directions. Along the south boundary of the campus runs Lancaster Pike (Route 30)—a busy four-laned avenue that connects the Main Line between Lancaster County (as well as Lancaster City) some 60 miles further west, to Philadelphia with a host of communities such as Radnor, Wayne, Paoli, and Malvern in between. Lying parallel about 300 meters to the north, runs the oldest set of train tracks in America—the famous Main Line itself. To be clear, the modern campus now extends beyond both these boundaries but the heart of the campus and indeed the original campus lies between the two.

St. Thomas of Villanova Church

One might presume that the presence of two such busy transportation corridors—one a veritable highway, the other a set of multiple and busy train tracks—would make Villanova feel like a parking garage amid a sea of vehicular motion. But interestingly, the exact opposite is true. Instead, the campus rests in a quiet solitude—a world set apart and guarded on both sides.

At the very center of campus stands the St. Thomas of Villanova Church. The structure can be more aptly described as a moderately-sized cathedral proudly positioned and, not surprisingly, on the highest point in the area.

A tree-lined walkway welcomes you to its front entrance some 100 meters from Lancaster Avenue. To the left, behind one line of trees lies a well-kept grassy area adorned by a large number of oak and tulip trees; to the right, beyond the other line of trees lies a playing field—a 400-meter stretch of grass ending at Ithan Avenue where the Field House can be seen in the distance to the east.

With the chapel as the center piece, a series of grey limestone buildings are attached. To the west lie the Monastery; St. Thomas (a freshman dorm and a wing of the Monastery); and Tolentine Hall, a large building housing classrooms, laboratories, and administrative offices. To the south, you discover Mendel Field—more green space before arriving at the Engineering Building, the Mendel Science Building,[3] and the Falvey Library. To the east lie more residences including St. Rita's, Alumni, Austin, Corr Hall, and further east, the famous quad Sullivan and Sheehan before reaching Bartley School of Business. In the middle of these buildings is the location of Kennedy Mall (the bookstore and the all-important post office) and the center of student activity, Dougherty Hall, the location of the student cafeteria.

Three features stand out: the consistent architecture and style of many of the buildings—namely the grey stone structures that emote dignity and a sense of permanence; the abundance of trees—there are trees everywhere standing majestically as guardians of the campus and protectors of those who pass under them; and the silence—it is *sooo* quiet. On any given school day, the grounds lie hushed save the hourly interludes when students pass from one class to another. But on weekends or holidays, it was just plain quiet. Any stray sound is quickly muffled and absorbed by the trees, and quietude prevails.

The Athletic Facilities

If you expected that a school with such a storied sports history in track and basketball during the 1966 to 1981 period would be replete with top class physical facilities, you would be taken by surprise. To paraphrase a famous Churchill quote: "The Villanova athletic facilities were modest to say the least and had much to be modest about." Or as Donal Walsh, one of Villanova's all-time great cross-country runners once said to Marcus O'Sullivan when he was being recruited: "It has nothing, but everything you need." Marcus went on the become a world class miler and is currently Villanova's head coach of men's track and field/cross country.

First the Field House. Interestingly, it had no name other than its eponymous function. Quiet rumors suggested that the building was the result of a donation from Al Capone in the early 1930s. Clearly Capone Hall, if at all contemplated as a name in view of the notorious and ignominious reputation of the alleged donor, was a short-lived consideration to be sure.

The Field House as seen from Lancaster Avenue

Located at the east end of campus, the Field House stands on the northeast corner of Lancaster and Ithan avenues. A stark and pseudo gothic-styled structure, it sits in relative solitude, effectively across the street from the main entrance to the university campus. It has a distinct feel of abandonment, as if the more stately and stylish buildings on main campus conveyed in some unknown language that "you don't just quite belong to the rest of us." So there the Field House sits by itself.

Constructed from rust-red brick with walls of considerable height, there is relief only by the rather imposing smokey-colored stained-glass windows. Furthermore, it has no apparent entrance. Oh yes, there are steps arising from Lancaster Avenue that lead to what appears to be several front doors. But these were seldom open. Of course, we soon found the one door that would be open most of the time—a small, inconspicuous entrance hidden in the southwest corner.

Once through that unassuming entrance, a small hallway leads you to the larger open area and the basketball court. But before you enter, and as you look to your left, you pass a tired little office containing two desks and barely enough room to allow two or three persons to stand. This was the track office. It was about as plain as an office could be—nothing denoted any sign or demarcation that this was the coaching centrum from which some of the most accomplished athletes in the sport had been guided. Its only distinguishing feature was the pile of Penn Relay plaques loosely stacked in a corner supporting more trophies precariously perched on that pile.

Crossing the end of the court leads you to the southeast corner and down the set of stairs. We are now entering the belly of the building. Straight ahead lies a narrow hallway that runs the length of the basketball court. Immediately you are greeted with a wave of odor—an unpleasant waft of dirty laundry offset somewhat by the ever so slight burnt smell of towels that you could hear circulating in the industrial-sized dryers. This was the cage—a dark, cellar type room to the left and home to two growly, elderly men (Charlie and his assistant Jim). Their task was straightforward: wash, hand-out, receive, and repeat. Namely, manage the essentials of our trade: a pair of socks, a T-shirt, a jock, and a towel. To be used and returned. Received before the workout and dropped off when you were done. Nothing more. Nothing less.

And now the hallway: a row of lockers to the left; a series of old packing trunks to the right. These trunks, effectively two feet by two feet by two feet and locked, were of the same ilk as those once used to ship goods by boat or train. These would serve as intermediary benches as we changed from our student dress to our running gear. These were the places we would sit after a hard run when we would linger, and the stories would begin. Or more likely, repeated. Interestingly and somewhat puzzling, we never saw what was in those trunks.

Opposite the cage is a short hallway that leads outside and to the track. But before you exit, you pass another small room—the physical therapy room. Back then, it looked more like an interrogation room—it had all the hallmarks of mystery and perhaps, even worse—torture: the basement location; concrete cinder block walls painted a lavatory green, and a single light bulb. Nothing but bare walls. Inside were two tables on which one could sit or lie down. And a whirlpool that saw little, if any, use.

In between the tables stood another piece of equipment that was used to emit some sort of rays—an ultrasound machine—or so we were told. No one was ever quite sure how it worked or what it might do. Nor did we ever receive any instruction on how it was to be used. On occasion, one of us might be brave enough to apply some cream to an injured area (an ankle, Achilles's tendon, or aching shin) and apply the mystery of the stainless-steel ultrasound apparatus for five to 10 minutes. Did it do anything? We had no clue. At least we were doing something.

As for the expertise of the trainer, that was limited to the taping of ankles and being the origin of lame jokes. The taping was done in such a way that you had no mobility whatsoever. One such experience was usually the first and the last. At least that was my experience. So much for physical therapy.

The "Boards"

Any analysis or understanding of Villanova Track would be remiss without a full exploration of the "boards," which were the board track on which we trained during the indoor season. The boards consisted of a banked track constructed of 4 inch by 4 feet boards. The structure comprised 11 laps to the mile (160 yards per lap). Indeed, they were the standard size track that would fit inside the ice surface of a typical North American hockey arena. The boards deserve special attention because they were unique and so particular to our Villanova experience.

The boards—11 laps to the mile

Villanova was the only school we knew of that had such an indoor track set up on the outfield—either on the football field or the practice field just north of the stadium. These were the legendary boards—a reference made with a mix of pride and fear. Pride, because we knew that training on this type of track—indoors/outdoors all at the same time, was something special. And we also knew about the great success former Villanova runners such as Ron Delany, Charlie Jenkins, Noel Carroll, Dave Patrick, and Larry James had clearly established, both as indoor runners, as well as becoming world-class athletes who trained on this very surface. The boards played a role in the making of other great athletes present or yet to emerge (Marty Liquori, Ken Schappert, John Hartnett, and Eamonn Coghlan, soon to be followed by Mark Belger, Don Paige, Sydney Maree, and Marcus O'Sullivan). Beneath that pride lurked a modicum of fear—we knew how tough these conditions really were: the cold, the wind, the snow that would have to be removed, and most significantly, the pain of those hard laps. Would we be able to withstand the routine? Would we make it? Would we beat the boards or would the boards beat us?

In some respects, the boards were a product of the times and perhaps not so unique in and of themselves. Indoor tracks of 11 laps to the mile were not uncommon. The '50s and until the early '80s saw the apogee of indoor track. Meets such as the Millrose Games in New York, the Boston Invitational, Cleveland Knights of Columbus, Toronto, San Diego, Philadelphia etc. were annual highlights—they drew sellout crowds. Here, the ladies dressed in their finest; men in their three-piece suits. The annual Millrose Games at Madison Square Gardens or the Toronto Star Indoor Games at Maple Leaf Gardens were nights to look forward to, and top of list for many socialites. This was the height of track and field. The excitement of seeing the best athletes in the world competing literally a few feet away was a spectator's dream.

But an indoor board track without cover or shelter, set up outdoors on a football practice field, subjected athletes to the ravages of winter, and nasty, unrelenting winds. Training on the boards had its own special ritual and distinct rhythm. There was a beat to the workout precipitated by the steady rumble of multiple feet pounding in the background. Hypnotic in its own way, it was like the drip-drip-drip of water torture—a quiet countdown to see how long you could last. There we warmed up in a state of waiting to hear what our workout would be. Waiting for the word from on-high became a ritual, hooded, gloved, fully clothed in thick sweats, ready to take on the wind and the monotony of the laps about to come.

A typical workout would be 10 times, three lappers (480 yards)—just a bit further than a ¼ mile. And so, the countdown began—three laps, two laps, one to go. Nine more to do. But first, a three-lap jog recovery running in the other direction. Then the turn around and away you went again: three laps, two laps, one to go. Eight more to do. Methodically the workout unfolded; seven more to do.... Aside from the steady rumble, the workouts were rather quiet; no one spoke; everyone was in their own zone of concentration; there was a unique intimacy—you, the line of runners you were part of, and the boards. The better runners took turns sharing the lead; no one passed unless the runner just ahead was starting to fall back. Each runner concentrated on keeping the pace; leaning on the turn; trying to get as much bounce out of the boards as possible. Six more to do; five more; now half done; using the turns to propel yourself forward if you were in need of an extra boost to keep the pace; four more, three, two ... and finally, one more three-lapper, the last one. But only the seasoned seniors and runners with exceptional conditioning ever got to this point without having to miss one repeat[4] or falling so far back that you were no longer considered part of the training group but just another straggler that was unlikely to go far both literally and figuratively.

No matter what the workout—whether these were five-lappers; or two-lappers, or some ladder combinations starting with a two-lapper, a three-lapper, a four-lapper, a five-lapper, and then down the same ladder; it was a countdown. The four- and five-lappers added an extra burn to the gut and took more concentration. The two-lappers, especially a workout that called for 10 such repeats, was a speed-endurance exercise—it took only a couple of these before your hamstrings started to burn and the pain of anaerobic overload arrived without showing any mercy.

The boards would emerge somewhere around the first week of December. But there were no formal workouts at that time. We were still "putting in the miles" with exams just around the corner. But each of us would slip over and give the boards a test run—a few easy laps; or perhaps a hard two-lapper or three-lapper. How does it feel? Oh, there is a good bounce here—a loose board there. Better watch out for that one—it could give at any time....

The real training for the indoor season began the day after January 1. Arriving from different corners of the continent or overseas, we were happy to return and see each other but with a certain reservation. We knew what was coming: Day 1 and the introductory 880-yard time trial! Jumbo wanted to see where we were at in terms of fitness. He would seed his top runners across three or four heats and the races were on. Usually there were few surprises. The top runners would win their respective heats. But on occasion, one of the runners would come through with an unexpected performance. The results would determine who would be running individual races and who would be on the Two Mile Relay Team. But we were all in the same pot—we were all judged based on that time trial. The stakes were high. We all knew it.

On occasion, during mid-season, a spot might open on this coveted relay team either due to injury or a meet schedule where one of the top performers running an individual event would not have enough time to recover for it. That meant another time trial—this time between two promising runners, usually freshmen. Now the pressure was really on. The rest of the team, as highly engaged bystanders, relished these time trials. This spectacle provided us the opportunity to witness firsthand the nerves and anguish of the chosen two, knowing that one of them was about to "make the grade" and move to the next level. With a notice usually no more than a day or two in advance, the tension built. Predictions abounded; bets would be made; catcalls and heckling intensified, and the two contestants avoided the rest of the team as much as possible. On the hour of reckoning, the boards were lined with fully-invested spectators: teammates awaiting the result; to collect their bets or claim the victory of prediction. Then the countdown began: the start; five laps to go; four; three ... he's making a move (or oh, he's dying) then two, then the final lap. A victor declared, head up, and ready for more. The vanquished, head down and accepting reluctantly, that today was not his day.

Supervising this seemingly circular madhouse was the ringmaster himself, none other than Jumbo Elliott. The routine was always the same; we would begin warming up around 3:30 p.m. jogging slowly, round and round. Around 3:45 p.m.—you would see a Cadillac Eldorado pull up in the nearby parking lot. Out stepped Jumbo dressed in his business suit, a winter overcoat, hat, gloves, and galoshes over his wing-tips if snow so required. He would make his way to the track and then to the hut shaped like a phone booth that could hold two—Mr. Pyrah would be waiting for him. A quick discussion and then Jumbo would chat to the leaders—Patrick, Liquori, later Hartnett, then Coghlan, and the workout would be announced. Quickly the word spread—often in whispers. No one spoke to Jumbo and Jumbo spoke to only one or two, typically the leaders. A few last strides and then workout began: three; two to go; one more; done. Every time you passed the hut, you would hear the split: 22; 44; 66; or in the case of two lappers: 21; 42....

Upon reflection, it was the boards where the real training took place and where the time was mostly spent—the easy introduction in December; the hard training all through January, February, and through to mid-March. A good 10 to 12 weeks in total. By comparison, training on the outdoor track might be a total of six to eight weeks. And not nearly as memorable.

Bottom line: If you survived the boards, you were ready for anything.

The Outdoor Track

Ironically, the most unremarkable facility at Villanova was the outdoor cinder track itself, located just east of the Field House. Simply put, it was a humble place[5]. Most high schools would have a facility equal or better. And much of the time, only the two inside lanes were suitable for running. After any rainfall, the east end of the track would be flooded and reduced to clay since the cinders would have long been washed away.

On occasion, the track would be leveled and graded but these occasions were rare indeed. During my entire time at Villanova (September 1970–June 1974), no track meets were hosted and at no time would the track have been suitable for competitions of any sort. The last major track meet held at Villanova was the inaugural Martin Luther King Games, May 1970, and this was the last time a major event considered cinders suitable for competition. Previously, Villanova hosted dual meets and occasionally the IC4As. Track technology had moved on while Villanova had not.

But we never complained. Intuitively, we knew that training on the cinders was more forgiving than the stories we were hearing of athletes training on all-weather tracks. We could put up with this. In truth, the cinders served as an incentive—it gave us something to look forward to—to compete on a synthetic all- weather surface—to put on the pin spikes and feel the bounce off a hard surface as we were warming up. Now we were really ready to race. And to win!

Again, the spring workouts were rather routine: 10 x 400 meters (always jogging the same distance for the interval); or 8 x 400 followed by 4 to 6 x 200 meters. Or occasionally, 5 x 800 meters—a tough workout that would really separate the men from the boys. We would take turns leading each repeat; as the workout progressed, the stronger runners would be leading more often. Few words were spoken; it was all concentration and business. Everyone in their own zone—all finding that delicate balance between pushing and relaxing. Or just hanging on.

Such was the routine from Monday to Thursday. Friday would be a rest day. Races on Saturday. An easy run on Sunday, and back to track on Monday. Nothing fancy, nothing complicated. And all under the observant eyes of Jumbo Elliott, who would arrive at the track as usual at 3:30 p.m.

The Running Loops

While Villanova University track was replete with characters (and strong characters at that), the running loops and their associated names had equal character: The Frolic; Tennis Courts; the Triple; Radnor 5; the Minga; the 3 ½. Each had their unique features. The first two—the Frolic and the Tennis Courts were typically afternoon runs while the other loops were shorter and tackled for morning runs. But they all shared the incredible ambience of the Main Line with winding shoulder-less roads, trees on both sides, large estates, beautiful homes, and the frequent emergence of streams running parallel to the roads on which we were running. In one place the stream actually ran across the road. No culvert or bridge. Nothing but running water and a set of stepping-stones—a good old-fashioned ford.

Typical road in the Villanova Area

The Frolic

The Frolic was a 10-mile loop south of campus that had such landmarks as the duck pond at mile six and the fabled Mt. F**K at the mile nine. Dave Patrick and his teammates founded this loop during the mid-60s. As Dave recalls, "I named it 'The Frolic' because every time I ran it, I would enjoy myself and have a good time. If I feel like walking, I'd just stop and walk. Or I'd stop by the duck pond and look at the ducks for a while."

He loves to tell the story about Frank Murphy (a recruit from Ireland) who one day spotted a short rotting log on the side of the road by the duck pond. He picked it up over his head and about 15 white mice came running out. Frank thought he was under attack and hightailed down the road faster than anyone had ever seen him run. Or perhaps ever thereafter, despite what became an accomplished career.

One of the first accounts I read about Villanova while sitting in my own high school library in Owen Sound, Ontario, Canada was about the Frolic. I found the article most intriguing: the school, the team, and about the athlete Marty Liquori, who was at that time, the number one ranked miler in the world. This is what I read in the spring of 1970:

> The snow along the side of the road has turned to between-storm ugliness, and the few flurries that fall do nothing to cover the gray. It is cold and the wind blows… but Marty Liquori is moving through the hills and woods of what all Villanova distance runners have come to call their Frolic Loop. In the summer it can be charming—10 miles by the backyards of some of the Main Line's most splendid estates, past a duck pond, a creek, goats, and cows and may include even a stop to pick wild apples. But in winter it turns depressing, and as Liquori reaches the top of the hill he says how later that afternoon, when he gets to that point he will swear at the top of his lungs, 'cursing the cold, cursing the wind and most of all cursing myself for being such a damn fool to be out there.'[6]

By the late 60s and early 70s, the Frolic was at the height of its popularity and groups of four or five runners would be seen leaving the Field House between 3 p.m. and 3:30 p.m. to take it on. The loop began by crossing Lancaster Avenue. Heading south on Ithan Avenue and about one mile in, you would enter a quiet neighborhood, pass a golf course with a bubbling stream to your right that kept us company for another mile. Then a right turn, up a hill, across a busy road, down another hill, another right, and now we were in farm country—much to the surprise of those who were experiencing the loop for the first time around. We would pass two dairy farms, which was quite astonishing given the prevalence of golf courses and posh estates typical of the area. For John Hartnett and me the only two farm boys at Villanova (and from dairy farms at that), we always looked forward to the farms. No matter what the pace might be, we could see the activity taking place: the seeding; the haying; the harvest—it was the closest we felt to home. And we always compared notes. Then we silently prepared for Mt. F**K, the prominent hill which proved to be the breaking point for many a runner. While groups of five would start, the last mile again on Ithan Avenue would often be witness to a heavy-breathing string of survivors.

The Tennis Court Loop

Mt. Pleasant Road was the backstretch on the Tennis Court Loop

About eight and a half miles in length, the Tennis Court Loop gradually became the more popular choice as steadily increased traffic on the Frolic made it dangerous given all the curves and lack of shoulders. The Tennis Court Loop offered a welcome reprieve. This scenic loop was actually founded by a walk-on runner (Phil Foley) and myself, in March of 1971 when the "big boys" were competing at the NCAA Indoors in Detroit. The loop was not totally original as it was effectively an add-on to another existing six-and-a-half-mile loop. The new loop became an extension from the backstretch into some neighborhoods that had not been earlier explored. We found the most interesting areas by mistake, the result of a wrong turn—I suggested that we call the loop "Foley's Folly" but Phil not being an assertive type, and myself as a lowly freshman, the name failed to stick for reasons now to be described.

The loop itself was a full of notable sights and incredible scenery. At the two-mile mark, you passed through the Bryn Mawr College campus. At three miles, you entered one of the most exclusive (and reclusive) neighborhoods in the Main Line—we would pass estate after estate including one called La Ronda—a Spanish-styled main house complete with stables and a gatehouse that itself was the size of a normal dwelling. Allegedly, the estate was built by and for the inventor of patent leather. More importantly, the loop was quiet and without much traffic—but all along the way, especially the last three miles, it led though an area of winding streets again all covered in large trees. Almost every property seemed to have a tennis court. Ergo the name.

The Triple

Perhaps the most notorious loop, the Triple, was a six and a half mile run better known by its full name: Triple F**K. Its distinguishing feature: a formidable hill one-half mile in length, with three stages, each stage progressively steeper. The climb started exactly two miles west of campus on County Line Road. But there was a way out—a quick left at the bottom of a steady decline that led to a more gradual climb. That became the Radnor Five, which was a popular morning run leading back to Lancaster Avenue.

Typical Residence on the Tennis Court Loop

The Triple left no one in a state of neutrality. Those who attacked the hill and defeated it would return with a discernable swagger and an ever-so-slight grin of victory: "I beat Triple F**K!" The expression would be emoted verbally or non-verbally. Those who fared less well would carry that unmistakable look of deflation as if to say: "I've got Triple F**K'd today." Again, the expression was likely to be non-verbal. Perhaps that was why most runners taking on the Triple chose to do so alone.

The Other Loops

The other loops, namely the 3½ Mile Loop and the Minga,[7] another five-mile run, had their own unique ambience and charm. The latter was an extension of the 3 ½ Mile Loop, which was also popular with the sprinters and quarter-milers. Many freshmen began their morning run routine on these loops. To no surprise, the middle-distance runners would be bemused by the sight of sprinters on the roads—to be sure they were never seen more than a mile and one-half from campus. But they too would be quickly immersed in the sea of green, the estates, and the quiet charm of the Main Line neighborhoods.

The Villanova Track Mystique

So, back to the question: What was it about Villanova and the surroundings that influenced the character and drive of so many great track athletes and teams that emerged to produce such a legend of excellence? Or perhaps the more interesting question: Would the very same group of athletes have produced the similar results in a different place or setting?

That makes for the asking of even deeper questions. Did the dignity, intimacy, and beauty of the campus setting have an influence or serve as a motivating factor? Did the simplicity of the athletic facilities converge to forge for the athletes a singularity of purpose to achieve no matter what the circumstances or difficulties of the moment? Did the unique and challenging conditions specific to training on the boards mold a unique resilience and special toughness? Did the ambience and the grandeur of the surrounding area inspire the pursuit, and achievement of even greater goals?

The answers to the last four questions are simply: yes, yes, yes, and yes. Villanova University is a special institution located in an astonishingly beautiful area. On arrival, you can immediately sense that this is no ordinary place. It starts with the quiet, dignified, intimate, and reflective ambience of the campus inspired by one of the most venerated saints in the history of Christendom—St. Augustine. Add the utilitarian functionality of the athletic facilities that did nothing but challenge athletes to a full menu of hard work and just getting on with it—especially the boards. Finally, the campus and the spectacular surroundings inspired in every season no matter how inclement the weather.

Together these ingredients produced the greatest collection of middle-distance runners ever to come out of a US university or college. Indeed, these same ingredients provided an almost mystical blend of elements that manufactured success with astonishing consistency.

No one really knew how these factors fused together and why they worked. But we all knew that it worked. But there was one critical ingredient yet to be added. That was the one man that everyone held with both awe and respect: Coach Jumbo Elliott.

3

Jumbo Elliott—A Character with Many "Colors"

"I am not a teacher but an awakener."

Robert Frost

Winston Churchill once described Russia as "a riddle wrapped in a mystery inside an enigma."[1] There is perhaps no better phrase to describe the legendary Villanova Track Coach, James Francis "Jumbo" Elliott.

From 1931, when James Elliott arrived as a freshman, to 1934 when he became track coach in his senior year, and to the day of his death on March 22, 1981, he was above all things, a mystery. Of course, as athletes, we all knew who he was. We had heard the stories and were fully aware of his legendary status. We knew about the multiple championship teams, the world record holders, the many Olympians. We could see the large portraits of Ron Delany and Charlie Jenkins, the two 1956 Olympic gold medal winners hanging in the stairwells of the eponymous field house. You could feel his presence when he arrived to meet with us, albeit an infrequent occasion. We all looked up to him. We all sought his favour—that moment when he might make eye contact and say something just to us as an individual. That was even more rare. There were those who thought they knew him better than others. Some thought they had a special insight or even a close relationship with him. But just when you thought you knew Jumbo, you would hear something either past or present that was completely new or surprising.

Did any of us really know Jumbo? What was behind this mysterious man who had such an enormous impact on his athletes and left such an enduring track legacy? In many ways, he was a human kaleidoscope in constant motion. Every time you looked, you saw a different color. And if 10 people all looked at the same time, each one would see a different color and be seeing a different part of him.

Jumbo, despite his nickname, was not a big man. He was medium in stature, a finely built man with slender arms and legs. *Sports Illustrated* in a feature article entitled "Nobody is Bigger Than Jumbo," referred to him as "lean, almost gaunt with skinny wrists and almost frail."[2] The name "Jumbo" was conferred thanks to a professional baseball player—a pitcher for the Philadelphia Phillies in the 1930s—a big man with the same name, Jim Elliott. That was the original "Jumbo." But the name stuck to the much more diminutive young man, a veritable speedster, from West Philadelphia. And while all his athletes repeatedly referred to him as Jumbo, they never addressed him as such. Instead, it was always "Mr. Elliott" and said with the greatest respect.

Villanova Track Coach James F. "Jumbo" Elliott

Both in manner and style, Jumbo manifested all the measures of a successful businessman. He drove a big shiny Cadillac Eldorado; he lived in a mansion located in Lower Merion, amidst an environ of opulent residences and estates which defined the Main Line; he had a beautiful wife and four children; he wore the best of clothes; he carried himself with a confidence and a swagger that would rival any type A personality at a business conference or noisy corner bar. Yet the young James Elliott grew up in a poor area of West Philadelphia; the area is called Lady of Victoria Parish but better known as "Shantytown." His father died when he was young, leaving him, his mother, and sister to fend for themselves in difficult economic times. He was a kid that started with nothing and earned his way from the bottom up.

The young Jimmy Elliott grew up in the streets. He discovered that he was both quick of wit and fleet of foot. He had speed. He could read the language of the street—and quickly learned when to run, when to fight, or if a good talk could settle the dispute. These qualities made him a natural leader and other boys were attracted to him. He became the leader of a motley collection of lads, some younger, some older, on the walk to school. The boys felt safe with Jimmy Elliott, the tough kid of Irish descent who seemed to have no fears.

In due course, his athletic abilities began to emerge. With his speed, he excelled in the sprints—the 100 yards; the 220 yards and the occasional one lap of the track, the 440 yards. And the Penn Relays in Franklin Field were just 20 blocks away. As a high school athlete, the chance to compete in Franklin Field left an indelible impression on him—to be part of the largest and oldest track meet in the world. He loved it and he loved how it made him feel special, and he wanted more.

In 1931, he was one of the first students to be offered a track scholarship to Villanova University. The Augustinian fathers recognized the value of sport to the school and thought this feisty, half-orphan kid of Irish descent was a worthy young man to support the nascent track program. In no time, his leadership skills were recognized. He was soon named team captain and by senior year he became the track coach as well. He was also the coach of the golf team, all the while as a student, and filling the role of trainer to the football team, if he was not already busy enough.

In 1936, he became one of the top 400 meters runners in the country but did not make the US Olympic Team to the Berlin Olympics. Through the process however, he befriended Jesse Owens, who was about to become the most famous track and field athlete in the world thanks to his four gold medals at those Berlin Olympics. He saw and heard about the discrimination that Jesse and other black athletes were experiencing firsthand. He started hearing more and more about the self-serving and egregious decision-making and imperious behavior that typified the sports organizing bodies of the day—namely the Amateur Athletic Union (AAU) and United States Olympic Committee (USOC).

In many ways, Jumbo Elliott epitomized mid-twentieth century America—a country which was, on reflection, the most amazing political, social, and economic experiment in modern history and since the Roman Empire. The United States was truly a land with no frontiers, no barriers, and was the dominant economic powerhouse in the world. As a country, it became the deciding factor, albeit reluctantly, in two world wars. Driven by a sense of destiny, exceptionalism, and a rapidly growing population, in just 170 years, it morphed from a struggling colony into the world's most powerful nation. Nothing was impossible, and there was little to be learned or needed to be learned from anyone else. After all, Europe had spent the first 50 years of the twentieth century and the better part of the past 500 years bent on destroying itself. Japan had done the same thing in the Pacific theatre.

By the late 1940s, the United States accounted for 40 percent of the entire world gross domestic product. It had become an economic superpower largely the result of its own geography and rapidly growing population. Jumbo reflected that prowess and sense of invincibility on stating from time to time, "when in Rome, do as the Ggg…damn[3] Americans do!" Flush with victory in both the Atlantic and Pacific theaters, it seemed that there was nothing that America could not do. There were no limits. The United States was the largest military power by far; it was the founder and perfector of mass production, the auto industry, skyscrapers, and the home of consumer innovations of every kind: telecommunications, electronics, television, and the movie and entertainment industry; the list goes on. As well, the Americans were leaders in the field of sports, both professional and amateur. What's more, the US college system, led by the NCAA, served as the breeding ground for major amateur sports such as track, swimming, rowing, basketball, volleyball, and gymnastics—all integral to the Olympic movement.

The 1950s Eisenhower era ushered in a period of prosperity never before seen in world history. While other parts of the world struggled to rebuild from the devastation of World War II, citizens of the United States saw their standard of living surpass what previous generations could only dream about. Eisenhower found the right combination of low taxes, balanced budgets, and public spending that allowed the economy to prosper. The federal decision to establish the Interstate Highway System was perhaps the most significant infrastructure commitment of the century. Now goods and people could move across the country in hours or a few days at the most.

There was no better industry sector than interstate highways for a salesperson of heavy construction equipment, such as Jim Elliott, to thrive. Jumbo had found his sweet spot. He knew that he could not only work harder, but he could also work smarter than anyone else. He applied his street smarts and his athletic discipline at full throttle. If the boss showed up a 7 a.m., he would be at the office at 6:30 a.m. He never stopped digging out prospects and making call after call. And when he missed a sale, he never dissed his competition. Rather, he would always wish the perspective customer the best, hoping things worked out for them. He played the long game, knowing that persistence and keeping the door open was critical to success. He knew from the streets in West Philadelphia that being positive, making friends, showing no fear, reading your customer, and assessing the mood that person might be in, were all critical to how he would relate and what he would or would not say. And he was well-liked. People enjoyed dealing with him. He was funny, he was informed, was always interesting, and was well-dressed, as if he was the most successful man in America.

Those qualities contributed to his success. Soon he rose to become the top salesperson. And he never let up. He never assumed that he could go into cruise control. He built and nurtured his relationships with clients and took nothing for granted. In due time, he became a partner in and then the owner of the business called Elliott and Franz, located in Norristown, just off Interstate 76, the Pennsylvania Turnpike, which ran from New Jersey to Pittsburgh and then further west.

The very same qualities that elevated Jumbo from West Philly to Villanova University, and then to success in the business world, defined his approach to track and field. He knew that it all started with having a positive attitude, working hard, and never giving up. Most important was recruiting, getting the right people with athletic potential and the right attitude from the very outset. No different than putting together a great sales team. Attitude was everything. He knew that recruits coming from hard-working backgrounds, with little or no luxuries, would be motivated to achieve. He also knew that kids living in comfortable climates in the south or California would have difficulty adjusting to the Philly winters and the conditions on the boards, which were so integral to the Villanova experience. He also knew the body type to go after—young athletes with slender arms and legs. Not too tall, not too short, with the strength and ability to run a good half mile and/or mile—ideally both. He sought out athletes with intelligence—good students. In the end, he knew full well that college track was only a temporary stage of a much longer life; real life began the day that the student athlete graduated. This was, indeed, the story of his own life. In the end, he was more delighted to hear about the success of a former athlete in business or as a professional, than a good half mile time at the IC4As. Most importantly, he knew that excellence breeds excellence. Good runners make for more good runners. Great runners produce more great runners. Now to the mysteries and the complexities of the man.

Jumbo never ran the mile. Yet he coached more sub-four-minute milers than any coach in the world. As well as legions of winning middle distance relay teams—two mile relays, sprint medleys, distance medleys, and four mile relays, and in the process set many world records and national bests. Jumbo's coaching produced several world-leading distance runners, NCAA cross-country champions, and championship teams. For more than 25 years he produced a string of world-class milers that put Villanova on the map as a centrum for middle distance running excellence.

He was never a full-time coach. One could even argue that he was not even a "coach" in the traditional sense of the word. Yet he was named "Coach of the Century" by the ICAAAA[4] in 1976. Coaching was in fact a hobby—a sideline to his successful business that sold heavy equipment to big construction projects and the building of highways, particularly the interstate. If he received a salary for coaching, that was quickly transferred back to the institution to support the track program. James Frances (Jumbo) Elliott was the most successful track coach in America, producing more national, world-record holders, and Olympians than any other coach in America. His teams included a bevy of world-renowned sprinters, 400-meter runners, pole vaulters, high-jumpers, and hurdlers.

One would expect such an accomplished businessperson would demand the best facilities for his national and world-class athletes. Yet nothing could be further from the truth. Jumbo's athletic factory was comprised of facilities that would not even match those of an average high school where the sport of track and field was not a priority. There were no indoor facilities; the outdoor track was a poorly disguised circular path of cinders; there was not even a proper locker room—just a hallway with lockers where the basketball, football players, and swimmers would pass through awkwardly on route to their own change rooms knowing full well that they had better "digs" than their track and field counterparts. *Sports Illustrated* described it this way: "The contrast between Villanova's archaic athletic facilities ... appeals to Jumbo's sense of humour and his up-by-the-bootstraps philosophy. Visitors usually ask what his teams do when snow blankets the 'indoor' track [the boards] 'We just give the boys shovels and put them to work,' he replies. 'It's good for them.'"[5]

Villanova track athletes were revered across the country for their poise and preparedness for races. Yet Jumbo held no pep talks. No last-minute gatherings before meets or major races. No reminders or special messages. Instead, he would slip quietly into the arenas (indoors) or the stadiums (outdoors). We knew he was there. But where? Probably in the stands somewhere. And if you saw him, it would be a simple "Howya feeling Champ?"

Jumbo was never seen wearing a track suit, or casual clothes for that matter. He was easy to spot at the track or in the stands dressed in the best of suits, tie, overcoat, and his ubiquitous wingtip shoes, which were always shined to the max. No jogging around the track with his adoring athletes for this man. Perhaps his sartorial proclivities stemmed from his experience as a sales representative for a clothing manufacturer early in his career. Whatever the cause or occasion, Jumbo knew one thing: first impressions are important.

It could also be presumed that a coach of such talented athletes would exercise considerable oversight over his prized assets. After all, these were his thoroughbreds, the best to be found. Yet we would never see him on campus. Nor would we ever see him following us in his car while running on the roads. Or checking on us as we made the rounds on the local golf course or some of our runs. Or bumping into us on the Lancaster Pike if we wandered off to Bryn Mawr to grab a bite to eat at Pizzi's or sneak a beer at Kelly's. The idea of Jumbo hovering over us or to check up on us was as remote to our imagination as our walking on Mars.

It was remarkable how little we saw of him. We would meet him early in September when all the athletes had returned from the summer break. It would be a short meeting. A quick welcome. A brief encouragement to keep it "nice and easy. Get in those miles—it's like putting money in the bank. And be sure to pay attention to your studies." That was it.

The next time we would see him would be the first Tuesday in October. Tuesday was track workout day as part of our cross-country program. There we would gather, warmed up and ready to go. Then it would be 20 times 440 yards—starting in 70 seconds with a full quarter jog. The next week it would be 20 quarters each in 68 seconds: then a week later, 20 in 66 seconds. By the end of October and early November, we would be running those quarter miles in 63 or 64 seconds.

To be sure, we would see him at our dual cross-country meets on Saturday mornings at Belmont Plateau, Fairmont Park. But usually from a distance. When the season ended in mid-November, no more Jumbo until the first week of January. Then it would be three or four times a week on the boards (Monday to Thursday) and for a solid two months. He would arrive at 3:30 p.m. We would be ready to go. At 5 p.m., the workout was over, and Jumbo left in his shiny Cadillac, often before we finished cooling down. With indoor season over, three weeks would pass and no sign of Jumbo. Back to the roads. Put in the miles. Nice and easy. More money in the bank.

Outdoor season and it was onto the cinders three or four times a week. Again 3:30 p.m. and we were ready to go. Now it was early April, four weeks to prepare for Penn Relays. By late May, the few athletes who qualified for the NCAAs were still on campus. The rest were gone for the summer. Not another word from Jumbo, until September, when the annual routine began again.

Then there was the mystery of his actual coaching. What was his program that it produced an unparalleled string of world-class milers for more than 25 years? Was there a magic formula that Jumbo exercised in a way unique to him and only to his athletes at the time? It will help to examine what was known about middle distance running beginning in the 1950s at the very time Jumbo began his legacy.

Emil Zatopek won an unprecedented triple at the Helsinki Olympics in 1952—the 5,000 metres; the 10,000 metres; and the marathon. At those same games, a promising British runner by the name of Roger Bannister finished fourth in the 1500 meters. He was favored to win (certainly the pick of the British press). But an extra round of qualifiers (heats, semis, and finals vs. the former regime of just heats and finals) left him tired and without his usual strong finishing kick. Two years later, he became the first man to break four minutes for the mile—an accomplishment that was considered humanly impossible. And an accomplishment that gained Bannister and the sport of track and field worldwide recognition.

What were Bannister and Zatopek doing? It was becoming well-known that interval training was key—namely taking the target distance such as the mile and breaking it down to shorter distances and running these at race pace. The most popular training distance became the quarter mile (or 440 yards) and running repeat after repeat with an "interval" of rest in between. The typical Bannister workout was 10 times quarter mile with a two-minute interval. Zatopek left people standing with mouths opened when it was heard that he would run up to 40 repeat quarters. And sometimes in army boots.

Meanwhile the Finns and Swedes introduced the idea of "fartlek" or speed play, typically one hour runs on forest paths or parks where runners would run at differing speeds for differing distances, all without watches and little supervision. This had been pioneered by the legendary Paavo Nurmi and essentially became the regime of Herb Elliott running on the beaches and sand dunes of Portsea near Melbourne, Australia, all under the tutelage of the eccentric Percy Cerruty. In 1958, Elliott ran an astonishing 3.54.5 mile at the age of 20 and became the Rome Olympic champion for 1500 meters in a new world record of 3.35.6—two years later.

Interval training had become the rage. In many ways it was a coach's dream training program. It allowed the coach to stand at the track, watch in hand and supervise the entire workout. The major questions being asked at the time were how far, how fast, and how many? During WWII, a German trainer named Waldemar Gerschler determined that he could get soldiers in shape within six weeks by having them run repeat 200 meters. You can be sure that Franz Stampfl, an Austrian but now living in London, England and the man who had advised Bannister, was paying close attention to those findings. They settled on repeat quarters instead. Interestingly, Marty Liquori suggested that much of Jumbo's understanding of interval training may have come from one of his own athletes, namely Fred Dwyer, in the mid-1950s. Fred had met Stampfl while in Europe in 1955. He came back to Villanova brimming with new insights, and suggested interval workouts. Ten years later, Fred gained national renown at Essex Catholic High School in North Jersey, coaching that same Marty Liquori who would become the third high-school runner to break the four-minute mile.

Other influential coaches included Mihaly Igloi, a refugee from Hungary who fled the 1956 repression by the Soviet Union and relocated to California. He ratcheted up interval training to another level and astonishingly, had his athletes run interval workouts sometime twice a day. Igloi's success became manifest with Jim Beatty, the first man to run a sub-four mile indoors coupled with a 3:55 outdoor mile. Another athlete included Jim Grelle, the Oregon grad who made the 1960 US Olympic Team. Then came the powerful Peter Snell, the Olympic 800-meter champion in 1960, winning again in the Tokyo 1964 Olympics when he doubled by winning both the 800 and 1500 meters. Both Snell and Murray Halberg were coached by Arthur Lydiard, who advocated a training regime built on long-distance running—up to 100 miles a week. A half-miler running these weekly distances was unheard of. These training regimes became well-known as more details emerged during that 13-year period from 1954 to 1967, which saw the world record for the mile fall from 3:59.4 (Roger Bannister) to a breathtaking 3:51.1 (Jim Ryun). Jumbo, as well as every other coach, was hearing about these programs.

So, what did Jumbo do? And here comes the genius of the man. He kept it simple. He focussed on two elements: miles and quarters. Put in the miles during the fall and early winter—not too few, not too many. But get them in. All part of the foundation ("money in the bank"). And when it came to intervals, his standard workout would be repeat quarter miles—usually 10 to 12 in total. Or three lappers (480 yards) on the boards. And when he was trackside, he watched his runners like a hawk. If the group looked good, sometimes it would be 15 quarters; if they were looking tired, it might be eight quarters followed by four to six x 220 yards. Occasionally, his pattern would be to run repeat half-miles; some of the stronger runners like Patrick, Liquori, Hartnett, Coghlan, and Maree thrived on repeat halves. But most of his runners preferred the shorter interval distances.

And it worked! Year after year, the Jumbo magic would crank out another star miler. By 1981, the year of his death, the list of runners running a sub-four-minute mile while still a student at Villanova looked like this: 1957: Ron Delany—3:57.5; 1968: Dave Patrick—3:56.8; Pat Traynor—3:59.0; 1969: Frank

Murphy—3:58.1; 1970: Chris Mason—3:59.9; 1971: Marty Liquori—3:54.6; 1973: John Hartnett—3:54.7; 1975: Eamon Coghlan—3:53.3; 1978: Phil Kane—3:59.4; Dean Childs—3:59.1; 1979 Don Paige—3:54.6; Mark Belger—3:58.4; Amos Korir—3:59.3; 1981: Sydney Maree—3:48.8. Not to mention more runners, such as Dick Buerkle and Ken Schappert, who broke four minutes after graduation or numerous more who were on the doorstep running between 4:00 and 4:03[6]. Villanova track became a veritable four-minute mile assembly line. While the boss was about somewhere, it was the workers on the floor who knew what to do. The skilled tradesmen showed the way; the newcomers were the apprentices learning by example, until it was their turn to pass on the knowledge and experiences to the next flight of incoming novices.

Not surprisingly, the track world drew comparisons between Jumbo Elliott and Bill Bowerman, University of Oregon Track Coach. This made for interesting discussion: Elliott vs. Bowerman; Villanova vs. Oregon; East vs. West. Two phenomenally successful track programs—each producing high quality runners. Villanova could boast Delany, Patrick, and Liquori; Oregon offered up Grelle, Burleson, and Prefontaine. Both coaches were of similar age: Jumbo was born in 1915; Bowerman was born in 1911. Both were known as having strong personalities—unique characters to say the least. But that is where the similarities ended. Elliott and Bowerman were completely different. And while they respected each other, it is evident that they did not like each other.

The Elliott vs. Bowerman debate is truly a comparison of the zeitgeist of East vs. West. Jumbo and Villanova from the East represented old wealth, the establishment, the center of political power, and the Big City. Bowerman represented the spirit of the West—the frontier, the terminus of the Oregon Trail, the breaking of new ground, the "leave us alone—we'll do it our way" attitude, the smaller, more rural population centers, lumber, fishing, and farming. Add to that a decided resentment of the East and what it represented.

In drawing the comparison further, Jumbo was a businessman; he was a part-time coach; he trusted his athletes to do the work that needed to be done as defined by his relative lack of presence on campus. Bowerman was a mountain man, a full-time coach, an autocrat who was always on campus, checking on his athletes and defined by his omni-presence. Jumbo had a take-or-leave-it approach with his athletes; Bowerman domineered over his athletes—it was his way or the highway, and the man took occasion to humiliate those who did not meet his standards. Jumbo would be seen in nothing but a business suit; Bowerman would appear from time to time in his birthday suit in the sauna ready to inflict the "rite of passage" to an unsuspecting athlete through the application of a hot key ring to the inner thigh of a new athlete in the sauna post-workout. It was a strange ritual whereby he would hide his ring of keys under a towel where it reached temperatures exceeding 160 degrees F, then sit next to his target and suddenly, his keys would be applied. The response was a shocked surprise to say the least, topped off with a lingering red welt that would last for several days.

In complete contrast, Jumbo Elliott had no time for such bizarre nonsense or rituals. Rather, he would leave his mark by being delighted with the success of his athletes after they graduated from Villanova. Nothing pleased him more than hearing about the ensuing business or professional accomplishments of his former athletes. Bowerman seemed to care little what happened to his athletes beyond the environs of Eugene, Oregon. Elliott called out the egregious and self-serving behavior of the AAU and USOC and was never named the coach of any national or Olympic team; Bowerman played up to them and was named "high altitude consultant" for the 1968 Olympic Team and Head Coach for the 1972 team. Yes indeed, they were different. They were completely different.

Yet, despite his reputation and coaching success, Jumbo never wrote a book. He never wrote a paper entitled the "ABCs of Being a Miler." In fact, to our knowledge, he never wrote a single thing, on paper, or on a blackboard—no workouts; no notes, nothing left behind except for the notes of conversations with Dr. Ted Berry to be titled paradoxically "Walk, Don't Run." But every athlete he coached remembers his words. He left a colorful litany of meaningful quotes starting with: "Live like a clock!" Regularity was everything, perhaps Jumbo's biggest golden rule. Do everything the same way at the same time: eating, sleeping, training, studying … everything.

One of his most memorable sayings was: "Run the miles, it's like putting money in the bank." And one of his very few instructions. Yet this statement defined the essence of building the necessary foundation for high level performance—the primary purpose of the cross-country season. Other famous quotes include:

"In college you can do three things: athletics, studies, or socialize. And you can only do two things well." This statement is perhaps his most famous and meaningful legacy. He repeated it often. He knew life was all about choices and the young athletes under his watch needed to be constantly reminded.

"Stop and smell the roses." Jumbo knew full-well how serious many of his athletes could be. Theirs was an attitude of all focus on running and no time to enjoy life—looking neither left nor right. He knew that relaxing, enjoying what was in front of you and the ability to relax were keys to success.

"Keep'em hungry." Jumbo loved to see his athletes run well and run fast. But there were times when the workout was going well and maybe just too well or too fast, and he would say "that's enough." Of course, the leaders wanted to do more. But Jumbo would rather have a rested eager horse the next day than a tired injured one.

"Handle yourself with class in victory and defeat." This was classic Jumbo, who was adamant in the belief that how you carried yourself, no matter what, was the true manifestation of character and class. He loathed hot-dogging. If you were good, you did not have to say anything, or worse still, engage in some foolish display. If you were having a bad day, well, wait until tomorrow.

"You do the running, and I'll do the thinking," This would come out when he saw one of his stars worrying too much, second guessing, or losing confidence about what to do. Coupled with this seeming simplistic statement was another side of Jumbo: his uncanny ability to both know the strengths of his own athletes and at the same time spot a weakness in a competitor. He knew for example that Jim Ryun, the world record holder in the mile and the 880 yards, the most feared miler in America, loved to kick. Thus, the slower the pace, the better for Ryun. Yet Villanova runners, namely Patrick and Liquori, would beat him repeatedly—Patrick in the 880 yards when he set the world indoor record in 1967 and Liquori in the mile at least three times leaving him ranked as the number one miler in the world in 1969 and 1971. The key: make a big move a long way from the finish. That would not only catch Ryun by surprise, but it would also tighten him up by taking the sting out of his great kick as he was now forced to chase. More about this in a later chapter.

And there were a couple of more zingers that were admonishments, and clearly targeted at offending parties:

"Get your Gggg…damn ass to the library." Jumbo demanded that his athletes do well in school. He would examine both mid-term and final grades in detail. He knew who the good students were and who was struggling. If the required C average to compete was not being met, he immediately acted and instructed accordingly.

"And get your Gggg…damn hair cut—you look like a horse's ass." Jumbo never subscribed to the late 60s and early 70s long-hair look. He did not want to be surrounded by a group of hippies on the track and certainly not when travelling as a team. The look had to be clean and business-like, void of whiskers, and always with a blazer and tie. Looking like professionals meant everything to Jumbo. Once, in the Philadelphia airport while waiting for a flight, Jumbo and the Villanova track team were enthusiastically greeted by the world's most famous personality and athlete, Mohammed Ali. He exclaimed loudly: "I saw you coming—you guys look like a million bucks!"

The fascinating thing about Jumbo was how his athletes viewed him and what they would say. Consider these remarks[7]. First the awe:

> "To me he was larger than life! If he said, 'Jump,' I would ask, 'How high?'"
>
> "Coming to Villanova, the quality of the team was so impressive. I had nothing but respect for Jumbo, the history, and the program."
>
> "Quite simple: he inspired confidence!"
>
> "We were scared of him. You thought what he said was Gospel. We were there to learn."
>
> "One of the best choices I ever made was going to Villanova.... Thanks to Jumbo".
>
> "I came because of the incredible reputation of Mr. Elliott and the runners who were there. In the beginning, I did not know what to expect. I wanted to learn as much as I could. I was a very curious person and asked a lot of questions—I think this bothered him."

Then there were those who saw Jumbo the businessman and his managerial style:

> "Jumbo was the consummate, no-BS businessman. He closed deals straight-up and clear, as he did with me to come to Villanova."
>
> "He coached like a businessman—very flexible, always adapting. He went with his instincts."
>
> "I was accustomed to detailed mentoring and instruction from my high school coach, so this was quite different. Later, I learned that Mr. Elliott had developed a culture that had been passed down from previous classes that we were no longer boys who needed 'hands-on' instruction. Rather, we were men who could figure things out for ourselves."
>
> "You would never see Jumbo in the morning or before 3:30 p.m. for that matter. Always arriving in his Cadillac, very business-like, in his suit, and his distinct pair of wingtip shoes. And he would expect you to be warmed up and ready to go."

Others saw the "father" in him:

> "I certainly feel that he took me under his wing on a personal level. The first couple of years he would have me over to his house for dinner and in my freshman year I spent Christmas there. Also, during the Christmas break and the summer months, I worked at his company."
>
> "When being recruited, I visited Jumbo's home. I met his wife along with members of his family. During the visit Jumbo did not pose any questions pertaining to track and running. His interest and focus of inquiry were all related to my own family, background, interests, and school. Jumbo knew my times and abilities from the record books and did not dwell on this aspect of recruitment. His line of questioning went well beyond the track."
>
> "I had a special relationship with Jumbo and at times I looked on him as my stepfather. The week I was about to leave home and come to Villanova, my dad passed away. I stayed home to get my family matters in order and joined Villanova a month later after school started. I had to sit out the season as I was behind in my classes and grades for the NCAA standards. My first two weeks in the USA was spent living in Jumbo's house as he kept a close eye on me as I made the adjustment to the new life at Villanova. Jumbo would touch base now and again with my mom to let her know I was doing just fine.
>
> "After a major meet, I was unable to run because of a deep bruise that I got diving for the line. He would come by every day to my dorm on his way to work to check on me. I'll never forget that kindness."
>
> "On one occasion he took me somewhere to shag golf balls. After seeing my swing, he shook his head and said, 'Hey Kid, stick to track.'"

Others commented on his intuition, that incredible inner sense he had:

> "He knew how to get you prepared for a race—the speed required. And the rest."
>
> "Jumbo just had that inner sense—he knew when to seek you out or not. He looked for the person that the rest of the team would follow."
>
> "He had been a runner—he would understand how you were feeling."

> "A few times each year when we'd have a team meeting, Jumbo often talked about life skills. He'd say something like, "You can only do three things: study, sports, or socialize. You can't do all three well; if you want to be successful, you can only do two." I remember him looking directly at me when he spoke his wisdom knowing there were a few of the guys in the room who were sweating and so glad he wasn't looking at them. I got the impression that by only looking directly at me he knew everyone was listening. I don't think Jumbo really thought I was burning all of the candles I could find. I could be wrong. It was a special relationship."
>
> "Jumbo never seemed to push you too hard in workouts. He expected excellence in racing, and he raced me a lot. If things didn't feel right, you could tell him so and he'd let you slide on a few workouts. He always seemed concerned with your well-being and energy level. If you were down, he'd sense it and work with it"
>
> "Jumbo has the special alchemy—he knew who to put on the teams and when to tell them. It was most uncanny. He could tell who was running well—you saw that at Penn Relays all the time. It was amazing!
>
> "He was direct in what he expected from me (and his athletes) and I remember how sternly he spoke to me before the half-mile race in the NCAAs that I would go up against Jim Ryun. Before the race he came over to me, put his hand on my shoulder, and stuttered (he did this especially when he wanted to emphasize his point) and said, 'Ch, Ch, Champ, I want you to go, go, go to the lead and improve your position.' So, clearly, he wanted me to take Ryun to task and if he was going to beat me, he would have to pay the price."

Or his generosity when he knew one of his runners might have little or no money to afford much of anything:

> "On more than one occasion he would slip me money to tell me to get a haircut. Usually at three or four times the cost of a haircut. Even though it was not the case, I liked to think I was one of his 'favorites'—that was the level of care he emitted to his athletes."
>
> "Jumbo once gave me $20 to take the train when he found out I often hitchhiked home from Philly. He told me to get a job so I wouldn't have to hitch."

And his aloofness:

> "I was always very quiet, so I rarely had any interaction with Jumbo. Honestly, I can't remember ever having a conversation with him; just 'Hello, Mr. Elliott.' That was all me, because it was obvious he was always available to speak with if you needed to talk to him."

> "I wouldn't say he was the warmest of coaches although he cared deeply; he left [warmth] to Coach Pyrah."

> "My interactions were fairly limited. There was never a plan laid out. It was basically a case of showing up and doing your workout. He never pulled me aside and said, 'Don't do this, or do more of that.'"

> "As the days and weeks went on, I was amazed at how 'hands-off' Mr. Elliott was. When we gathered for interval workouts, he would give orders on what to do, but there were other days, when we didn't see him at all. The upperclassmen organized the training runs and I just followed along."

> "In simplest terms, it was a complex, distant relationship. Like every athlete, you wanted to be noticed by Jumbo. But he had his favorites, and he very rarely singled anyone, albeit the occasional conversation with one of the stars."

These comments are but a sampling of the commentary offered when talking with my former teammates about Jumbo. And the more conversations one might have, the more details would come forward. There were other athletes who were not the stars but trained daily, ran all the cross-country races, and endured the boards, but never had a conversation with Jumbo the entire time they were at Villanova. He might say, "How's it going Champ," but nothing more. And there were also detractors, top prospects who did not fit in or adjust to his style or personality. They would fall into two categories: a) the overly-sensitive and b) the over-thinkers. And heaven help the person whose personality intersected both these domains.

Jumbo did not hold hands. He did not supervise, console, or make any effort to empathize with an athlete who was not performing, or who needed daily affirmation. To quote one of the high performers, "The strong became stronger and the weak fell away." Nor did he have the inclination or the time to debate or even discuss his training programs. He knew they worked. The results were there for the reviewing. He only needed to sell what he knew would deliver results. You could tell that he gravitated to those athletes who exhibited the same personality traits that defined him: the street smarts; the positive attitude; the playful banter; the wit; the "let's get on with it" attitude; and most of all, keep it simple. If you did not like his program, you had the choice of four directions if you chose to exit.

But he had a soft side that did on rare occasions emerge. One of those times that vividly stands out took place with the passing of Ken Schappert's father in 1976. Ken grew up in the Bronx, just a few blocks north of Yankee Stadium. His father drove a fuel truck, worked hard, and cheered on the Villanova team whenever he could. There were no parents in New York City prouder of their son and Villanova Track, than the Schapperts. This was a dream come true—to have their youngest son attend such a prestigious university and be part of such an accomplished track program.

The Schapperts loved Jumbo and Jumbo loved them. The easy rapport and acute street savvy that Kenny and Jumbo shared was evident from afar. But the sudden and unexpected death of Kenny's father, who was still in his 50s, shook both the Villanova Track Team and Jumbo. It occurred in early February, just before the Millrose Games to be held in Madison Square Garden. The team, including Jumbo, arrived en masse to pay their respects to Mrs. Schappert, Ken, and his family. That night the affection that Jumbo had for Ken and the Schapperts became evident. The tears flowed freely, and Jumbo held nothing back. It was a night that Ken and the team would never forget. (Much more about Ken Schappert in a later chapter).

I only witnessed the soft side of Jumbo once during my four years at Villanova. After a promising freshman year, and mid-way through my sophomore year, I suffered a serious foot injury (bone spurs in my ankle) requiring orthopedic surgery. Afterwards, not being able to run for several months, I did everything I could to stay in shape, taking up some serious circuit training that included several weight exercises (light loads with many repetitions). I quickly put on about 10 pounds, all in my chest and shoulders. It was late spring when he saw me at the track and immediately started yelling, "What the hell are you doing? You look like a Gggg…damn football player." I was very upset—all I had been trying to do, unbeknownst to Jumbo, was find substitutes for running. He sensed my distress and immediately softened. We then had a quiet conversation and he encouraged me to go home for the summer and gradually build up my mileage. Of course, I did not want to let him down as I quickly built up to 100-mile weeks and went back down to my lithe 160 pounds.

So, who was the real Jumbo? The answer: all the above. In essence he was a reflective prism that responded to the full spectrum of colors and characters directed at him: businessman, salesperson, coach, father, wit, street fighter, mentor, admonisher, teller of a harsh truth, unsympathetic hard-ass, generous spirit who was concerned about your mother or father … he was all of these things. And as the kaleidoscope continued to turn, you might find another attribute or two. He was indeed a coach with many colors who could relate to all kinds and characters. He could bring out the best in almost anyone.

Jumbo with his two star milers: Marty Liquori and Dave Patrick

To fully describe and understand James Francis Jumbo Elliott as a coach, mentor, or inspiration, would be a body of work beyond the scope of this undertaking. Perhaps best to follow the man's own advice: "Keep it simple." It comes down to a set of relatively straightforward factors: first, anything is possible; strive to be the best; select the right people; always present yourself and those you work with as winners; work hard and never give up; everyone can be beaten; never count yourself out; take time to "smell the roses"; expect ups and downs; and above all, adopt a positive attitude and believe in yourself. For when that happens, success breeds more success. That is what made Jumbo Elliott the unmatched track coach of his era. Truly the "Maker of Milers, Maker of Men[8]."

But one more ingredient was integral to his success and the success of the Villanova track program. That was the critical parallel contribution of his assistant coach, Jack "Mother" Pyrah. Without the nurturing "mother," would Jumbo have had the same success?

4

Villanova's DMR Streak Begins: The Patrick-Messenger Era

"We were a team without class or color, committed to being the best and having fun along the way."

Dave Patrick

Dave Patrick's introduction to track and field could hardly be called a gentle entry. The Baltimore-based teenager originally planned to go out for soccer when he entered Kenwood High School in the 10th grade. But a discussion with his older brother Len, who suggested cross-country instead, changed his mind. With Len's encouragement, Dave decided, "This is what I'm going to do."

The first week of workouts were to run four miles straight every day, which he did with dogged determination. But by the Friday, his calf muscles became so sore that he did not run a step over the weekend. When he showed up for the workout on Monday, his coach asked, "What did you do over the weekend?" Dave replied, "I told him my legs were so sore I didn't run a step." Visibly irritated the coach retorted "Cross-country is NOT a five-day-a-week sport! If that's what you want, you better go out for another sport, like soccer." Dumbfounded at the response, Dave felt there was no other place for him to go. He wanted to be the best at something. Deep inside, he knew that running was his strength.

So, it began—the commitment to running and a new regime of hard work—not a strange condition to the aspiring runner. Hard work was standard fare within the Patrick household. "We came from a humble, blue-collar background. My father worked at Bethlehem Steel—all he did was work. And my mother, no matter how tough things got, never complained."

Meanwhile, another sprightly youth arrived at Kenwood High that same fall. Charlie Messenger was a bit shorter in stature than Dave, but equally as determined. Although from different middle schools, they had met earlier playing baseball on opposing teams. Both were highly competitive, hated to lose, and were always looking to get one up on the other. And now they were on the same team. And both had run the mile in the ninth grade—Dave ran a 5:32; Charlie ran a 5:33. And it didn't take long before Dave and Charlie were fused as teammates and the pursuit of the same goal—to be the very best they could be. And the immediate focus was simple—beat the other guy.

Dave's brother Len, seven years older and a former state champion in the half-mile, was instrumental in influencing Dave's mental approach to the sport. "He was everything you wanted in a big brother and more—the consummate cheerleader and on-site photographer. I was getting ready for my first race—a triangular meet at Kenwood against two good teams and top runners. That night, and before the race my bowels were really loose, showing the effects of my nerves—simply scared on what was to come. Before the race, my brother comes over and says 'Dave! You can do this! You can beat these guys. They are no better than you. Like you, they put their pants on one leg at a time.' Dave recalls his reaction: 'Wow, I never really thought about it, but he reiterated the importance of believing in yourself and that he would be on the course and at the finish rooting for me. So, the gun goes off, I take the lead and stayed there the whole way to beat the favorite by a couple of strides. That day, my brother made an impact on me that would serve me well for the rest of my life.'"

The Patrick-Messenger duo continued to grow in prominence. The two pushed each other—you would hardly see one without the other. So too came the wins, numerous one, two finishes, including a big win at the 1964 Penn Relays High School Distance Medley Relay, which the pair won in record time coming from far behind. To win this race against all the best high schools from New York, New Jersey, and Pennsylvania was no small feat.

It had not been an easy win. Dave's memories some 57 years later remain clear: "We were not one of the favorites although we had two really good runners. Archbishop Malloy in NYC was clearly the team to beat. What's more, the race started badly. Our half-miler was spiked on the first turn and ended up running 2:08 on the slow cinder track—about six seconds slower than normal. At that time, we were way back, like 11th place. Our quarter-miler picked up a couple of places with a 54 quarter and handed to Charlie. Charlie swept around the track picking up places with his 3:08 ¾ mile and handed to me around fourth, down about 50 yards behind the Malloy anchor."

And now words from what would become trademark Patrick: "I lasered my eyes on the Malloy runner and finally caught up with about 330 yards to go (incidentally the place in Franklin Field where the Villanova team sits)[1] and decided to try to take the lead. I fought for about 50 yards until he finally gave in, and with my 4:14 anchor we set a new DMR championship record, received the plaque and those coveted Penn Relays watches. What a day to remember! So exciting. Little did I know that this would be far from the last time I anchored a team at Penn."

To add to this victory, on the very next day in the inaugural running of the Penn Relays high school boys' mile, came another one, two finish. Dave won in 4:15.4 and Charlie came in second just a step or two behind. That made Dave and Charlie two of the most sought-after recruits in the United States.

While Dave was known as the miler, Charlie clocked the second fastest two-mile in high school history (9:09), second only to the legendary Gerry Lindgren from Washington State, who ran an unbelievable 8:40.0 indoors. Shortly thereafter, *Track & Field News* dubbed them the nation's best one, two distance punch in high school. And they were determined to stay together.

Many schools came a-calling—the leading contenders being Penn State, Georgetown, and Villanova. The Penn State University (PSU) visit came first—the two eager recruits visited the school in State College, ran with the team, and as Dave recalls: "We distinguished ourselves on the track. I don't remember much about the rest of the visit except for going to my first frat party, and that was fun. But later, PSU offered me a full scholarship and then told Charlie that they would get back to him later."

On discussing this offer, Dave said to Charlie: "Don't they understand that if we both don't get full scholarships, we are NOT going to Penn State?" That was the end of those negotiations. Charlie still chuckles to this day with great satisfaction about coming back to Penn State in his senior year, four years later. On that visit, he arrived in a Villanova uniform for the annual cross-country dual meet. He left with the course record. "That made me feel good. It really did," recalls a smiling Messenger. "You didn't give me a scholarship? OK, now I have your course record."

The Villanova visit was quite different. Dave and Charlie visited the campus, were hosted by the Villanova Track Team including Tom Sullivan, Vic Zwolak, Al Adams, Jimmy Orr, and Noel Carroll and stayed overnight. Dave goes on to describe: "These guys, in our minds, were legendary. Vic was the NCAA individual cross-country champion. And Tom, Al, Jimmy, and Noel held the world record for the indoor two mile relay. These guys were salt of the earth, so genuine, so supportive, and open to share the Villanova experience."

The next day, Dave and Charlie worked out with Vic Zwolak and stayed with him every step of the way. It was the end of the indoor season, and the workout was on the legendary boards. Afterwards, Vic told them that none of his Villanova teammates would run workouts with him. They felt on top of the world. Brother Len had already told Dave in order to become the best you have to be with the best and be coached by the best. That advice stuck with both as they reviewed other college offers, including Georgetown, who bent over backwards to recruit the dynamic duo. But Villanova and Jumbo Elliott were in a different class. And the choice was easy.

On Penn Relays weekend a few weeks later Dave, Charlie, and the Kenwood team won the HS Championship of America DMR. Immediately thereafter, Georgetown offered both boys scholarships. But it was too late. Dave now recalls that offer with a certain irony: "Two years later (1966), Georgetown was the favorite in the Penn Relays DMR—the year that our streak started!"

Summer passed, and now came September 1964. Despite the positive recruiting visit the previous spring, Dave's introduction to Villanova, like his entry to high school, was also far from easy. Whatever discomfort he experienced on his first introduction to cross-country, the Villanova initiation was much more challenging. In no time, Dave was in shock and visibly distressed: "The first time I stepped on campus, it was overwhelming. We were coming from a regular public school to a private school; from a coed school to an all-boys school[2]; to a Catholic school, while we were Protestants and maybe the only ones."

And it only got worse: "Everything was different! This was a huge step up for us from an academic perspective. We were overwhelmed by the freshman orientation. We had to wear beanies, bowties, roll up our pants two or three times, and sing the Villanova Alma Mater or spirit songs when confronted by upperclassmen. It was eye-opening! Not to mention having to wear a coat and tie to all classes. This was a seismic type awakening, and the adjustment was a big challenge for sure."

So much so, that two weeks later, Dave had had his fill. He was desperately homesick, having never been away excepting the odd occasion. Feeling disoriented and very much out of place, he called his parents and asked, "Is it ok if I transfer to the U of Maryland—just down the road from Baltimore?" They said that was fine with them. Immediately Dave spoke with Charlie, who then called his parents and asked the same question.

Dave Patrick and Charlie Messenger as unsettled freshmen

The answer came back "Absolutely not! You've made a commitment and you have to stick it out." As Charlie now surmises, "If my parents had said 'Yes,' that would have been it—we would have been out of there. No more Villanova. We would have been running for Maryland!"

College life soon took on its own rhythm and Dave and Charlie began to settle in. It became a routine of attending class, training, and studies. At that time, there was a "natural" divide on the track team. It was the varsity runners in one camp and the freshmen in another. Freshmen were not eligible to compete and by virtue of this exclusion, a separation, though not intentional, existed. As Charlie put it: "Those guys (the varsity runners) were like men. Especially the Two Mile Relay Team, who had set the world record in 1964. We were still boys growing up."

Charlie remembers one run early that fall with the varsity runners at the beginning of the cross-country season—they took him on the infamous Triple (the 600-meter hill with three stages—each progressively steeper) yet unknown to the eager freshman. It was a foggy day and the first two miles, mostly downhill, came easy. Then the hill, which Charlie chose to attack. But the fog obscured what lay ahead. By the time stage two of the Triple emerged, he was beat, only to be left behind by the chortling men as they disappeared into the fog while ascending stage three. Welcome to Villanova.

Freshmen had their own races during the cross-country season. Not surprisingly, this new group of freshmen would often train together, hang out together, study together, party together. Many also roomed together. And the long-established bond between Dave and Charlie, so very normal for them, provided a social gravity that drew in the remaining freshmen like Ian Hamilton and Craig Nation. It was like a foundation, something you could count on. "We genuinely liked each other; we had each other's back. We pulled pranks on each other, we laughed with and at each other. We played pinochle until three in the morning. The track team was our family." So much so that dating (a rare occurrence to be sure) also became a family affair. As Charlie put it: "If one guy got a date, he would make sure that there would be three friends in addition to his target of interest for the rest of his teammates."

Dave Patrick reflects on those days: "You could have complained about a lot of things. A big adjustment was getting used to the terrible food. The portions were small, no extras in terms of drinks, salads etc. And if you didn't get there by 6:15 p.m., you didn't eat. That meant going to the Pie Shoppe and using our Pie Shoppe tickets (15 cents) each to grab a burger and a shake. But we did not care. We were happy to be there—like my mom, we never complained."

This led to another ritual for the team—the evening gathering in the Pie Shoppe. Jumbo Elliott knew that runners needed fuel beyond the three meals served in the cafeteria. Hence the fourth meal, made possible by the provision of Pie Shoppe tickets to athletes on scholarship. Each person received 30 tickets a week—enough for a burger or a hoagie, and a drink each evening. And at 8:30 p.m., the convergence of track athletes from all directions would occur. Like cows heading for pasture after the evening milking, they would appear, some as singles; some doubles, and perhaps the odd triple—from the dorms to the west; from dorms to the east; and from the library about 200 meters to the north. At 8:25 p.m., the Pie Shoppe would be quiet. Five minutes later it was filled with 15 to 20 hungry runners looking to fill their stomachs yet again. But they did not do so quietly, as the full measure of verbosity and jocularity would abound without restraint. Settling at three or four adjacent tables, it became a ritual of non-stop theatrics, cracking jokes, playing tricks, testing each other, finding the openings, the weaknesses, one-upping the one-uppers. Night after night. This was when the characters were shaped, the feats magnified, and the bonds of friendship deepened to levels that remained for life. And a legacy that would be passed on to subsequent team members for years.

Incoming freshmen were also quick to learn about the importance of the Penn Relays. Not only was it the oldest and biggest track meet in the world (started in 1895 one year before the modern Olympics in 1896), but it was also Jumbo Elliott's showcase. First to his own backyard—West Philadelphia—in the early days as an aspiring school boy, but increasingly to the national and international stage as his coaching reputation grew. The meet had hosted such famous athletes as Jesse Owens in the 1930s and in 1951, Roger Bannister, who would become the most famous middle-distance runner in the world, the first man to run a sub-four-minute mile, and the man who would run and win the Benjamin Franklin Mile. Dave summed up the importance of Penn Relays this way: "At Villanova, there are three seasons: indoor track, outdoor track, and the Penn Relays. Furthermore, when you are a committed runner, you dream about running in the Penn Relays. In any conversation invariably on track you will hear the question: 'Did you run in the Penn Relays?' We soon realized that we could be a small part of such a worldwide known event that attracts runners from everywhere." And Jumbo knew that was the time to shine.

But in 1965, the best that freshmen could do was observe. There in the massive domain of Franklin Field sat Dave, Charlie, and the rest of the frosh, in the precise area where Dave had made the big move in the DMR the year before as a high school senior. "We watched the varsity team win at Penn and it permeated into our consciousness. It got under our skin and left us saying—'I want to be on a winning team.'" That year, Villanova won the Championship of America Collegiate Two Mile Relay thanks to a full roster of seniors (Jim Orr, Al Adams, Tom Sullivan, and Noel Carrol) and the Four Mile Relay (Dave Hyland, Jim Orr, Noel Carroll, and Tom Sullivan). The tradition of winning had been clearly established. And Dave, Charlie, and the remaining freshmen could hardly wait to play their part.

Penn Relays 1966

With all the seniors graduating that spring of 1965, the big question being asked was this: Could Villanova win even one Penn Relays Championship? Frank Dolson from the *Philadelphia Inquirer* expressed it this way: "For 11 straight years, Villanova has won at least one major championship at Penn Relays. To make it 12, a group of sophomores must rise to the occasion! To keep the streak alive will need top performances from its young stars."[3] Dolson also referred to Patrick, Hamilton, and McCafferty as "youngsters," pointing out that Georgetown had several outstanding distance runners. Meanwhile Charlie Messenger was having an off-season and would have to wait another year before his star would shine.

Dave and his teammates were now fully versed in Villanova's Penn Relays history: 11 straight years with at least one win—five distance medley relay wins; a pair of two mile relays, and an unprecedented streak of seven mile relays—by far the most outstanding series of performance in the history of the relays. The pressure was on.

"It was the Villanova tradition, and just knowing that we just don't lose at Penn," Patrick said. "And when we donned the Villanova singlet, it was all business.

We committed to excellence in a fierce way and left it all on the track. You did not want to let any of your teammates down and how you run is in full display. I was just hoping that the team could stay close."

Dave describes that first race in detail:

> It was surreal, waiting in the bullpen, getting ready to anchor in rainy, cool conditions that would make the cinder track even more challenging. The favorite was Georgetown. Yes! The same school that wanted Charlie and me after our performances at Penn our senior year in high school. The anticipation was a bit unnerving but not enough to distract or affect our goal to get the victory and those coveted gold watches. Sure enough, Georgetown had built a sizable lead and by the time I got the baton there was a 40-yard deficit to make up. I methodically made-up ground and could hear the crowd and our teammates urging me on. And before I finally caught them with about 330 yards to go but not knowing how much I had left. Should I just wait and try to out kick him down the straight to the finish line? I decided to go for it early and was able to get to the finish line with lots of room to spare running the fastest mile relay leg ever at the Carnival in 4:04.6. The feeling of hugging my teammates was unforgettable and would fuel my desire to anchor more team wins!

The time of 9:46.4 for the DMR was a new meet record—seven seconds better than the old one. Now the overall Villanova winning streak at Penn Relays stood at 12 years in a row. With Friday's work done, it was onto the Two Mile Relay the next day. That meant another rematch with Georgetown, again the favorite and anchored by the NCAA half-mile champion Ricardo Urbina. Distressingly, conditions only got worse. It rained all day, and the track was now even muddier. Simply, it was "Mud City." McCafferty, Nation, Hamilton, and Patrick knew they had a fight on their hands, and it would take a supreme effort from every runner to come away with a victory.

Dave Patrick, followed by Frank Murphy

The first three legs were separated by no more than five yards when Patrick received the baton a few yards behind Urbina. Patrick's memory remains clear:

> The race was on, and I knew the pain to endure ahead of me was real if we were going to beat Georgetown. Urbina had a high kick, and the cinders were pounding my chest with every stride. As I moved closer, the cinders were hitting my face and eyes at the quarter pole, so I dropped back a couple yards to avoid them. I did not have the confidence that I could overtake him with 330 to go so I decided to wait until the final straightaway to reach down for whatever I had left. The crowd on the turn sensed a sprint to the finish and I knew they were rooting for us. I also knew I did not want to get right next to Urbina and give him a chance to gain an additional burst of energy, so I decided to go as wide as possible and beat him to the wire. I remember getting to him with five yards to go and just getting by as he dove to the finish line. Yes, it was a surreal feeling that our team was able to come from behind against favored Georgetown and get four more gold watches.

Little did the Villanova foursome realize that Georgetown proceeded immediately with a protest claiming that Patrick did not cross the finish line with the baton in hand. According to their dispute, he had dropped it a yard before the line. Since there was no video replay, it was Jumbo's word against theirs, and his statement declared that Patrick threw the baton behind after finishing. The next day, the newspaper photo showed the baton laying before the finish line. But it was a moot point. Georgetown had been soundly beaten. They just did not want to accept that. As Dave puts it: "I don't know for sure what really happened, but it is possible that after following Georgetown for 875 yards, the sheer excitement of passing them may have been cause for me letting to go of the baton early." He concludes, "for the record, let's go with 'I threw it behind me.'"

The 1966 Penn Relays reached its finale with Villanova winning both the Distance Medley Relay and the Two Mile Relay. But it was the DMR that made the biggest headlines. The winning time of 9:46.4 was a record and broke the previous mark of 9:53.9 set by Yale in 1961. Although the Villanova Wildcats' record would be broken the next year, 1966 marked the final year that races were held on the old Franklin Field cinder track. Villanova's time of 9:46.4 was considered to be the equivalent of a mark which might have stood until 1975 when Villanova would re-write the records books once again.

In 2016, the 1966 Villanova DMR Team were inducted to the Penn Relays Wall of Fame: "This is phenomenal," said McCafferty, the half-miler. "The people at the Penn couldn't be nicer. We are so excited. They are taking care of us. Fifty years.

It's changed a lot. But it's been wonderful." He and his teammates beamed as brightly, recalling the great victory much as they had 50 years earlier, the day of the actual win.

Patrick explains the wins (and those yet to come) this way:

> Wearing the Villanova singlet was inspiring, and you knew that everyone on the relay was willing to spill his guts to win. We were not only in the best form we could be so early in the year, but our mental approach was also at the very highest level. In addition, the worse the weather conditions, the better, for heaven knows training on the boards for three months prepared you for the worst. Forty, fifty-degree weather with winds did not affect us in the least. We endured tougher conditions and those cool spring temperatures while other teams that came from warmer states had another obstacle to overcome.

Penn Relays 1967

How quickly a school year passes. Now the Villanova "youngsters" were really starting to roll as they tore up the collegiate cross-country and track world in progressive order. The 1966/67 season began with a bang with the cross-country team—Patrick, Messenger, the Irish speedster Frank Murphy, the gritty Dubliner Des McCormick, and the quiet but exceedingly tough North Philly boy Tom Donnelly—winning the IC4A Cross-Country Championship. A week later they accomplished what a group of essentially half-milers had never done before: they won the NCAA Cross-Country Championships. That was a real highlight and most unexpected.

The indoor results were even more impressive. Patrick ran his first sub-four-minute mile (3:59.3) with a win at the NYAC Indoor Meet in Madison Square Garden. As the newest member of this exclusive club, the win established Patrick as a world-class miler. Three weeks later, after the team won the indoor IC4A Championship with ease, it was time to take on the best collegians in the country at the NCAA Indoors held at Cobo Hall in Detroit. That meant going head-to-head with the most prodigious runner in history, Jim Ryun of Kansas—the first high schooler to break four minutes and the world record-holder for the mile. That previous summer, Ryun ran a 3:51.3 mile, a full two second improvement on the old record and a time considered "out of this world." And it was going to be head-to-head in the 880 yards (the indoor half mile)—a Patrick vs. Ryun duel. Not to be overlooked was the fact that Ryun also held the outdoor world record in that event with a blazing 1:44.9.

Patrick wasted no time. At the sound of the starter's pistol, he sprinted to the lead. He had one simple instruction from Jumbo: "Take the lead and improve your position." To this day, Dave has no idea what that meant. All he could do was run as hard as he could. And that was exactly what he did. Unchallenged as the leader, exactly 1 minute and 48.9 seconds later, he won easily—setting a new world indoor record. And Ryun was more than 15 yards, a full 2 seconds behind—not even in the race.

Penn Relays were now a month away. The Villanova team looked stronger than ever. The former sophomores were now a group of confident upperclassmen. But the health of a track athlete is like the weather in the mountains. You never know what is going to come next. And sure enough, what could go wrong was going wrong. Ian Hamilton, the trusty and experienced half-miler, and a runner you could count on to run a solid three-quarter mile, came down with mononucleosis. And a virus was going round—Patrick was a veritable coughing machine. He could hardly run the 3½ mile loop without feeling like a bag of disease. The week before, at the Queens-Iona Relays in New York City… the team looked terrible: Manhattan College won the Distance Medley; Fordham won the Four Mile Relay; and Georgetown won the Two Mile Relay, with Villanova in a losing position each time.

What's more, the new $200,000 tartan track in Franklin Field now rated as "superfast," created a new surge of interest from colleges across the United States. Abilene Christian had just run 9:45 for the DMR at the Texas Relays—a full second faster than Villanova had run the year before. And Georgetown and Fordham were stronger than ever. Time for fiercely proud Texans to teach the "East" a lesson.

Enter Charlie Messenger. For two years now, Charlie had been itching to get back to the Penn Relays. He knew the feeling of what it meant thanks to winning the high school DMR three years previously. Freshman year was exciting but how exciting can sitting in the stands be when you would rather be running? And sophomore year had been a real drag. While it was thrilling to witness his teammates and especially his closest friend win two races, not being part of the winning teams when you know it could well have been you on those teams and in the thick of things, left a feeling of emptiness and frustration that was never filled. Furthermore, Charlie was getting tired of being considered just a "two-miler" and a good cross-country runner. He knew he had speed and he wanted to prove it.

The DMR started at the usual Friday afternoon time—3:00 p.m. Tom Cushman with the *Philadelphia Daily News* described the Villanova team as being "in a state of unhealthy determination."[4] Patrick was wheezing and coughing. Everyone was worried. Now it was up to the team to perform no matter what. That would start with the feisty but unproven Dubliner, Frank Murphy. The leadoff leg went smoothly, and it was fast. Frank was looking good and handed off a yard behind Fordham running a very respectable 1:50.3, the fastest first leg ever. Bill Heidelberger ran his predictable 48 second quarter. Now over to Charlie. If you thought that Dave Patrick was competitive, wait until you watched Charlie—he was every bit as competitive, maybe more. With much to prove and two years of pent-up frustration, Charlie ran the best ¾ mile of his life—2:56 and passed the baton to Dave Patrick with a clear lead. Dave knew what he had to do—he had room to spare, and he could take it a bit easy. Sure enough, the Fordham runner soon loomed on his shoulder and passed. From then on it became a waiting game.

To quote from the *Philadelphia Daily News:* "there was a challenge from Fordham, but Patrick cut in the afterburner with 220 yards to go."[5] The win was a breeze and the headlines the next day read: "Villanova Wheezes to D-M Crown."[6] As easy as the win looked, Patrick was overcome with a coughing and hacking spell that did not go unnoticed. Cushman went on to write: "Patrick sounded like a one-man hospital ward with his post-race coughing and sneezing." Unbelievably, the overall time of 9:39.6 was a full 7 seconds faster than the previous year's record performance. Again, to quote Cushman, the win was "primed more heavily with antibiotics than confidence."

Meanwhile Jumbo kept looking at his stopwatch. "This must be wrong! They could not have run that fast." Sure enough, Charlie's fast ¾ mile was the decisive leg after Murphy had set the table. Dave's 4.04.8 mile made for a winning team time that entered new territory.

But Villanova's efforts at the Penn Relays were far from over. In many respects, the DMR win was simply the appetizer to the main event on Saturday. First, the Four Mile Relay. Once again, the Villanova foursome which now included Charlie Messenger went to work. Dave made it look easy as he had to ensure the win with a leisurely 4:10 mile but save himself for one more race—the Two Mile Relay, only a couple of hours away.

On this day, the legend of Dave and Charlie grew even larger. This time it was Villanova and Fordham all the way. The first three legs were literally shoulder-to-shoulder but the third runner, Charlie Messenger ran an unbelievable 1:48.8. Two-miler did you say? That gave anchor Dave Patrick more daylight. But a fresh (and healthy) Jack Fath, the Fordham national class half-miler, was not going away quietly. He kept coming and coming and off the final turn, he pressed ahead.

Dave tried to hold him off with all the strength he had left but it wasn't enough. Collapsing at the finish line, he fell like a dead man and did not move for 10 minutes. The headlines read: "Patrick Collapses, Villanova Loses 2-Mile."[7] When he finally revived, Dave released the full manifestation of all the phlegm and infectious substances he had been carrying. When the press cornered Jumbo immediately after the race and Dave was back on his feet, he muttered: "If he had been healthy, we would have won by 40 yards."

Meanwhile, a satisfied Charlie Messenger pocketed his two new gold watches with great pride. Finally, another Penn Relays watch after three long years! And he had proven what he knew all along—he could run a great half mile as well as a great mile. And he knew one more thing. If his dear friend and long-time teammate had been even half-healthy, he would have been bringing home a third watch.

Ten weeks later (mid-July), Dave Patrick was still not feeling well. Now back home in Baltimore, he made an appointment with his local doctor. Within minutes came the diagnosis: "Dave, you have serious tonsilitis and we need to take them out immediately." After the operation just a few hours later, the doctor came by with a certain urgency in his voice: "Those were the largest most infected tonsils I had ever seen." The recovering Patrick was now relieved but also carried some regret. To be sure, those infected tonsils cost the Villanova team a third Penn Relays Championship. And he also missed the opportunity to compete in the Pan American Games being held in Winnipeg, Manitoba, Canada that very week. Ah, the merits of hindsight and a much-delayed diagnosis.

Penn Relays 1968

1968 is considered one of the most tumultuous years in American history. Most of the attention was focused on the Vietnam War. Without question, the year began badly with the Tet Offensive catching the American Military completely off-guard. For two years, the public had been told repeatedly that the war was all but won. Tet shook public confidence to the core. Every day, the counteroffensive grew and so did American casualties. A bewildered and increasingly sceptical American public began to realize that imminent victory was fantasy, far from reality. So much for a quick end to this perplexing and seemingly pointless war.

Then came a series of disasters that went from bad to worse. First the assassination of Martin Luther King; then the declaration by President Lyndon Johnson that he would not seek a second term; then the assassination of Robert Kennedy; and all the while the rise of the anti-war movement, the Yippies, the Weathermen, the

Black Panthers, waves of civil unrest from coast to coast; followed by the ill-fated Democratic Convention in Chicago in late August. Meanwhile the international scene saw riots in Paris and Mexico City while the Soviets marched into Prague to crush the fragile green shoots of a fledgling democratic movement.

The world of track and field was equally tumultuous. It was a year of highs and lows. And the Villanova track team found itself riding the wave of social and political discontent whether it wanted to or not. That fall, the team repeated the NCAA cross-country win, consolidating its position as the best running program in the nation. And on February 17th, the now seasoned and highly regarded Patrick anchored the Two Mile Relay in Louisville setting a new world indoor record—7:24.6 (Hamilton 1:51.6, Messenger 1:53.2, Murphy 1:49.8, and Patrick 1:49.1). It was a great accomplishment. But it was the night before, on February 16, 1968, when the Villanova team did not run, that really made the news.

Dave Patrick takes over from Charlie Messenger

February 16th was the New York Athletic Club (NYAC) Indoor meet in Madison Square Garden—perhaps the most prestigious athletic club in the United States, hosting in the most prestigious venue in the nation. Dave Patrick, now a sub-four-minute miler, was the star attraction. And the mile was the feature event. New York track fans conditioned with more than 10 years of Villanova superstars including Ron Delany, Freddie Dwyer, Charlie Jenkins, Noel Carroll, and Don Bragg would come out in droves. The programs were printed. Dave Patrick was on the cover. What could be better?

But there was a problem. The NYAC, a bastion of "high society," had rules: *Negroes and Jews need not apply.* Simply, they were banned from ever becoming NYAC members despite the club's focus on track and field. Granted they could compete. *But don't stop by our posh facilities on the edge of Central Park—you are not invited.*

With the civil rights movement in full force, and leaders such as Dr. Harry Edwards at San José State and the high-profile Mohammad Ali banned from the sport for refusing the draft into the army, African American athletes had had enough. The sport of track and field was replete with discrimination exhibited by the treatment of such stars as Jesse Owens in the '30s and more recently toward Bob Hayes, John Carlos, Lee Evans, Tommie Smith, and Bob Beamon. It was the time to take a stand and possibly boycott the Olympics all together. This was the moment to take the first all-important first step.

Villanova had some of the country's top sprinters, led by Larry James, who was a leading Olympic contender in the 400 meters. James as well other black athletes including Erv Hall, Lamotte Hyman, and Hardge Davis felt strongly that they needed to support the boycott.

A concerned Dave Patrick, who always sought fairness and justice, met with Jumbo. "What do we do?" Jumbo, who had his own experiences with a discrimination of a different kind from the track establishment, gave his usual straightforward response. "Call a team meeting and I'll support you whatever you decide." The team voted 17–0 by secret ballot to boycott the meet. "I know because I counted the votes," Patrick says. "There were two reasons. We thought the New York AC was doing itself an injustice by not letting Negroes in the organization. We also thought that we have such a great team feeling that we didn't want to take a chance and split any views. We functioned as a team, and we should go or not go as a team. We decided not to go. Although some athletes might excel more than others, the team unity is what we strive for. It was tough for me since that was the race last year that I ran 3:59.3, my first sub-four-minute mile." Dave also informed me that he was dating the meet director's daughter at the time. Villanova's decision meant that romantic adventure was not going to end well.

Villanova's choice not to participate sent a loud message. Track and field needed to change[8]. Dave Patrick, together with Larry James, placed team and brotherhood above all. They were not afraid to take this stand. But had the price of this action been fully paid? There remains another part to this story. But first let's examine the rest of the indoor season, Penn Relays, the outdoor season, and preparations for the Olympic Trials.

There is another sidebar to the February 1968 saga. Upon returning from Louisville, Dave finally went to the Bryn Mawr hospital. His foot had been bothering him for weeks and was limiting his training. Submitting to x-rays, an astonished doctor soon returned and said: "Your foot has been fractured! That's the bad news. The good news is that it is almost healed" showing Dave the gray line where the fracture was now fusing. "If you have been able to run up until now, there's no reason why you can't keep running now."

Patrick was now firmly established as America's top middle-distance runner. Two weeks later, he topped off the indoor season by winning the NCAA half-mile for the second year in a row. This time was slower (1:52.0) than his world record effort the previous year, but right on his heels came Frank Murphy just 1/10th of a second behind and getting stronger every week. Further, the relay teams also looked strong with wins in the Mile Relay, the DMR, and a close second behind Harvard in the Two Mile Relay. No one was concerned with the second-place finish. Villanova runners typically ran several races in addition to the relays while other teams went with fresh runners. All in all, the relay wins added more points for the team as Villanova crushed the University of Southern California (USC), the odds-on favorite to win the NCAA Championships. Dave still smiles with the memory: "USC were predicted to double up on the second-place score—they didn't know what was in store for them as we crushed them in reverse almost doubling their score on them. Our black athletes knew we were all in this together and the possibility of five major wins at Penn Relays was a mere month away." Time to get ready.

But then came April 4, 1968—the assassination of Dr Martin Luther King in Memphis, Tennessee. Shock waves reverberated across America, which also put the Villanova track team in a tailspin. Just two days later, on April 6, they were scheduled to compete in Knoxville, Tennessee in the much-anticipated dual meet against the University of Tennessee. It was already being heralded as a battle of two college giants: Villanova vs. Tennessee—both top ranked in the country.

What to do? Could this contest proceed oblivious to the tragedy that had just occurred? Could they ignore the rising racial tensions in view of the large contingent of black athletes on the Villanova team? How should they react to this tragedy? Once again Jumbo asked Dave to summon a team meeting not unlike the one that had taken place a mere two months earlier in advance of the NYAC boycott. And once again, Dave sought for unity.

The choice was simple: stay home or go? After some discussion, the team members came to a consensus: they would not be intimidated by this tragedy but instead show unity, strength, resolution and most importantly, courage. They were prepared to stand up even in the face of this horrific event. Patrick summed up the feeling: "The Villanova track team did not see color as an issue. We were unified and in effect colorless. We were a team focused on being the best we could be and having fun along the way. The NYAC decision paved the way for the decision to run in Tennessee because everyone genuinely cared for each other, respected each other, and we knew that together this tragedy was not going to stop us."

To be sure, Tennessee had a formidable team, well-balanced with sprinters, middle distance runners, throwers, and field men. All in all, they had depth in every event. By comparison, Villanova had great runners but only two competitive field men—a great pole vaulter in Vince Bizzarro, and a top-notch javelin thrower in Jim Shillow—but Villanova really had no depth beyond its actual track athletes. Dave admits "in the back of our minds we wished we were travelling to Eugene to take on Oregon, but the testy relationship between Jumbo and Bowerman would not let that happen."

The very next day, the Villanova team flew to Knoxville for the much-anticipated dual meet. Evidently, the word was out that the BEST running team in America was coming to town. Upon landing, an eager press awaited the team, keen for interviews and fresh insights. Surprised by the welcome, the Wildcats survived this unexpected gauntlet and finally boarded a bus transporting them to their place of lodging at the University of Tennessee. On arrival, Larry James stood up and said, "I don't know about you guys, but I am NOT going to be the first person off this bus!" The team burst out with laughter and with that statement Larry single-handedly broke the ice. Jocularity aside, this in no way diminished his and the concerns of several other black athletes (Erv Hall, Hardge Davis, Lamotte Hyman, Bob Whitehead, and Handsome Wearing). The tensions of the times gave them good reason to be extra cautious knowing full well that as black athletes they were far from welcome in Tennessee or elsewhere in the "good ole" south.

Saturday arrived. Tension at the Tom Black Track was palpable. The track, situated in a bowl, held an estimated 10,000 spectators, many more than had been anticipated as people were packed cheek by jowl on the grass on all sides. This was not just a competition between two powerhouse teams. This event had a decided racial undertone. It was the white southern Tennessee sprinters lined up against the northern Villanova black invaders. More specifically, it was their nationally-ranked and champion Richmond Flowers (yes, the same guy that played defensive back for the NY Giants) against Erv Hall. It was their nationally-ranked Hardee McIllaney versus our rising sophomore Larry James. And it was the Villanova stable of top class-middle distance runners and two field men against the exceptionally talented and deep Tennessee squad with strength at the full range of track and field events.

So, the dual meet began. First, Erv Hall, Villanova's superb sprinter, managed to beat Richmond Flowers in the hurdles, the 100, and 220. Then, Larry James decisively beat Hardee McIllaney in the quarter mile, so much so that his time of 45.2 seconds for 440 yards was a mere .3 seconds off the world record. That earned Larry the moniker "The Mighty Burner"—a term he would carry for life.

Dave Patrick followed this display of sprint victories by taking the 880 yards to defeat Tennessee's NCAA Champion Larry Kelly. And Villanova just kept winning: they swept the mile, the two-mile, the 440 hurdles, and one more time Captain Dave Patrick re-emerged to run a leg on the winning mile relay team. As he vividly recalls, "What a memory ... how many times does a miler find himself running a leg on a 3:09 mile relay!" Villanova took the pole vault and the javelin but somehow still managed to lose the meet. Tennessee swept all the other field events—their depth was too much to overcome. To ensure victory and at the very last minute, the Tennessee hosts inserted an event called the 35 lb. weight throw. Jumbo roared, "Hell, we didn't have anyone on the team that can even pick up 35 pounds!" But for the Villanova team, the loss was just fine. They came for a higher purpose: to do a job and show Tennessee and the track and field world that they had a stable of runners that could and would not be denied. How do you win every running race, sweep several events, and lose the meet? Simple, compete in a meet in which added events tipped the scales to help the home team win.

Next day, the headlines summed up the meet perfectly: "*Villanova Wins Track —Tennessee Wins Field.*"[9] Further, the press reported that the 10,000 lucky spectators were treated to a track meet "for the ages." But more importantly, unknown to the outside world, the Villanova team grew in strength, spirit, and love for one another—an underlying zeitgeist that would define the essence of the team's spirit for years to come. After this experience, Villanova was one step closer to making the upcoming Penn Relays a track meet for the history books.

The 1968 Penn Relays witnessed the greatest set of performances ever displayed by a college track team. To no one's surprise, the Villanova DMR Team anchored by the now incomparable Patrick won easily on the Friday. This time, Frank Murphy demonstrated his considerable ability with a 2.53 leg on the ¾ mile, bringing the baton from behind and handing off to Patrick in first place. Patrick, operating under one simple instruction by the savvy Jumbo Elliott, "just run to win," played with the field. The Harvard team, who had beaten Villanova the week before at the Queen's Iona Relay, took the lead on lap two. But Patrick sat and waited, waited some more, and then with 250 yards to go, made one big move to win easily with a mile time of 4:05.3.

But it is what happened on Saturday that left everyone—spectators, athletes, and coaches—spellbound. First came the Four Mile Relay. The Villanova foursome—Ian Hamilton, Tom Donnelly, Charlie Messenger and the emerging star, Frank Murphy, won easily. Little did the crowd know that this race was almost a no-show for Villanova. Just minutes before the race, a frantic search for Murphy ensued. Where was he? Just in time, Charlie spotted Frank in the stands dispensing the full measure of his Irish charm to a female admirer. Clearly, he felt no need to warm up for his upcoming mile. But warming co-ed hearts was another matter. Dragged to the paddock but with the young lady's phone number written on his spikes, Frank waited his turn and did what he needed to do to bring the team home. Win number two.

Then came the Sprint Medley, which included Larry James, Irv Hall, Bob Whitehead, and Dave Patrick with another win. Shortly thereafter came the Two Mile Relay, when the fearless foursome, the world indoor record holders, went to work: Craig Nation, Charlie Messenger, Frank Murphy, and Dave Patrick simply outclassed all other teams and chalked up another win. Now one major Championship Relay Race remained—the Mile Relay. Could Villanova win an unprecedented fifth championship race?

Commencing at 5:30 p.m., the ensuing 3 minutes and 6.1 seconds remain as one of the most memorable moments in Penn Relays history. It came down to two teams: Rice University from Houston, Texas; and Villanova. After three legs, it looked all but over. Rice had it in the bag. Their anchor man took the baton a good 10 plus yards ahead of a trailing Villanova team. Then one of the most unbelievable sights ever to be beheld in the sport occurred. Larry James blasted from the very start. On the first turn, he started closing the gap immediately. Unbelievably, that gap continued to narrow on the backstretch. The crowd was going wild. Could this be true? When was James going to die? Had he gone out too fast? But he just kept going, and with 220 yards to go, he sailed right on by the lead runner. Surely the Rice anchor would respond. But their relative speeds never changed, and by the time James entered the final stretch, he was now clear by a good three yards. And when he hit the finish line, he had gained another seven yards. People looked at their stopwatches in disbelief. Had this just happened? Then came the now-animated voice of Jack O'Reilly on the public address system, more excited than anyone had ever heard. "Ladies and Gentlemen, the winner of the Championship of American Mile Relay and anchored by Larry James with a time of 43…." The crowd roared so loud that the split could not be heard. Nor did it matter. It was the fastest 440 yards ever run in the history of track and field. Larry James's 43.9 split was beyond imagination.

Villanova had done it. The winner of five Championships of America Relays—the Five Peat. Under the leadership of Dave Patrick and Larry James, this group of athletes who two years prior were an unknown and unproven group of sophomores had just accomplished something never done before.

Craig Nation hands off to Dave Patrick

In retrospect, Dave commented, "I don't think I fully grasped how amazing our team was at the time. I knew we accomplished more than any team in 1968 (five championships at Penn, NCAA Cross-Country Title, NCAA Indoor Title, numerous world records). By holding those meetings back in February and the vote to boycott the NYAC Games in 1968 was a stake in the ground, a catalyst to embolden our team to reach another goal including the NCAA indoor track championships."

The wins kept on coming. Dave won the NCAA 1500 meters on June 15th in Berkeley, California in a personal best time of 3:39.9. Then on June 30, 1968, Patrick won the US Olympic Trials in the 1,500 meters at the Los Angeles Memorial Coliseum with a time of 3:43.6, thus securing a spot on the Olympic Team for Mexico City. With Jim Ryun, the world record holder for both the mile and 1500 meters, sidelined with mononucleosis, the win positioned Dave as the country's number one miler and ranked top five in the world. With his Olympic Team position now secured (and assured by the US Olympic Committee), Dave's thoughts moved toward the Olympic Games coming up in October. It was no longer a case of making the Olympic Team, it was now about winning a medal and the possibility of taking the whole enchilada—the gold medal itself.

But two challenges lay ahead: first, getting ready to run at altitude. Mexico is situated on a high plain more than 7,300 feet above sea level—unknown territory for most runners excepting those living and training in east Africa, who were just beginning to enter the world stage. Second, build fitness to compete four months beyond July which meant extending the normal summer track season by almost three months. Together with Jumbo, Dave devised a simple plan: continue to work hard, keep putting in the miles, lots of intervals, then taper beginning mid-September with the objective to peak in October. That meant working hard through the second set of trials that were to be held in early September when the remaining members of the team would be selected, including the two additional 1500-meter runners. His only requirement was to "demonstrate" fitness in the meantime.

Then a sudden and most unexpected development occurred. Less than two weeks before the second set of trials, Bill Bowerman, serving as the "High Altitude" Consultant to the US Olympic Committee (USOC), convinced his peers and betters to throw out the Los Angeles results. The premise and the basis of his argument? Altitude conditions were so different that any results at sea level (i.e., the first set of Trials) should not be considered. Bowerman put the proposition before the athletes and called for a vote. Of course, the number of athletes eligible to vote vastly exceeded the number of first-place finishers. Almost all the athletes saw their chances of making the team increase by a factor of 50 percent. Instead of two positions per event to be selected, all three were now open.

The real reason for this sudden shift in policy will never be known. Head Coach Payton Jordan was away for the weekend. Nor was Jumbo present at the committee meeting to speak on Patrick's behalf. His views on the self-serving short-sighted practices of the USOC and the AAU were well-known—he was effectively a persona non grata although he had single-handily produced more Olympic athletes than any other coach. And who had disrupted the track scene earlier that year? Who had given the boycott of the NYAC meet more credibility than any other team in the sport? Villanova University and Team Captain Dave Patrick.

1968 Olympic Trials Final, with Marty Liquori and Dave Patrick leading on the backstretch

And then there was Bowerman—he despised the East with its eastern establishment that included Villanova and Jumbo Elliott. Furthermore, he had two athletes contending for positions in the 1500 meters. Liquori, the talented Villanova freshman, appeared to be adapting well to altitude and was looking very strong in workouts at the Lake Tahoe training camp. With Patrick's assured selection pushed aside, the chances for his University of Oregon athletes to qualify increased considerably. Patrick could be beaten since it was well known that he had not been resting up for the Tahoe Trials. Thus, the possibility that his two runners could claim two of those three coveted positions. Without the input of either Jordan or Jumbo, the meeting might never have taken place or may have turned out differently.

Patrick went to the starting line in Lake Tahoe feeling as unprepared as he ever had been for a high-level race. Even though he had run the fastest semi-final the day before, he was tired. "It felt like being in the wrong place at the wrong time," Patrick recalls. "Physically, I knew I wasn't at my best. Mentally, I knew I was nowhere near my best. I remember being unsure of what to do or how to run that race. That had never happened to me before."

The worst outcome that a runner can experience, unfolded. Dave finished fourth. It was won by Jim Ryun, now recovered from mono and with his usual "big" finish; second went to the Villanova freshman Marty Liquori just a ½ second behind; and third went to Tom von Ruden. Dave finished a full 20 meters back—the only race that he had lost all year. He was devasted. Perhaps the only solace to this travesty was the poor placing of Bowerman's athletes—one finished fifth; and the other, who had been a favorite, finished dead last. Bowerman had been right—his runners were not able to beat the Villanovans, no matter the conditions. But that did nothing to console Dave.

To this day, the outcome and the back-room politics that left Dave Patrick off the 1968 US Olympic Team remains one of most controversial and flawed decisions in the sport. Dave went from being a named member of that team, a bona fide medal hopeful, to sitting on the sidelines. In one single moment, his hopes, aspirations, and dreams dissipated like the rising mist from the fields on an early summer morning.

"I thought it was a travesty. It never should have happened," said Erv Hall, Patrick's teammate at Villanova, who went on to win the silver medal in the 110-meter hurdles at the Mexico City Games. "Dave had won the event at the initial Olympic Trials. He had already earned his way on to the team. I thought what happened to him was really not fair."

Patrick had a difficult time dealing with the result. He stopped running for about a year. He turned down the chance to serve as an Honorary Marshal for the Special Olympics. He blamed himself for disappointing those close to him. And now a college graduate, he had to find his way in the working world. There was no such thing as the ability to earn a living as a professional runner. The desire and the passion for running that defined him were gone. He never returned to competitive running. Twenty-two years of age and his track career was over.

"There was no way that decision would fly in this day and age. It wasn't a fair vote," Marcus O'Sullivan, a four-time Olympian for Ireland in the middle-distance events, who now serves as the Villanova's Head Track and Field Coach, said of the decision to throw out the L.A. trials and make Patrick requalify for the team. "You'd have attorneys fighting on your behalf. It was an injustice. The USOC let the system fail."[10]

On a happier note, some 40 years later, at a Sheraton Hotel in Philadelphia, not far from the Penn Relays, witnessed a reunion of Villanova's 1968 powerhouse track team that produced five Olympians. Patrick helped put it together. Unbeknownst to Patrick, Payton Jordan, the coach of the US Track Team in '68, was invited to attend. During the presentation, much to Patrick's surprise, Jordon made his entry, and was called by Marcus O'Sullivan to the podium. Jordan's address was short: He called Dave Patrick to join him and officially named him to the US 1968 Olympic Team.

The emotions came pouring out. Those who were present, including O'Sullivan, had tears in their eyes. "I'll never forget Payton Jordan, at 91 years of age, telling me, 'There isn't a day that goes by that I don't think about the injustice that was perpetrated on you,'" Patrick said. "It was pretty touching." For Patrick, the moment finally provided some sort of closure for a wound that will never completely heal.

For those of us who came after Dave Patrick, we have grown to appreciate the foundation that he built while at Villanova. To be sure, there had been comradery, commitment, and great achievements on the team before. But Dave, together with Charlie Messenger, forged this to a deeper level. He was the pure manifestation of what happens when you apply commitment and hard work with motivation and talent. Dave Patrick arrived as a promising but not exceptional high school athlete; he left as a superstar winning every major race and becoming a contender to be the best in the world. He embodied a sense of fraternity fused by common goals; he precipitated the formation of an inspired brotherhood founded on the principles of justice, fairness, and standing up for what was right. He demonstrated a winning spirit to overcome all obstacles at a time when everyone wondered whether Villanova could win even one Championship Race at Penn Relays; with indefatigable confidence he led the team to win an unheard of five championships at those same Relays.

Most importantly, he crafted a "culture of certainty" by leading a team that truly "touched greatness" and in doing so, left a history, a destiny, and a legacy that lasts to this very day. For the past 50 years, a Villanova track athlete in any situation need only ask one question: "What would Dave Patrick do?" The answer to that question would undoubtedly result in doing the right thing, the right way, and through hard work, produce a winning result in the process.

Now in the fall of 1968 with the departure of Dave Patrick, the torch of greatness had been passed to the precocious, cocky, and classy 19-year-old Villanova freshman now a sophomore. It was the second week of October and he had just made the Olympic 1500-meter final in Mexico City. Marty Liquori, one of only three athletes to run a sub-four-minute mile in high school, stepped onto to the world stage.

5

The Streak Continues: The Liquori-Mason Era

"Running at its core is all about time management—a big reason why so many runners leaving Villanova have successful careers."

Marty Liquori

When running, most of us would visibly manifest the stress on our faces and bodies, but not Marty. The tougher the circumstances, the greater his tranquility. There was something special about Marty Liquori. When the going got rough, at that critical point in a race or when the workout reached that inevitable breaking point, a seemingly angelic cloud would enshroud him. He would literally glow and transcend as he made his big move, and these big moves defined him as he became one of the greatest milers of his time. Photos capturing the finishes of his races display that sublime look of calm followed with triumph.

Marty Liquori arrived on the Villanova campus in September 1967. He was truly one of a kind; the first East Coast American high schooler to break four minutes for the mile. And he was a Jersey Boy—cool, tough, and fearing nothing. He was another of the Jersey Boys prototypes like Frank Sinatra and Frankie Valli. Living in the shadow of the Big Apple and closer to an even rougher Newark and Paterson, what choice did a young boy have? He had to be as tough or even tougher than those guys. And cool. *Sports Illustrated*[1] would later describe Liquori's demeanor this way: "It wasn't a swagger really, but more a look or a smile or a manner that implies he is doing something 18-year-olds aren't supposed to do. It is also bell-bottoms, Gucci shoe buckles, turtlenecks and the model-type girl in the jump suit." Jumbo Elliott said, "and he's my cool cat." But Liquori was also smart. Marty displayed an analytical side that he applied not only to his training, but also against his competitors. He was constantly assessing and determining how best he could gain an edge. Where is the opening? Where are the cracks?

Liquori wins with ease

Upon entering high school, Marty wanted to play basketball, but chafed at the structure. He wanted more control of his destiny. Running proved to be a better choice. Under the experienced watch of Freddie Dwyer, himself a graduate of Villanova, another Jersey Boy, and a 4:00.8 miler during the Delany era, Marty's talent began to emerge. He started putting in the miles and the results showed. First, a 4:18 mile as a 15-year-old sophomore; then a 5 second improvement in his junior year, despite some injuries; followed by his senior year running 70-mile weeks including hard intervals. That produced a 4:04 mile at Penn Relays when Marty anchored the high school distance medley, followed by a 4:01.1 in Compton in early June; another 4:00.1 in San Diego. Could he get any closer and break that four-minute barrier?

Then came the evening of June 23, 1967 on a fast, crushed brick track in Bakersfield, California—a one-mile run for the ages. There were two stories: first the winner—Jim Ryun runs a new world record mile in 3:51.1—an astonishing time, leading from start to finish and coming through the half in 1:59. His last quarter was clocked in a blazing 53 seconds. In the second story, Marty Liquori in seventh place, runs 3:59.8. Now Marty became the third high school athlete to break four minutes.

Shortly afterwards, the three Oregon athletes in that same race (Jim Grelle, Dave Wilborn, and Roscoe Divine) took Liquori to meet the imperious Bill Bowerman, Coach of the University of Oregon Track Team. The conversation was short—it was evident that Bowerman was not interested in this cool Jersey Boy. He preferred West Coast types. After a brief conversation, he basically told Liquori to stay in the East.

But Jumbo Elliott wanted this kid. By the summer of 1967, he had already produced two sub-four-minute milers (Delany and Patrick). Here was his chance to take this young runner, who was already a sub-four-minute miler at the age of 17. Just think what might be possible. After the banal meeting with Bowerman, who had treated him like an out of place school-boy, Liquori decided that Villanova was the place for him, and Jumbo was his kind of coach. He liked Jumbo's style and admired his already stellar reputation in producing results. Liquori reflected: "He had the reputation and I really connected with him. He had it all: wit, showmanship, salesmanship, Irish blarney, parental discipline, instinct, and knowledge. This was the place for me."

Chris Mason in the lead

Meanwhile, across the Atlantic in Sheffield, England, another young athlete contemplated his future. Chris Mason, now 18 years of age, had run a very respectable 4:08 mile. Like most British youngsters, he played football (soccer) and followed the league tables closely. But when he ran in the local school's cross-country race a couple of years earlier, he finished in the top 10 without any training. Then he started to win and quickly established himself as a top junior in track. But where to go next? Sheffield was a gritty industrial town located in Yorkshire. Considered the north of England, it is an area replete with coal mines, steel factories (the home of stainless steel), metal fabrication shops, and no-nonsense hard-working people. Chris Mason was tough. Growing up in Sheffield was one thing; enduring the weather was another. Summers were tolerable but winters were grim. Not much snow, but icy, damp winds across the Yorkshire Moors blew right through a person. More than once, Chris needed to warm up all his extremities after cranking out repeat quarter miles on a beat-up city-run cinder track.

Sheffield was also the home of Joe Cocker, who lived about a mile away and held a job as a gas fitter before his unmistakable voice brought him fame as a rock star. On occasion, Chris would see Joe riding the last bus home from work. Years later, Sheffield became known worldwide as the location of the famed *Full Monty*—a depiction of Sheffield life in the state of industrial decline that had afflicted much of northern England already in the mid-60s.

There were athletes from Sheffield as well. Just 10 years earlier, in July 1957, a local by the name of Derek Ibbotson from nearby Huddersfield, broke the world record for the mile with a 3:57.2. Affectionately known as the "Four Minute Smiler" thanks to the omnipresent grin he wore when racing, Ibbotson served to inspire other young athletes with the message that you did not have to come from Oxford or Cambridge to become a world champion. And in 1956, a youngster by the name of Sebastian Coe and his family moved to Sheffield when Peter Coe, a metallurgical engineer would run one of those local factories. Seb would electrify the track world some 20 years later by first joining the Hallamshire Harriers, the same club that gave Chris his start.

The easy path for Chris, like most of his British counterparts, would be to settle in, get a job, and continue his track career through the club system. But Chris was not certain that this was the path for him. He knew of the opportunity for scholarships in the United States as an option. He had heard of the "Irish in America"—Ron Delany, Noel Carrol, and Frank Murphy. What did he have to lose? Chris decided to write Jumbo Elliott a letter. In retrospect, it would be the most important letter of his life. He received a letter in return and after exchanging some newspaper clippings to verify his track times, a scholarship offer followed. Chris was on his way to Villanova where his life would change forever.

Liquori and Mason formed the core of the incoming freshmen group in the fall of 1967. They joined a seasoned Villanova track team led by Dave Patrick, a man clearly on the rise. Chris Mason recalled those early days: "I had no idea what to expect. The second day I went to Jumbo's house for dinner and thought that all of America was like the Main Line. Until I went to Franklin Field through West Philadelphia, a rough neighborhood to say the least."[2] The Patrick-Messenger gang took them in, showed them the ropes, and quickly introduced them to the running loops. Chris remembered that "it was mostly the Frolic in the afternoon and the DPM in the morning." He laughed as he recalled the DPM, or the Dave Patrick Memorial 3 ½ mile loop made famous by one of Dave's allegedly rare morning runs.

Liquori and Mason were quite different. Marty the American had a worldly, savvy style. He knew the Philadelphia area; he was not far from home, and he had very clear goals. Running sub-four for the mile was one thing but making the 1968 Olympic Team and becoming the best miler in the world were the next mountains to conquer. He came to Villanova as an already "Big Man on Campus (BMOC)." He had a car—a Thunderbird; he had a parking spot on campus; after having difficulty sleeping because of the "sleep talking" Mason and a third roommate—a late-night card player, Jumbo arranged for him to have a single room in the dorm usually reserved for upperclassmen. He had a snazzy wardrobe—Levi slacks, Izod shirts, and stylish penny loafers. You would rarely see Marty in blue jeans. He loved music and had a stereo with a full stack of the best and latest albums. And he had a TV at a time when such a device on campus was a great rarity.

Chris Mason

Chris the Brit, on the other hand, was just happy to be there, adjusting to life in America and surviving classes in the high-class suburban environment. He lived in the freshman dorm with two roommates. He wore jeans and sneakers. He barely had enough money to afford laundry and the occasional hoagie from Campus Corner—the infamous local fast-food joint. But he also loved music—he introduced the team to groups other than the Beatles and the Rolling Stones, including such novels acts (at the time) as Joe Cocker, Eric Burdon and the Animals, the Who, the Kinks, and Cream with Eric Clapton. Yet everything was new. It was a big change from industrial Sheffield. Fortunately, both freshmen did not have to worry about competing in a serious way that first year. They were not yet eligible and instead they learned the ropes from the varsity athletes. They both worked hard day in, day out. Marty soon earned the reputation for hard workouts, but Chris would stay with him every step of the way.

While 1968 was a tumultuous year for the United States, it was an ideal time for Liquori to get ready for goal number two: the upcoming Olympic Trials and Mexico City later that fall. Dave Patrick, clearly a favorite and the man to beat, was busy week in, week out competing on the college track scene. That April, both freshmen took in the Penn Relays as spectators and witnessed Villanova's historic five Championship Relays of America wins. Marty was no stranger to Penn Relays. He was fully aware of its history and importance as a major track event. He had been schooled by his coach Freddie Dwyer and had heard about Villanova legacy. What's more, he had gained first-hand experience. North Jersey was less than two hours' drive from Franklin Field. It was on this track that he anchored his high school team distance medley twice: first as a junior when coming off an injury he was beaten by Jim Jackson with Boys High School from NYC; and again, as a senior, but this time he ran a spectacular 4:04 mile to win the race and to "blow away" that same Jim Jackson who at the final exchange, led by more than 100 yards. That result signaled that Marty was on the rise and a force to be reckoned with.

But for Chris, the whole experience was a complete eye opener: "I first heard about the Penn Relays as a freshman in 1967. I lived for one semester in a dorm room with two other track members and the 'currency' they and the rest of the freshmen on the team held was how their high school teams had performed at Penn. The talk on the team about the '68 relays quickly focused on winning all five relays. This apparently had never been done. As a freshman, I was not able to compete, so I was not paying much attention and had no intention of attending. It was Marty who encouraged me to go and at least take in the Saturday afternoon portion. This occurred when I was preparing for final exams, and I wanted to get ready for them. I was pleasantly surprised at the atmosphere and the size of the crowd. Everything was building towards that final event, the Mile Relay. I can still hear the roar of the crowd and the bellowing voice of the announcer giving Larry James's split. All you heard was '43…' as the announcer let us know we'd just seen the fastest 440 yards ever run in the history of track and field with James's 43.9 split. For myself, I thought, 'Welcome to the Penn Relays.'"

The remainder of 1968 and early 1969 is the story of the Liquori ascendency. That is a full story in and of itself. Suffice it to say, that during the next 12 months, Marty asserted himself as one of the country's top track stars. First, he ran a series of very competitive mile races on the West Coast, barely losing to Jim Ryun in Eugene, Oregon (3:59.0 to 3:59.3). Then it was off to Lake Tahoe, the high-altitude training camp and location for the second set of Olympic Trials. He responded well to altitude training and was peaking just in time for the trials that September. The trials were structured to emulate the Olympic Games schedule—heats, semis, and finals. The AAU, with input from the USOC, considered this to be the realistic and fairest way to select worthy team members. For Liquori, it was step one: make the semi; step two: make the final; step three; finish in the top three. Liquori successfully reached each step coming off a slow first half in the final, to kick with Jim Ryun, who sliced through the field from last to first in the last lap. Liquori finished second and Tom von Ruden followed him; all three were selected for the US Olympic Team. At the Olympics he progressed steadily, moving through the heats, the semis, and becoming the youngest runner in the field to make the final. But the year and all that hard work caught up to him. Plagued by a stress fracture in his foot, he could barely run and finished dead last. Nevertheless, he had the best view in the house as he watched Kip Keino scorch the field to win in a new Olympic record of 3:34.9. While disappointed, Marty quickly evaluated his performance from a broader perspective. After all, making the Olympic final just weeks after his 19th birthday was no small achievement. And he had sent a clear message that this was just the beginning of bigger and better things to come.

That following March at the NCAA Indoor Championships at Cobo Hall, Detroit, Liquori really made his mark. It was a head-to-head contest with Jim Ryun in the mile. Both had met the previous day in the two mile, a race that had not gone well for either runner. Liquori finished a disappointing sixth place, scoring no points for the team, while Ryun dropped out early in the race saving himself for the mile. Jumbo was furious and protested that Ryun had quit without cause and should not be allowed to run. But Jumbo's protest was to no avail.

Ryun had an unusual plan—rather than his typical wait and kick approach, he went out fast and tried to burn a tired Liquori. Liquori stayed with him through a 60-second quarter and then went by him as they passed the half in 2:03. Liquori continued to lead for next five laps until Ryun came up to him on the final turn. They finished in a dead heat—each with the identical time of 4:02.6. Some say that Liquori had out-leaned Ryun. But the victory was given to the reigning world record holder and NCAA mile champion who was the sentimental favorite. You could hear Liquori thinking, "This will be last time Jim Ryun beats me." Without knowing how prescient such a thought really was, it was time to get ready for Penn Relays.

Penn Relays 1969

The incredible five championship win in 1968 led Tom Cushman with the *Philadelphia Daily News*[3] to raise this question: "In an unprecedented display of overall excellence, the Wildcats ran off with five Relays of America titles ripping up records and leaving the opposition frustrated on every front. Could the Cats do it again?" Jumbo replied, "Not likely. We lost Dave Patrick and Ian Hamilton, two key seniors who gave us a lot of depth."

Now it would be up to two sophomores to fill the gap: Olympian Marty Liquori and England's Chris Mason. Villanova also had Frank Murphy, now a senior and running better than ever. Everyone knew that Liquori would be carrying a big load: the DMR; the Four Mile Relay and the Two Mile Relay. But Chris had no idea what was in store: "I was totally surprised when Jumbo took me aside on the Tuesday before Penn Relays and told me I would be running three races. Up until that point I figured one or two races at the most. Given the results of the prior year I was nervous and scared at the same time. Probably more scared of dropping the baton than anything. I did not want to be on a team that did not continue the streak of five championship relays from the year before." Again, a hint of Jumbo's insight. He had seen the hard work that Chris had been doing, saw his strength, and knew full well that he would be able to handle the load, even as a first-time sophomore.

Despite the usual seeming chaos that characterized the warm-up area, Mason was ready to go for the DMR at 3:00 p.m. on Friday for the leadoff 880 yards. Exactly 1 minute and 52 seconds later, he handed off in second place to Lamotte Hyman. While spotting the University of Tennessee a good six yards, he was still in good position. Lamotte, a reliable quarter miler, held his ground with a 47.3 effort; then the irrepressible Frank Murphy took over. Frank made it look easy as he breezed around on his first lap. Two laps and precisely 2 minutes and 57.1 seconds later he handed off in the lead to Liquori, who teased Howell Michael, a former high school competitor and now with William & Mary University, allowing him to catch up. But the outcome was never in doubt. Coming off the backstretch into the final turn, Liquori opened up and quickly gained 25 yards to establish a gap that never decreased. His time: 4:02.9; the overall team time of 9:38.2 was just .3 seconds off the record set the year before. Win number one. And now the DMR streak stood at four.

Day two at Penn Relays was another one for the track history books. First came the Four Mile Relay—with leadoff man Tom Donnelly, who churned out a 4:10 mile; Dick Buerkle followed with a 4:07.9. Tom Donnelly, hard-working, quiet, and highly respected, known more as a cross-country runner, did his job running with the leaders.[4] Dick Buerkle, who would become known as the most successful walk-on in US college history, ran a personal best. Both Tom and Dick were critical pieces to the Villanova team, adding greatly to the comradery and deep friendships.[5] Anyone having trouble with classes could rely on Tom, who was the consummate mentor. Dick won everyone's admiration because of his steady improvement starting as a no-name freshman to becoming a key cog in the Villanova running machine. An incessant prankster, Dick played tricks on his teammates all the time keeping things loose. But it was all business today. As the baton was passed, Chris simply did what he had to do: run a solid mile (4.08.8) and exchange it in the lead to a waiting Liquori. Three Penn Relays' first timers anchored by the young man who would soon be the best miler in the United States. Running conservatively, Liquori focused more on saving himself for the upcoming Two Mile Relay than he did on winning the race with a leisurely 4.11.2. That came easily and the win was a piece of cake. Win number two.

Now for the Sprint Medley. Larry James, the Mighty Burner, took full control in the opening quarter, passing the baton to Dave Fender and then to Hardge Davis, each running a solid 220-yard leg, anchored by the wily and experienced Frank Murphy, who was just flying and won easily with a winning margin of seven yards. Win number three.

Next up: the Two Mile Relay and enter Andy O'Reilly—a feisty New Yorker of Irish descent, an engineering student, and the designated leadoff man. Andy was one of those incredibly consistent teammates you could rely on day in, day out. He had great foot speed and guts to spare. And he knew no matter what happened in the opening relay leg, he was passing to the most reliable threesome of middle-distance runners in the United States: Mason, Liquori, and Murphy, who would anchor for the second time that day. This time Frank, no longer distracted by his romantic proclivities with female spectators as he had been in the previous year, left all other teams in the dust, winning by more than 30 yards. The race outcome was never in doubt. Win number four.

Finally, the coup de grace: the Mile Relay with Hardge Davis, Andy O'Reilly, Lamotte Hyman, and Larry James running as if it were just another ordinary day at the office. With the world's second fastest 400- meter runner of all time on anchor, Larry James made the race look like a walk in the park. No last lap heroics required this time and another easy win as Larry finished ahead of his nearest competitor by a good 12 yards. Win number five.

The Wildcats had done it again. Winners of five Championship Relays of America for the second year in a row. An unheard-of result. What was considered impossible one year ago, had just happened again and this time it seemed all too easy. Marty was not that surprised given his in-depth knowledge of the relays and knowing how strong the Villanova team really was. Chris could not believe it. Not only had he expected to run only one race, but he had also just run three, with three victories at that.

Now the bigger issue for the Penn Relays as a Relay Carnival was not whether Villanova would win. Rather it became a question of who would be willing to come and compete with them? Gordon Forbes from the *Philadelphia Inquirer*[6] mused, "there were some wild bell bottoms and turtlenecks, but nothing swung like the Villanova track team. Winning four races on Saturday by ridiculous margins—25 yards in the 4-Mile; 30 yards in the 2-Mile; 7 yards in the Sprint Medley; and 12 yards in the 1-Mile. And the DMR on Friday." Was there simply a lack of competition?

Yet the 1969 track season was just getting started. First the IC4A's at the end of May where Villanova dominated, winning virtually every track race including Marty's win in the mile. Then two weeks later at the NCAA Outdoor Championships in Knoxville Tennessee, Liquori and his teammates Frank Murphy and Chris Mason shocked the track world in the men's mile. Once again, it came down to a Liquori–Ryun showdown. Ryun the favorite, had gone four seasons in college without a loss. But with one lap to go, Liquori led after a slow 3:03.5 ¾ mile time. Then he exploded, hammering the last lap and never letting up. He fully expected to be passed by Ryun at any moment. But that did not happen, and with his 54 second final lap, he hit the tape in 3:57.7. Ryun was almost a full two seconds back in 3.59.3 followed by Frank Murphy in 3:59.8, and Chris Mason in seventh with a 4:02.8. Not only had Liquori finally beaten the world record holder, but he was also now clearly the best miler on the US college scene. And there were three Villanovans in the top seven—a unquestionable display of middle-distance strength. Jumbo Elliott could not have been prouder.

A week later at the AAU's, Liquori met Ryun once again, this time in Miami. The conditions were hot and humid. Everyone was waiting for this race—the pre-race jitters were evident across athletes and spectators alike. Would Ryun avenge the loss from the previous week? The race began with great anticipation. Then to everyone's surprise, Ryun dropped out before they hit the half-mile mark. He'd had enough. Marty went on and won easily in 3:59.5. Shortly thereafter, Ryun announced that he was retiring from the sport. The disappointment of his silver medal at the 1968 Olympics, combined with the non-stop pressure he experienced every time he stepped on the track, left him exhausted. Plus, as a newlywed, he faced a new set of interests and obligations. Meanwhile, Marty headed for Europe and beat the best that the cradle of track and field could throw at him. In the Europe vs. Western Hemisphere meet, he led at the bell and continued leading to the finish unchallenged, beating the European Champion, Italy's Francesco Arese, and Germany's 1968 Olympic bronze medalist in the 1500 meters, Bodo Tummler. By summer's end, with the world's fastest 1500-meter time of the year, and his wins over the world record holder, he was named Number One Miler in the world by *Track & Field News*. Marty had achieved his third goal—to be the best in the world.

Penn Relays 1970

The 1970 indoor track season unfolded seeing win after win for Liquori: the prestigious Wanamaker Mile at the Millrose Games; the IC4A's; and the NCAA's. He was now the undisputed top miler in America. As Penn Relays approached, the same question posed in 1969 arose: can Villanova win five major championships?

Jim Tuppeny, Head Coach at the University of Pennsylvania (and former assistant coach at Villanova until 1967) simply said: "They have a good shot at it, provided they run scared." Liquori and Mason were each slated to run three races and they were feeling confident.

This time the University of Texas El Paso (UTEP) came to town competing at the fabled Penn Relays for the first time. With a bevy of top distance runners including seven Australians, a Brit, and a lanky American named Kerry Ellison who had run a 4:02 mile, a boisterous Coach Wayne Vandenburg thought they had a chance to unseat the Wildcats. The previous week, the UTEP Miners won the DMR at the Texas Relays with relative ease in a time of 9:40.1. Frank Dolson, who referred to Vandenburg as the "perpetual talk machine" and the "mouth that roared," listened patiently knowing full well that a Villanova schooling was about to take place.[7]

April in Philadelphia can bring the best of weather and the worst. Friday, April 24th came in as one of those bad days—wind, rain, cold. That morning, the Villanova DMR Team comprising Wilson Smith, Greg Govan, Chris Mason, and Marty Liquori met—they had planned to go for a new record but with the poor conditions, it was decided that a win would suffice. Wilson and Greg were new to the team. Both sophomores, Wilson hailed from West Virginia, and he embodied the best attributes for which that state is known—small town friendliness, unfailing politeness, and a grit embedded in its people as deep as the omnipresent coal. He was a 1:50 high school half-miler, one of the best in the country, and a heck of a cross-country runner. Greg, the 400-meter man came from the Big Apple—he was cool, cocky, always carried that mischievous glint in his eye, but was equally as friendly. Greg had all the attributes of Larry James when it came to a smooth running style.

Cushman described the weather forecast: wind, rain, and another Villanova hurricane. He then added: all were correct.[8] The outcome was never in doubt. Wilson, with a 1:51.5 opening half-mile, handed off in third; Greg floated his single circuit in 47.0 picking up a position handing off in second; Chris ran his usual workmanlike 2:56.1, ¾-mile, handing off with a good eight-yard lead to Liquori, who finished with a 4:03.9 mile. The time: 9:38.5, a mere .6 seconds off the record set by Patrick et al. in 1968, despite the weather. As for UTEP, the Miners never had a chance. They stayed with Villanova for the first three legs but ultimately finished third behind Maryland. Liquori was clearly in a class of his own. The somewhat muted Vandenburg, who expressed disappointment with the race mused, "Maybe our first three runners are equal to theirs. But nobody has a better fourth man than they do."

Meanwhile, the DMR winning streak for Villanova now stood at five.

The Sunday headlines, the day after the full day of relay races said it all: "Villanova Scores 3rd Relay Sweep!"[9] What was once considered impossible, had become commonplace. With much improved weather, the day began with the Four Mile Relay. This time a new Villanova rookie (a sophomore) Davey Wright led off. Coming from Newcastle, England, Davey was now the second Brit (or more affectionately known as Limy) to join Chris Mason at Villanova. And he arrived with great promise having run 4:03.8 as an 18-year-old. Davey ran with an unmistakable bounce (and a smile) as he did what every leadoff man needed to do—hand off in the top three. Over to the now experienced and ever improving Dick Buerkle, who followed with a 4:05.5 mile. Then to Chris Mason: it was now a game of saving himself for the Two Mile Relay—and he sauntered the four laps in a pedestrian 4:14.9. Finally, Liquori playing the same game as Chris, outkicked the Georgetown anchor, winning by five yards but only needing a 4:11.2 mile to dispose of this pesky rival.

But the afternoon had just begun. The Sprint Medley came next with Larry James setting the table with a 46.3 first lap and the lead. Hardge Davis and Lamotte Hyman quickly dispensed two quick 220-yard legs; now the seasoned Andy O'Reilly took over. Not having the star power of some of his teammates, Andy had proven his ability by consistently running top quality half miles on numerous two mile relays. Now it was his turn to bring it home which is exactly what he did with his 1:50.1 anchor. Win number three.

The Two Mile Relay proved to be the bigger contest. As Andy O'Reilly put it: "we were sitting ducks for any team that was fresh. I was dead and so was everyone else." Wilson Smith, back for a second time, led off—this time in 1:53.3. The "dead" O'Reilly, clearly ecstatic but exhausted with his big Sprint Medley win and only one hour rest, managed a 1:55.5. Mason came back with his usual competitive 1:51.2, and finally, over to Liquori. This time, UTEP really meant business. With the UTEP anchor Greg Jones running sub 1:49, Liquori dug deeper than he had for the previous two races, running one of his very best half miles ever in 1:48.1 to win by seven yards. A delighted Jumbo assessed the win with this statement: "He showed his class in that win....one thing about Marty is his ability to sustain his speed over a long distance. He can do that like no other runner I have ever seen." Win number four.

Which left the last race of the meet—the Mile Relay. Hardge Davis—47.3; Greg Govan—47.4; Lamotte Hyman—47.2; and Larry James—46.0 made easy work of it. While a speedy Rutgers anchor made it interesting, James was never challenged. Win number five.

The "five-peat" had been completed for the third year in a row, and the future looked bright. Mason and Liquori were juniors. Wilson Smith and Davey Wright were sophomores. The only seniors leaving were Larry James and Dick Buerkle. With Greg Govan to replace Larry James and a new crop of half-milers and milers such as Billy McLaughlin, Karl Kinscherf, and Rick Kell coming along, Villanova looked indomitable.

Penn Relays 1971

The 1970 school year began with a new crop of accomplished middle-distance runners. The cohort included Les Nagy, from the steel town of Youngstown Ohio; John Hartnett, a farm boy from County Cork who just won the European Junior Cross-Country Championships in March; Ken Schappert, the top half-miler/miler from New York City; and me, another farm boy and the current under-18 Canadian one-mile recordholder and Canadian Junior 800 Meter Champion. All three—Les, Ken and I—had clocked 4:09 for the mile. Only two other high schoolers in America had run that fast—Joe Savage and Tony Colon—both headed for Manhattan College, which was now coached by Freddie Dwyer. Add to this group of Villanova freshmen, one Brian McElroy, the fastest American high school half-miler in 1969 (1:49). Brian McElroy, heralded as the next Jim Ryun (both in speed and physique) had gone to the University of Kansas to emulate his track doppelganger. However, the suburban Long Island resident found rural Kansas much to his disliking, and after a year and a half, transferred to Villanova and arrived in January 1971.

Once again, the Villanova Track Team went from strength to strength, winning the NCAA Cross-Country Championship beating out Oregon by a point (both freshmen Les Nagy and John Hartnett were on that team). Liquori continued his winning streak, winning every race he ran—repeating wins with the Wanamaker Mile, the indoor IC4A, and NCAA one-mile runs.

Significantly, 1971 would be the first year when freshmen would be allowed to run. No more varsity-freshmen divide. And Jumbo would make full use of that enhanced latitude. There were limitations, however. McElroy had to "redshirt" for a year and Hartnett, while showing promise as a miler, came down with a leg injury at the end of the indoor season.[10] But Nagy, Schappert, and I were in—the first crop of freshman to carry the Villanova colors at Penn Relays.

After 15 consecutive relay wins, what was in store for Villanova this year? Reporter Tom Cushman suggested, "This is the year that Penn Relays comes back to earth. With Larry James, Hardge Davis, Frank Murphy, Dick Buerkle and Dave Patrick all consigned to the record books, the reservoir of great quality that allowed Villanova's great teams to sweep 15 championships has become considerably less by comparison."[11] Jumbo remained cagey but it was clear that there were to be no early concessions. His two main horses, Liquori and Mason, would be ready to carry heavy loads.

Being named along with Les Nagy to Four Mile Relay came as a big surprise to me. Ken was named to run two races—the Two Mile Relay and the Mile Relay. We were all feeling the pressure. I for one had never been to the Penn Relays—it was all completely new to me. My introduction came on Friday, April 23rd, my first time to Franklin Field to watch the DMR.

I peered through the crowd and there stood my teammates, pensive, nervous, just itching to get going. The members were the repeat of the 1970 team. Wilson Smith—the affable half-miler who made it very clear to all that he was from West "by God" Virginia; Greg Govan—our smooth striding quarter miler; Chris Mason—the gritty, hard-working sub-four-minute miler; and Marty Liquori—our superstar, the number one ranked miler in the world. in his usual cool, aloof, sublime manner. Everyone knew that Villanova was the favorite. This should be an easy win.

The half-milers were now on the line. Once the starters made sure that all the runners were in proper position, it was the crouch, the gun, and off they went. The usual jostling around the first turn unfolded and things quickly settled down. Wilson Smith looked comfortable—he could run a 1.50 for the half mile any day of the week; twice if he had to. All he had to do, like last year, was stay out of trouble and hand off in the top three. For that matter, all the first three runners had to do was get the stick to Liquori. And he would do the rest. We all knew that.

But suddenly, Wilson was struggling. As runners circled the track for the second time, you could see on his face that he was in distress as his stride became markedly clipped. He had clearly pulled something. But thankfully, he kept going. Now he was close to the back of the pack. You could hear a change in the noise of the crowd—it shifted from the sounds of a carefree cheer to the tense expressions of yells and urgings on. Even the running race commentary delivered by the velvety voice of Jack O'Reilly showed signs of strain as he tried to hide his concern and partiality to the school he openly admired.

Meanwhile the waiting Greg Govan, our quarter-miler, kept shifting further to the outside lanes on the starting line. He had been in second position after the pack passed the finish with one lap to go; then fifth; now he was being guided to 10th … 11th … 14th. Chris Mason, who would be up next, appeared uncharacteristically anxious and wore a look that none of us had seen before.

Though almost 50 years ago, the memory remains fresh in Chris Mason's mind: "I realize there were a few close calls to the DMR streak, but the closest came in 1971. Needless to say, by the time I received the baton from Greg, we were well back. For some reason, the leaders never took advantage of the situation. I was able to catch up to the lead pack with a lap to go when I heard Liquori yell not to give him a lead. But I did just that." The DMR streak remained intact. Chris had run his usual 2:56 ¾ mile, able to catch the pack and command of the race. Marty did the rest with a 4:04.1 mile, easily outkicking Manhattan's optimistic Savage who thought for a brief moment that he might actually beat Liquori when he passed him on the second lap. That was but a dream.

Win number one. And the DMR streak now stood at six.

Saturday was a glorious sunny day. Despite a sleepless night brought on by my experience the day before seeing firsthand the thrills and pressures of Penn Relays, I led off the Four Mile Relay. My instructions were simple: stay out of trouble and don't let anyone get away. The race passed in a flash and four laps later I handed off in third with a 4:12 mile, just behind the leaders. Nagy followed with a 4:11 and established a 20-yard lead. Davey Wright bounced his way through the third mile with another 4:12, passing the baton to Liquori. The work had been done; the tensions passed; the doubts gone. Marty just needed a 4:08 mile to seal the win. Win number two.

One hour later, Chris Mason returned to the track to anchor the Sprint Medley. He was tired. South Carolina was fresh and hungry. Despite getting the baton in the lead, Chris was up against a bona fide half-miler—Bob Kaczka, the South Carolina anchor who ran 1:48.5. Chris managed a 1:49.9 but it wasn't good enough. He lost by six yards and felt badly. This was the first Villanova relay loss in four years, after 17 straight wins since 1968. As Chris describes it, "I had to run harder in the DMR on Friday than I was expecting, especially since the qualifying rounds of the Sprint Medley coming up an hour later. In the final, I was outsprinted and the possibility of winning five Championship Relays of America for a third time was broken. I never asked Jumbo why he put me (not a true half-miler) as the anchor on the Sprint Medley."

Then one hour later, the Two Mile Relay Team went to work. This time the freshman Ken Schappert led off in 1:54.3 and handed off in the lead; Davey Wright for his encore performance ran 1:52.6. And one more time, Chris Mason now running his fourth race, managed another 1:50.1. Three teams were in the battle: Manhattan, UTEP, and Villanova. Marty Liquori ran a steady first lap; then on the backstretch, he made his move. Once again, Joe Savage dug in as deep as he could, but Liquori managed to squeeze out a lead and maintain it. Coming off the turn, the lead was narrow, but Liquori held off the surging Savage. His time: 1:48.7. Win number three.

The Mile Relay Team, so dominant since 1955 finally met its match. Schappert led off. But three teams were stronger and despite Lamotte Hyman's heroic efforts, Adelphi College, University Tennessee, and Temple University all finished ahead of Villanova.

There are a couple of sidebars to this storied era. Firstly, Marty Liquori never lost a single relay while at Villanova—he had nine straight wins. Chris Mason experienced only one loss—the Sprint Medley in 1971. Almost 50 years later (2018), at a track reunion, Chris met Wilson Smith for the first time since his graduation in 1972. The first thing Wilson said, "I owe you an apology for having made you run so hard in DMR that Friday knowing that you had to qualify in the Sprint Medley and run the final the next day." Chris responded in his usual humble style "in retrospect, not being a true half-miler, I would have been outkicked anyway by the South Carolina runner who was a true half-miler."

But Chris still wonders why Jumbo chose him to anchor that team. All these years later, it is clear to me why Jumbo made this choice. Chris was his strongest "horse," second only to Liquori. He evaluated his stable of runners and distributed them where they best fit. He could use a couple of freshmen such as Nagy and myself on the Four Mile Relay with Liquori as anchor—he did not need Chris there. He needed Liquori to assure wins in the DMR, the Four Mile and the Two Mile relays. That left the Sprint Medley. And who was his strongest half-miler at the time, someone who could run four races? None other than Chris Mason.

There is, however one unanswerable question. Despite Liquori's heroic runs and unassailable record at the Penn Relays, he was never named Performer of the Meet. Was the resentment among the University of Pennsylvania Ivy League brass that pronounced regarding Villanova, Jumbo Elliott, and his astonishing record? Or perhaps it was payback time from Jim Tuppeny to Marty Liquori. In speaking with Marty, he informed me that he originally accepted a University of Pennsylvania scholarship offer in 1967, much to the great delight of Tuppeny, who had just begun his coaching career at this Ivy League school. What a coup that would have been for "Tupp" to recruit an athlete of Liquori's calibre. But Marty changed his mind and went with Jumbo Elliott and Villanova instead. Perhaps that change of mind remained all too fresh in Tuppeny's mind and what might have been.

Just three weeks later, the 1971 track season was about to witness what track aficionados call the best mile race ever run in the United States. It took place on Sunday, May 16, 1971, at Franklin Field. Once again it was a Liquori-Ryun showdown. Two years had passed since they'd last met—Liquori now carried the mantle of the world's number one miler. But the "retired" Ryun was back. Resuming training in the fall of 1970, we heard firsthand accounts from Brian McElroy about how well Ryun's training was progressing. In early 1971, Ryun tested his fitness indoors and promptly tied the world indoor record for the mile in 3:56.4. Clearly, he was fit and ready for more.

That "more" came with the second hosting of the Martin Luther King Games founded by Bert Lancaster. Heralded the "Dream Mile," it featured world record holder Jim Ryun set in 1967 vs. the 1969 number one ranked miler in the world, Marty Liquori. It was truly the best vs. the best—the era of the epic contest, taking place just four months after the monumental heavy-weight battle between Mohammed Ali vs. Joe Frazier—the former world champion against the new world champion. The best vs. the best—like War Admiral against Sea Biscuit; the Triple Crown Winner vs. the "pretender" in the Match Race of the Century, in 1938.

The sports world was all atwitter. This was a match made in heaven—the best possible match-up you could ever imagine. The tension was building each day as sports writers hunted down both Ryun and Liquori, looking for new angles, new stories. It was West vs. East; the quintessentially "good" small town against the big "bad" city; the shy country boy vs. the cocky city tough guy. It was the military-styled Bob Timmons vs. the sophisticated businessman Jumbo Elliott. Any difference or contrast that could be found, was mined, refined, accentuated, and exacerbated.

Back on campus, exams were over and the only ones left were the track team who still had several meets to prepare for. We could feel the rising tension. We had never seen Liquori so aloof, lost in his thoughts. His usual banter, quick retort, and swagger went amiss. We all knew it was best to leave him alone.

The weather that week was great—the temperatures were warm, and our workouts were going very well. On Wednesday, we ran a time trial half-mile in the low 1:50s on the beat-up cinders. It felt easy. By Thursday, several of us decided to slip away to the Jersey Shore for a brief respite. We ran, played whiffle ball, relaxed, but most of all, we talked about the upcoming race. Could Liquori take Ryun again? Was Ryun back to his old form? How would the race progress? Who would make the first move? Views were split on who would win.

Liquori beats Ryun for the first time in 1969: NCAA Mile

Then came Sunday May 16th. What had been a splendid week of weather, suddenly dissipated. Shockingly, the day greeted us with a bitter cool wind and intermittent rain. Instead of the usual temperatures in the low 80s, it was barely 50 degrees Fahrenheit. We could not believe it. Dressed as if it was a cool fall day, we shuffled into Franklin Field and settled into the usual northwest "Villanova" corner, to endure the meet (and the weather) in progress, not paying much attention, nor for that matter able to recall a single event. We were there for one reason: to see the Dream Mile. Finally, the call came. The runners gathered at the starting line surrounded by more photographers than were present at the Olympic Games. The field included Byron Dyce, Joe Savage, Morgan Mosser, Denis Fikes, Sam Bair, Reggie McAfee, and a couple of Villanova teammates: Davey Wright and Brian McElroy. Ryun and Liquori were positioned side by side in lane one. And would you believe, a false start? At last, a clean start and immediately you could sense that the pace was slow. Joe Savage, the Manhattan freshman, led as they passed the first lap in 61 seconds. Liquori was in fourth and Ryun was near the back of the pack. Nothing much changed for the next half lap and then Ryun started to move steadily to the front. But it was still slow. Liquori moved behind Ryun and the timer yelled out the half mile split—2:03. 2:03! What were they doing? That would be a time for a high school race.

But wait. You could see Ryun gradually picking up the pace. And then to our (and everyone's surprise), at the top of the back stretch, a full 750 yards from the finish, Liquori burst into the lead. What was he doing? This was his big move and he was making it early. Really early. We could not believe our eyes. Now everyone was standing fully focused on just two runners. Those last 750 yards became a flat-out race between two great milers. Every step of the way.

Liquori was flying. His beautiful smooth stride being matched step for step by the more upright angular gait of Ryun. The ¾ mile split came in three minutes flat—a 57 second lap (maybe slightly faster). It was now truly a two-man race. The rest of the field lingered far behind and were forgotten. Down the backstretch. Liquori led Ryun into the final turn. Then coming off the turn, Ryun moved up to Liquori's shoulder and pulled even. Liquori looked ever so slightly to his right and dug deep one more time. He edged slightly ahead, and it was shoulder to shoulder down the entire stretch. Finally, the slightest amount of daylight appeared and Liquori squeezed ahead. He had won. The time 3:54.6 meant that the last half had been run in a blazing 1:51. The crowd was breathless. Such a contest had never before been seen. The remaining runners straggled to the finish line like forgotten bystanders.

The Dream Mile was over. But what made this race so special was the intensity and the length of the battle that had been fought. Many mile races will see a front runner move steadily away from the field with the matter being settled early; or a runner making a big move from 500 meters out and lead all alone; or a sprint finish with the real racing taking place over the last 250 yards or the last straightaway. This had been a full-out 750-yard battle. And Liquori had done it once again, beating Ryun for the third time (plus one dead heat). Each time he found a way to outrace a runner who seemed unbeatable. Each time he took the "sting" out of Ryun's feared kick. Liquori was now undisputedly the best miler in the world.

All these years later Marty Liquori now expresses a more philosophical and reflective perspective. Could he have run faster? Probably. In retrospect, the world record was within reach. On May 17, 1975, Marty ran a 3:52.2 mile, second to Filbert Bayi, who did indeed break the world record that day with a time of 3:51.0. He muses that the American college system, Villanova included, implicitly focused on indoors, outdoors, dual meets, relays—all in all, a great deal of racing that required one to be in competitive shape for months on end. As he traveled abroad, talked with most if not all the world leading milers, he could see that the intense competitive approach characteristic of the United States, was not what other countries were following. Fewer races, breaking training into distinct blocks would have made for even higher quality performances. And perhaps less injuries, which were the bane to his career, particularly at critical times.

The Liquori-Mason era deepened an already rich track history at Villanova. First, Jumbo knew from the very outset that recruiting Marty Liquori was a game changer. And indeed, it was. Liquori demonstrated that a Villanova runner could be number one in the world. But he also showed that a runner with a better time could be beaten. Everyone had their weaknesses—it was a case of knowing your

The Dream Mile 1971: Marty Liquori finishes in glowing style

strengths and applying it to those weaknesses. With clinical precision, Liquori would take apart the world record holder time after time.

Secondly, Jumbo was willing to take a chance. On the basis of a mere letter and a set of press clippings, he'd brought Chris Mason on board. And what an addition. Mason's work ethic amplified the team spirit and commitment already present. His consistent hard work, high-quality performances combined with the care and attention he paid to the other athletes, me included, was invaluable. Chris's unassuming and selfless style truly made a difference.

Finally, the Jumbo relay formula of three strong runners and one superstar proved unbeatable—it started with Delany, Jenkins, Carrol, further proven with Patrick, Murphy, James, and now Liquori. The graduation of James in 1970 and then the subsequent loss of the Penn Relays Mile Relay in 1971 also meant that future wins in this event were no longer assured. And with the middle-distance powerhouses of Liquori and Mason now about to graduate, who would step up and take on the leadership mantle next?

6

Hartnett-Schappert: A New Generation Takes the Lead

"My job was simple. Have three great teammates to give you the baton in the lead and just keep it there."

John Hartnett

"Overbrook, Meryan,[1] Wyndwood…Ardmore, Rosemont…?? Nova, St. David's, Wayne…." The exhausted and completely disoriented young Irishman cocked his already strained hearing in the direction of the exceedingly indifferent train conductor. Somewhere in that indiscernible blur of station names, he prayed there was a "Villanova." But that was far from certain. Or clear. He had no idea what the conductor with his thick South Philadelphia accent was saying. Finally, he drew the courage to ask and directed his quiet Cork-accented inquiry as best he could. "Is Villanova on this line?"

"Yes," he was told, "two more stops."

It had been an incredible journey—everything that could go wrong had gone wrong. It started with the departure from Shannon Airport in the west of Ireland. No sooner had the aircraft left the ground than it sucked a bird into one of the jet engines. That meant an immediate return to the airport, landing just in time before it seized up entirely. "Good thing my mother didn't see this happen!" He thought, "She would be worried sick."

And then came the delays. One hour turned into three. Then it was announced that the aircraft could not be repaired. That was after another six hours. Finally, another aircraft from Dublin was summoned and the anxious young man along with 130 other exhausted passengers set off across the Atlantic, more than twelve hours behind schedule, for JFK Airport, Long Island.

Yes, John Hartnett the farm boy from Ballyhooly, County Cork was on his way to Villanova University. Little did he know that he would be the next great Irish miler to leave a legacy at the school that had become such an icon in the hearts and minds of aspiring Irish schoolboys. Afterall, while he was an accomplished cross-country runner, track was almost secondary. Yes, a few three mile runs on the track here and there. But certainly not the mile. And to be sure at this very moment, the mile was furthest thing from his mind. All he could think about were the sad looks of his family as they waved goodbye, thinking they might never see him again.

Meanwhile, at JFK, the designated pickup man Billy McLaughlin, from Yonkers—a Villanova junior and one of New York City's leading high school runners in 1968—had lost hope. There was no information and no sign that any flight was to arrive from Ireland. Billy returned to Yonkers and was long "between the sheets" before the designated flight even left Ireland. So much for a greeting party.

Ken Schappert to John Hartnett 1973 while Dave Wottle watches

On his arrival at JFK, John somehow made it to Penn Central Station, thanks to an Irish priest he had met on the flight. From there he found the train to Philadelphia. But that was not the end. It meant climbing out of one train at the 30th Street Station and then finding the right commuter line—one of many choices in a busy train station. The final leg of the journey was the Main Line—and now at last, he was approaching the legendary Villanova University a full two days after his scheduled arrival. No one knew where he was. And he knew no one at Villanova knew him (except his fellow Corkman Donal Walsh, who was not scheduled to arrive for a few days). Everyone was just a name on paper or a muffled voice on a bad phone connection on the only phone available to him located some two miles from the farm—an outdoor phone booth located in the center of Ballyhooly.

It was September 1970 and John Hartnett had finally arrived. He was the most unlikely of freshman. He had already passed his 19th birthday, but no one (except Jumbo) knew that he had left school at the age of 15 to work on his uncle's dairy farm. Jumbo the ultimate salesman, assuaged the worries of the Dean of Admissions with his usual no-nonsense style. He simply said: "Not to worry. His school records were lost in a fire. He'll do just fine."

Fortunately, Jumbo's reputation for selecting outstanding athletes, almost in all cases excellent students, had been firmly established. But John was totally unaware of the internal "arrangement." The prospect of being a student at an American university, not to mention this school fabled for the Irish, thanks to Ron Delany, terrified him.

John's credentials were noteworthy indeed: Irish Junior Cross-Country Champion; winner of the European Junior Cross-Country Championships in 1970; fourth in those same championships in 1969, which were won by England's Dave Bedford who had in the meantime become the world record holder for the 10,000 meters. There was no question that this kid from rural Ireland could run. And thanks to Donal Walsh from Cork City, some 30 kilometers distant in the home country, now a Villanova sophomore and a prodigious cross-country runner in his own right, the connection had been established.

John grew up on the family dairy farm just south of Ballyhooly. It was like one of hundreds of dairy farms in County Cork as well as across Ireland. Like many Irish families, life was hard. And money was scarce. At the age of 15, John started working at his uncle's farm. The days were long and full: early morning milking; cleaning and feeding chores; the evening milking; and the seasonal routine of seeding in the spring, haying in the summer, harvesting grain in the fall. Day in. Day out. Work until 9 p.m. And little to no hope or change in sight.

Somehow John found the opportunity and the motivation to run. A local club, the Grange Fermoy Athletic Club, and Sunday competitions provided some relief from his daily duties. First some local races, then the County Championships. Then the All-Irelands. Though he had little time to train, with his light frame, his ease of movement, and most of all, his fierce determination, he began to taste success. And that taste raised the ante for more success. The fourth-place finish in the spring of 1969 at the European Junior Cross-Country Championships in Edinburgh behind the winner Dave Bedford crystallized his goals. Now only one finishing position would satisfy him.

But the long days of hard work and squeezing in late night workouts led to injury that fall of 1969. He could not run for several weeks. And time was running out.

Fortunately, he recovered, and his coach knew enough about running to suggest fast track to regain fitness. No time to build a base. Speed endurance all the way. Repeat 200 meters. That would be the formula.

Repeat 200s. At least three times a week. But not on a manicured track in the full light of day. No, John had a full day's work to put in first. And milking was not done until 8 p.m. at the earliest. And Ireland in winter sees the darkness fall early and hard. It's pitch black by 5 p.m. The only solution was to run the 200s on the pasture—on the most even ground he could find near the family farmhouse. And with the help of two lanterns—one at each end of the field. At 9 p.m. at night. "The first night I ran 14 repeats. I was beat. A week later I hit 20 and couple of weeks later I did 30. When I came in that evening, my sister saw me smiling. I was the happiest man in Ireland—I knew I was getting in shape."

In short order John won the County Championships, then the All-Irelands and then off to Vichy, France for the European Juniors to claim the goal that he set out one year prior. Simply put, John charged to the lead and cleaned up—the first Irish junior to win this prestigious event. Suddenly he was an international star. His photo appeared in *Athletics Weekly.* And he was on Jumbo's radar thanks to Donal Walsh.

Meanwhile, that week in September, on 181st Street, Bronx, New York, a young Ken Schappert packed his bags to start his Villanova career. He could not be more excited. He had no idea who would be joining him and little did he know that an Irish recruit from Ballyhooly was passing through New York City at that precise moment. And the differences between the Bronx and Ballyhooly could not be greater. In Ken's case, more people lived within five miles of his home than the entire population of Ireland. And he would see more cars pass by on the streets over a period of 30 minutes than John would see in the County Cork countryside over an entire year.

To say that Ken was an active kid would be an understatement. He was always moving, playing games, looking for trouble, and at times, causing trouble. Like many kids in the Bronx, he played many made-up games mainly because they either played in a school yard or in the streets fighting traffic and parked cars. "We played a lot of stick ball, basketball, and softball. Handball was another game … that was played often. All you needed was a wall, some chalk to make the lines and you had a game." And follow baseball. While other boys across the United States and Canada like myself would be following the mighty Yankees (Mickey Mantle, Roger Maris, Whitey Ford) on the radio, Ken and his friends could literally hear the cheers from Yankee Stadium, just a few blocks away.

And he was quick. In the fourth grade, Ken won a 50-yard and a 220-yard dash, which at the time he thought of the 220 as a distance race. He was not only fast on his feet, but he was also quick with his wit. No matter the comment made, Ken's lightening response would catch everyone off-guard, particularly the protagonist, who would often be left speechless. And it was usually funny. Very funny. But Ken had another critical skill—he knew the streets. He knew what smelled of trouble and what did not. Most importantly, he knew when to run and when to fight. Both, he did very well.

In grade nine, Ken attended Bishop Dubois, a Catholic High School located in Harlem. As he recalls: "I was one of the only two Caucasians who tried out for the track team. At five foot two inches, I was way too small for basketball, and we had no football team." But like Dave Patrick, it was not an easy start. Ken struggled with getting good grades. "Mom and Dad were paying tuition for me to go to Bishop Dubois, whereas my two brothers always went to public school. At a teacher meeting that year Mom said to one of the teachers who was the assistant track coach that if my grades didn't get better quickly, I was off the team. He begged her not to do that and worked with me to get my grades where they needed to be." Never shying from a challenge, Ken soon had the grades he needed and to allow him to purse the sport that he had fallen in love with.

A distance runner by the name of Tony Carrion, who had run 9:20 for a two-mile, took a liking to Ken and tucked him under his wing. Ken started doing workouts with him and by his sophomore year, his talent started to show; he broke two minutes in the half-mile and ran a sub 4:30 mile. Junior year he followed with a 1:55 half-mile and 4:20 mile. During the winter of 1970, Ken won two prestigious Eastern States races: the indoor 1,000 yards and the outdoor 880 yards in 1:51. Interestingly, New York City in the late '60s was replete with national-leading high school runners: Hector Ortiz, Dennis Fikes, Tony Colon, Mike Keogh, Brian McElroy, Marcel Philippe, Joe Savage, and the Lovette brothers.

His senior year was a big one. That spring, Ken joined the aforementioned group of elite runners: a 1:50.1 half-mile at the Glen Locks Memorial Games followed the same day with a 4:15 mile. Plus, a great run at the 1970 Penn Relays in the high school DMR which became an all-New York City affair. Ken, who had been selected to run the open mile chose to join his teammate Cliff Bruce, a 1:52 half-miler, instead. Ken recounts, "that race was huge for me. I ran one of the fastest anchor legs up to that time in 4:09 and we went from seventh to third behind Power Memorial with Tony Colon, and Rice High School with Denis Fikes."

Now the question of what college to attend? With all those great New York City and North Jersey high school runners, the competition was intense. Fred Dwyer had just taken over as Coach at Manhattan College. He was intent on building a program that would rival Villanova and gained favour with Joe Savage, Tony Colon and Mike Keough. And Freddy didn't stop there. He recruited Cliff Bruce as well. Ken was devastated. "We were best buds and always talked about going to college together. When Dwyer recruited him over me, I was heartbroken." From that day forward, Ken was determined to kick Manhattan ass and show Freddy that he chose the wrong guy.

But Villanova was not Ken's first choice. The University of Tennessee was interested and offered him the usual campus tour. It was off to Knoxville via Atlanta. But who should Ken meet in the Atlanta airport terminal when transferring to his Knoxville flight? None other than Jumbo Elliott and the entire Villanova Track Team on route for the annual Tennessee-Villanova Dual meet. Less than 20 minutes into the flight, Jumbo invited Ken to come up front and sit with him. They got along famously and after his Penn Relays performance a few weeks later, Ken Schappert was on his way to Villanova.

John Hartnett and Ken Schappert joined two other freshmen recruits that fall: Les Nagy from Youngstown, Ohio and me from Owen Sound, Ontario, Canada—both 4:09 milers. Word quickly spread that a major Villanova-Manhattan rivalry was in the making. But that was far from the minds of this group at the time. The newly-arrived freshmen found their surroundings and the setting to be a big change from where they had each come from. There was a lot to adjust to. John faced the prospect of going back to school for the first time in four years—a university at that. And Ken, the inner-city kid, described the beauty of the campus and the mansions located on the running loops as a "completely different world." Add to that adjustment, the diversity he found on the team: Irish, English, Canadian, West Virginian, Jersey, Pennsylvania, Maryland ... all very different from the neighborhood he'd grown up in.

Then the daily routine: breakfast; classes; five miles in the morning; lunch; more classes; eight to 10 miles or a track workout in the afternoon; dinner; the library; the pie shoppe; and finally, bedtime. Some days may have differed somewhat, but most days were much the same. Then to the boards for the indoor season; a few freshmen two mile relays; and the occasional individual race. There were flashes of brilliance for Hartnett, such as his second place IC4A freshman cross-country finish behind a surging Bob Wheeler from Duke who had run a 4:10 mile in high school; making the team that won the NCAA Cross-Country Championships when Donal Walsh chased a dying Steve Prefontaine to capture second place; and an 8:16 indoor 3,000 meters in Madison Square Garden. Meanwhile Ken showed his speed and his tenacity by running the quarter on both the IC4A and NCAA indoor mile relay teams after having a solid cross-country season.

And Penn Relays 1971? John was the only freshman recruit that did not run that year when freshmen were first eligible to compete. Nagy, Schappert, and Bouma were all part of winning teams. But sitting in the stands as a spectator was the first time that John realized the importance of Penn Relays to Villanova: "Up until then, I didn't have a clue what they were or what they meant. But watching the teams and watching Jumbo and reading the Philly papers, you just knew that this was a big deal."

Penn Relays 1972

The year 1972 brought with it a change of season. Frank Dolson described it as "the year that Penn Relays came back to Earth." [2] There were no big stars left at Villanova. Marty Liquori had graduated. And Chris Mason, the reliable workhorse, was gone. And no heir apparent.

IC4A 1972 Cross-Country Championship with John Hartnett and Donal Walsh in the lead

The press predicted that the Villanova era at Penn was over. *The Courier-Post*[3] (Camden, New Jersey) forecasted that Villanova was in grave danger of losing every championship race. A win every year since 1955 including three five-win sweeps. And the six DMRs in a row was also in jeopardy. With no Liquori or Mason, who would step up now? Davey Wright, the promising 4:03 miler as an 18-year-old, now a senior but going nowhere fast, went from one injury and setback to another. Nagy was injured. Bouma was on the sidelines after undergoing orthopedic surgery to remove bone spurs in his ankle. And now McElroy came down with a sudden injury the week prior.

But Jumbo played his cards close to his chest. He knew that though the team lacked experience, it did not lack guts. When it came to the DMR, the all-important first race, it would be Ken Schappert leading off, Greg Govan running the quarter, Tom Gregan, the latest Irishman to arrive at Villanova handling the ¾ mile; and John Hartnett on the anchor. This time, Villanova was not the favorite. Duke University would be anchored by Bob Wheeler—the 1971 NCAA Indoor 1,000-yard champion and second to Liquori in 3:59.9 at the Outdoor

NCAA Championships. And the University of Pennsylvania had a stacked team including Dennis Fikes and Karl Thornton—both men were getting dangerously close to sub four-minute mile territory.

Tom Gregan, the newest man on the team, added to the Irish pipeline joining the team that previous September. In 1971 at the age of 18, he caught the attention of the track world by running 3.43.5 - 1500 meters at the British AAAs. Only one person had run faster at that age—that was the great Jim Ryun. Now with a few months of America under his belt he asked, "Mr. Pyrah, are the Penn Relays important?" Pyrah's jaw dropped as he could not believe what he was hearing: "Important? You better ask Jumbo that question!"[4] Not only did Gregan not know much about Penn Relays, but the whole experience was also totally new: "I was overwhelmed by all the activities outside the stadium with all the vendors selling stuff. The crowds were immense, and I had to figure out where to find a place to go and warm up for my race and not be late trying to get back into the stadium for the race."

Schappert led off with a solid 1:51.2 half mile and in his usual gutsy style handing off in the lead to Govan with both Penn and Duke in hot pursuit. The Penn runner Bruce Collins ran a blazing 46.4 to take the lead as Govan passed in second place to the rookie Gregan: "My number one goal was not to mess up the baton exchange with Govan running at great speed—that exchange area was just a crazy place to be. But the first 10 yards into the race I settled down to business. Running for Villanova in the Distance Medley, we knew our team was respected and I made sure that no one on the track during the race was going to push me around or interfered with the change-over." Gregan lived up to his billing and ran a brilliant 2.55.5 behind Penn's Denis Fikes who maintained the lead throughout. Now it was up "to the two-miler" John Hartnett to go to work.

The University of Pennsylvania team had long yearned to beat Villanova at the Penn Relays. They had not won a race since 1961 and with the addition of Jim Tuppeny as coach in 1967, also the Penn Relays Director, the former Villanova assistant coach wanted nothing more than to show up Jumbo and those annoying Villanova runners. We did not know at the time that Tuppeny thought he had Liquori locked up on a scholarship and losing him to Jumbo hurt then and it still hurt. Now Karl Thornton embodied all that pent-up desire and frustration and took off. With Tuppeny yelling, "Slow down," he barreled on running 56 seconds for the first lap, reaching the half in 1:57. This suited John perfectly because he knew only one thing: run hard. By the third lap, Thornton was tiring, and John made his move. He knew full well that Wheeler was not far behind. Wheeler kept closing but it was too late for the Duke anchor. Hartnett, whose nickname was "The Duke," held him off with a 4:03 mile, his fastest yet. Wheeler's 3:59 had closed the gap to just two strides passing Thornton in the process who faded to fourth as Manhattan took third. But our Villanova Duke had beaten a pressing Wheeler Duke, although to be clear, there was precious little room between them.

With a rookie freshman, two unproven sophomores, and a senior, Villanova had done it. Another win for the Distance Medley Relay, and not only a win, but a new meet record—the time of 9:35.9 beating the old mark of 9:37.5 also set by Villanova in 1968. Jumbo was ecstatic: "Honestly, I was surprised … I never thought we had a chance, but the kids were great."[5] He had actually gone on record saying that Villanova would not win anything that year. But Jumbo had delivered his magic one more time. The *Philadelphia Daily News* reported it this way: "Elliott making the habit of making the right moves at the proper time. The new crew had proven him right!"[6]

With the winning streak still in hand (seven straight DMRs and a win every year since 1955), the main event on Saturday was still to come. First, the Four Mile Relay. And what an eclectic team: all foreigners—three Micks and a Limey. First came Donal Walsh followed by Davey Wright—a study of opposites. Donal the feisty Cork City man loved to mix things up, playing the hardnose hood, as he cast the aura of an IRA insider at a time when the "troubles" were escalating.[7] He was as tough a lad as you would find. But he was a cross-country runner and a three-miler and more accurately, a six-miler. On a good day, Donal would be pressed to break 60 seconds for a quarter mile. On the other hand, Dave Wright or "Gall Blimey" as we would call him, was erudite, reclusive, and eccentric as only a Brit from Newcastle could be. On occasion, we would see Davey standing on Lancaster Avenue opposite the Field House, book in one hand, a cup of tea in the other, a shawl fashionably wrapped around his neck, hitchhiking all the while reading a novel.

I remember clearly a highly spirited and almost violent exchange between Donal and Davey in the locker room over British incursions in Ireland. It came very close to blows as an infuriated Davey slammed his locker in response to the snarly rapid-fire attacks from the surly Corkman. Now the two national prototypes—one Irish, one English—were joined as Four Mile Relay team members. This time Jumbo decided that his young four-minute equivalent miler should anchor and the two-miler Hartnett, would run the third leg.

But where was Davey? It was 12:30 p.m. and an exasperated Jumbo started to roar. Red faced and flailing at Mr. Pyrah, Jumbo released a string of invectives that would shame the most hardened navy officer. The race was one hour away, and Davey Wright was nowhere to be found. Chris Mason, to be sure the only spectator in Franklin Field with eight Penn Relays' watches, reported that Davey was supposed to meet him at 11:30 a.m. on campus. But he had not shown up, so Chris had left without him. Mr. Pyrah rolled his eyes and said, "He's a 4.0 student, but when it comes to catching a ride or the train, who knows?" Then at 12:50 p.m., Davey walked in—in a foul mood and in a New York Athletics Club (NYAC) sweat suit. His gear was still in Mason's room. "But I left the door open!" said Chris. Then Gregan disappeared. Jumbo raged again but at 1:17 p.m., with 13 minutes to spare, he suddenly re-emerged. Meanwhile from somewhere, a set of Villanova racing shorts and a singlet for Davey was found and with 10 minutes to spare, the team reported to the paddock. Jumbo looked like a man just released from a cage.

Ken Schappert takes over

The first three legs were relatively uneventful. Walsh, Wright, and Hartnett all did their job—staying with the leaders and at some points, even leading. Finally, Hartnett gave Gregan a 20-yard lead. But the inexperienced Gregan seeing himself as the next Jim Ryun, thought a wait and kick strategy would win the day. And it was all going so well until the last lap. As Penn, Villanova, Manhattan, and Duke dawdled for three laps passing the ¾ mile mark in 3:16, we all knew that a storm was brewing. This could be trouble. Then the storm burst. Wheeler took off like a shot and was not to be caught. Thornton died a little less this time, and Gregan scrambled in disbelief finishing in third place. No watches for Villanova as Bob Wheeler expounded to the press: "We finally cracked the Wildcats!"[8]

Later that afternoon came the Two Mile Relay. This time, Schappert was called to anchor. Following Rick Kell, Billy McLaughlin, and Wilson Smith, Ken received the stick in fifth place, a good 35 yards back of the leader Willie Thomas with the University of Tennessee. By the end of the first lap and a blazing 49 seconds later, Ken had passed all four anchormen and took the lead running as hard as he possibly could. As he passed Willie Thomas on the backstretch, he remembered some advice he had heard: "If his head is leaning to the left, pass. If his head is leaning to the right, watch out." Too late! His head was leaning to the right and Ken passed him anyway. Then came the final straight. Unfortunately, Ken's opening quarter caught up to him and the hard charging Willie Thomas beat him to the line. Upon reflection, Ken recalls: "This was one of my worst defeats while attending Villanova University! I felt so bad that I lost that race; you could not imagine. A few minutes after the race Jumbo comes up to me laughing with that cackle of his saying it was the gutsiest race ever!"

Thus ended, Penn Relays 1972. Only one Championship of America Relay for Villanova. But it was the DMR—the seventh win in a row. And two new stars were born—one from the Bronx and one from Ballyhooly—both with two more years to show what they could really do.

Penn Relays 1973

The 1972/73 school year began quietly for the Villanova track team. The year 1972 was of course the Olympic year—the ill-fated Munich Games that went down in history as a great tragedy. Ironically, the Germans hoped to present the country and the event as the paragon of restoration and happiness post the savagery of WWII. Unfortunately, and sadly, these goals were far from realized.

Hartnett made the Irish team running the 5,000 meters. But it did not go well for him and he failed to move beyond the qualifying heats. Meanwhile Schappert ran 1:47.6 – 880 yards that June and qualified for the US Olympic Trials but did not make the final.

In 1972 a capped Dave Wottle[9] rose from being an obscure Ohio-based unknown to run an electrifying Olympic 800-meter final. Passing the bell in last place, Wottle ran the exact same pace for each 200 meters. He started passing on the backstretch and steadily worked his way through the entire field as all the other runners were actually slowing down. With 10 meters to go, the number one ranked Russian Yevhen Arzhanov remained between Wottle and the lead. Then in the final meter, Wottle edged ahead by a whisker with a time of 1.45.86. The gold medal was his and Dave Wottle complete with his now famous cap, became an international star.

The exuberance of that September 2nd win by Wottle, and the games themselves, were completely subsumed by the tragedy that took place just three days later. For all of us who were so deeply invested in the sport, the Black September hostage taking and the death of the eleven Israeli athletes, was an unspeakable disaster. It cast a pall on the sport. We all returned a few days later to Villanova in a somber mood. John Hartnett had lived through the entire unfolding of the tragedy—he was even more quiet than usual. Gregan was putting in the miles hoping that

1973 would deliver a better outcome for his mile aspirations than the previous season. But a new spark had arrived—a young spirited Eamonn Coghlan from Dublin, Ireland. Delighted to be at Villanova, Eamonn could not wait to tear up the cross-country paths and take on the track world. (Much more about Eamonn in the next chapter.)

Nevertheless, there were highlights. In January 1973, we were visited by two of England's most accomplished runners: Brendan Foster who had finished fifth in the Olympic 1500-meter final; and Ian Stewart—the bronze medalist in the 5,000 meters, who had out-leaned a fading Steve Prefontaine after his courageous push over the last mile of that race. Brendan and Ian were delightful company. I was still nursing a sore foot now 11 months after surgery and could not join John as he hosted the Brits for a "nice" run that sunny afternoon. They chose the Tennis Court loop. Waiting at the Field House, I had barely walked to the weight room, pushed a few bench presses, gone for a drink of water from the trusty fountain, and they were back. To be sure, that had to be the fastest Tennis Court run ever—8 ½ miles and 40 minutes later. John looked worked-over but had a satisfied look on his face. That might have been his best run over the course of the winter.

Schappert had a singular goal that indoor season: win the NCAA indoor half-mile. An audacious goal to be sure—he had his own teammate Brian McElroy to beat, not to mention Chicago's Mike Durkin and Marcel Philippe from Fordham, one of the top half milers in the United States and now an Olympian albeit for France. At Cobo Hall in mid-March, Jumbo told Ken "go with three laps to go and don't look back" (the half mile being 5 ½ laps). Ken did just that and while Durkin and Philippe were eyeing and elbowing each other, Ken bolted and ran away with the race finishing in 1:50.1, followed by Roger Chadwick from Nebraska in 1:53.0—almost a full 3 seconds back. Interestingly, that was the second fastest time ever run on that track—the fastest being Dave Patrick's world record of 1:48.9 in 1967.

Meanwhile, John Hartnett was putting in the miles. He had found his groove. His indoor results were nothing special but that was not his focus. Job one: getting strong. So began what I termed as the infamous Hartnett "Five Frolic Weekend"—the Frolic on Friday afternoon, twice on Saturday and twice on Sunday. With lots of sleep, additional naps, and multiple meals in between—the runs were smooth, consistent, and he seemed tireless.

Penn Relays 1973 presented a new challenger. This time, Bowling Green State University, home of the Olympic 800-meter champion Dave Wottle announced they were coming to town. Reading between the lines, one could only interpret this as an outright challenge—the opportunity to teach the Villanova Track Team a lesson. And they were going to do this in high drama: first run the Four Mile Relay at the Drake Relays (Des Moines, Iowa) the Friday before; and then immediately fly to Philadelphia to repeat that effort against Villanova on the Saturday. Schappert with his usual super-extroverted style, rubbed his hands together vigorously and gleefully erupted: "We are going to kick some butt." Hartnett grinned and nodded agreement. But you could tell he was not yet so confident. But first the Distance Medley Relay on Friday needed to be taken care of.

John Hartnett "Running in the Rain" 1973

Friday was one of those miserable spring days in Philadelphia. Tom Cushman described Franklin Field as the world's largest floating track and the anchorman should be a swimmer, not a runner.[10] But the DMR and its 3:15 p.m. start would not be delayed. Brian McElroy led off in the pouring rain with a 1:50.9 half and the lead; freshman Jack Garniewski ran a journeyman 48.6 quarter mile; then Schappert took over with a 2:58.4 ¾ mile handing John a 35-meter gap to the good. With Penn's Denis Fikes and Fordham's Marcel Phillipe in hot pursuit, Hartnett left no doubt—57; 1:58, 2:58. Phillippe went out in 55 seconds and seeing that little ground was being made, started to fade. With a lap to go, John was so far ahead that Cushman wrote "he could only be caught if he drowned!"[11] Hearing his teammates yell, "save yourself", John slowed to a 67 last lap and literally walked over the line with a 4:05 mile. Job done. Win number one. And the DMR streak now stood at eight consecutive wins.

When Hartnett was asked afterwards about the conditions, he just smiled and said "in Ireland I've run in much worse weather. I don't mind it at all." As the Wildcats toweled themselves dry, their thoughts turned quickly not to celebrations, but what lay ahead. Now for Saturday and the showdown with Dave Wottle and Bowling Green.

Saturday, April 28, 1973, was the day that the Villanova Four Mile Relay Team entered the world of celebrity. Dave Wottle and his Bowling Green teammates had just won the Drake Relays Four Mile Relay on the previous evening and were now here in Philadelphia to show Villanova how it was done. *Sports Illustrated* had sent their photographers and writers; the press including the *Philadelphia Inquirer, New York Times, Washington Post, Chicago Sun-Times* among 30 other newspapermen clambered close to the start line all eager to get a unique spin on the showdown. McElroy was quoted as saying, "We have to give Hartnett a 20-yard lead, at the very least."[12] Everyone knew that Wottle had speed and John did not. So, it was up to the cocky freshman from Dublin, Eamonn Coghlan, to get things started. This was his first Penn Relays, and he loved the excitement and the atmosphere. With a 4:09.9 effort, his best mile time ever, he handed a 25-yard lead to McElroy who was then caught by the Bowling Green's second man; they handed off one, two but Schappert let the Bowling Green runner do the work. The pace was easy and Schappert waited for two reasons: he was saving himself for the Two Mile Relay; and he knew he could out-kick this unsuspecting pretender whenever he wanted. With 300 yards to go, Ken exploded. His last lap, a scorching 53 seconds, opened up a 90-yard lead. The gap made for a great picture in Sports Illustrated—the Schappert-Hartnett exchange with a dejected Dave Wottle looking up the track as his own teammate was just entering the home stretch. John took off. It was 59, 2:01, 3:02 and the gap did not close. He finished with a 4:03.2.

Tom Gregan anchors with Bob Wheeler (Duke) and Greg Fredericks (Penn State)

Afterwards, Wottle lamented, "I didn't think they'd ever beat us by as much as they did." To this, Frank Dolson added this concluding remark: "But then again, he never heard one of Jumbo Elliott's Penn Relays pep talks."[13]

The race was not even close. Bowling Green proved to be paper tigers, finished 14 seconds back. The *Philadelphia Inquirer* wrote, "Villanova's four-mile relay team—looking very much like the early Beatles savors Penn Relays Victory."[14] Yes, the Beatles cum Villanova Four Mile Relay Team were front page news and with their good looks and brilliant athleticism, the fab four captured the hearts of young and old that day.

But the "Beatles" were not yet done. There was another set to play. Once more, Jumbo made one of his famous last-minute moves with his final selections for the Two Mile Relay. This time it was putting in the two-miler, now one-miler, John Hartnett as the leadoff man. He knew that John was on a roll, and this was a safe move. But before the race, it was bedlam in the small dressing room. Both Hartnett's and Schappert's spikes were missing. Fortunately, Ken borrowed a pair from Marty Liquori who had just stopped by. And John borrowed a size 11½ from a veritable stranger. And to Jumbo's prediction, John showed his steady hand and ran 1:53.7 for the half-mile (his fastest by far); Gregan followed with 1:52.1; McElroy with a 1:50.3; and finally, Schappert who finished the race off with a 1:49.6. This time he beat Willie Thomas, from Tennessee, whose head was leaning left by a good 25 yards—a very satisfying result. Villanova, who had been described before the meet as "washed up," had won three Championships of America. Villanova was back!

The 1973 track season was still young. John Hartnett knew that a sub four-minute mile was not far off. Sure enough, on May 12th in Raleigh, North Carolina he broke the magic barrier with a 3:58.3. After this race, John returned to the Villanova campus. Exams were over and the only ones on campus were a few track stragglers with lots of time on their hands. John used that opportunity to really put in the miles: five to seven in the morning; either 10 miles or a track workout in the afternoon; and then after dinner another easy three miles to finish off the day. One week in early June he totaled 140 miles; we were witnessing this in amazement. It seemed that the more miles John put in, the stronger he got. John was the type of runner that could run 100 miles a week, not do a stitch of speedwork and step on the track and run 60, two minutes, three minutes, four minutes—a four-minute mile like it was an afternoon jog. But now he was doing solid speed work as well.

Then it was off to Eugene, Oregon with no rest from those big mile weeks to where Steve Prefontaine and Dave Wottle had been working together to organize a fast mile race. Both were having issues with the AAU and plans for a European tour. They decided, "let's go for a world record here." That effort took place on June 20th at the fabled Hayward Field. The word got out and with short notice over 12,000 spectators packed the stadium. And to be sure, they got their full money's worth. What a fine race. Fast from the start, Prefontaine led Wottle for the first three laps. But just a step behind was Hartnett all the way. In the last lap, Wottle took over and finished in 3:53.3. In second was Prefontaine in 3:54.6. And there was Hartnett just a half-step behind in 3:54.7.

John Hartnett, the shy Irish cross-country runner had just entered "miler stratosphere." The number of sub 3:55 milers were few and here he was, now ranked the fifth fastest miler in the world in 1973. The Villanova track team without question had a bright future: a world class miler; a NCAA 880 champion; and a stable of top-class milers who were ready to take on the world. And we knew one more thing. It was just a matter of time before the world record of 3:51.1 would fall. If John could run a 3:54 while running between 120 to 140 miles a week and not even be a bona fide miler, just imagine what a miler (John included) could do.

Penn Relays 1974

A year in college, just like a year in life, goes by in a flash. The 1973/74 year picked up speed and the weeks were flying by. First the cross-country season. While the team included John Hartnett, Tom Gregan, Eamonn Coghlan, Steve Dorsey, and me at long last injury-free, John Hartnett was the only serious contender. He won the IC4As convincingly.

That season was Schappert's turn for injury, and it forced him to the sidelines. Two months later at the Olympic Invitational at the Nassau Coliseum, Long Island, the first indoor meet, John dropped an 8:26.0 two-mile, which proved to be the fastest time in the world for the entire season. Then in Cleveland, on February second, the rapidly improving (and cocky) Coghlan with his mid-calf length striped red and white socks, took on Dave Wottle, only losing by inches in the mile. Both were clocked in 4.03.9. Coghlan started grinning at the end of the race, signaling there's a lot more yet to come. Unfortunately, Schappert's injury persisted, and it became evident that his entire year would be lost.

One week later, John Hartnett was invited to compete at the Toronto Star Indoor Games—the one mile proved to be a crack field including the 1972 Olympic champion, Pekka Vasala from Finland, John Walker from New Zealand who two weeks earlier broke the world outdoor record for the 1500 meters with a 3:32.4 second only to the new world record holder, Filbert Bayi—3:32.2; and

Marty Liquori, the number one ranked miler in the world in 1971. Taking his usual nap that afternoon, John woke up feeling dreadful. It was one of those too long naps when you wake up feeling both groggy and disoriented. A few hours later, he lined up for the start feeling a bit better but knowing full well that the very best in the world stood to his left and to his right. And they had speed to spare. After a steady first half in two minutes, John made the only move that he had—go to front and push. With five laps to go, he took over and ran for his life. No one responded and John broke away becoming the first person in Canada to crack the four-minute mile barrier indoors with a 3:59.6. Byron Dyce, the perennially competitive runner from New York City was a full second back in 4:00.8; followed by Walker in 4:01.3; Liquori in 4:02.2 and Vasala in fifth with a 4:02.6. John Hartnett had just beaten the best in the world. He returned to campus with his usual low-key humble attitude, but you could tell in his eyes that he knew now anything was possible.

John Hartnett leads world class field: Bryon Dyce, Pekka Vasala, Dave Wottle, and John Walker

Two weeks later at the IC4A Championships, a two-day competition, Villanova ended the first day with zero points. Manhattan College and the ever-abrasive Fred Dwyer were poised to repeat the championship the team had won in 1973. Then the most amazing thing happened. Jumbo described it, as I recall, this way: "It was like taking the scattered pieces of a puzzle on a table, throwing them on the floor and having them all end up in place." First John Hartnett won the two mile in 8:32.2 with Kevin McCarey in third; then Tom Gregan ran the gutsiest race of his season and won the mile in 4:00.6; then Eamonn Coghlan, not wanting to end the Irish winning streak, won the half mile in 1:51.7; then the Distance Medley with Phil Kane, Greg Eckman, myself, and John Hartnett (in that order) took another first. Meanwhile a fourth-place finish in the Two Mile Relay (George Mackay, Charlie McCarthy, Tom Gregan, and Eamonn Coghlan) gave Villanova a total of 29 points. No one saw this coming. Manhattan College could only come up with 27 points. They were not happy. We had fun celebrating—it came as a complete surprise and were joined by the injured Ken Schappert who was perhaps the happiest person on our entire team. We had beaten those "Manhattan" guys who had overlooked him four years prior and he was simply delighted.

A week later, our team of seven athletes headed off to Detroit for the Indoor NCAAs. We were a modest group and had a lot to be modest about. John won the two mile in 8:33.6. But the rest of the performances were rather un-noteworthy—we finished fifth in the DMR with a 9:52.7 (Jerry Bouma, Greg Eckman, Eamonn Coghlan, John Hartnett), and that was about it. Eamonn did run the fastest leg for the ¾ mile with a 2:56, but neither he nor Gregan ran well enough in their respective individual races to score any points for the team.

April loomed on the doorstep and time to get ready for Penn Relays. As usual, the sailing was anything but smooth. This time Hartnett experienced a mild case of sciatica and had to take a couple of weeks off in the middle of April. Jumbo was coy about the readiness of the team. But Coghlan, Gregan, McElroy, Bouma, and McCarey were all healthy. Jim Tuppeny predicted that the competition for the 1974 version was the best yet and he predicted several records would fall.

Penn Relays week at Villanova is a time of the mystic, mystery, and nerves all mixed with the alchemy of the most successful coach in track history. Who is injured? Who is running well? Who has the guts no-matter what? What brew will Jumbo stir this year?

Having been a non-contender for two years, I was eager to be part of that mix once again. But Jumbo had several proven horses: John Hartnett, coming through time and time again, and of course, now a 3:54 miler; Eamonn Coghlan, now knocking on four minutes for the mile—not afraid of anyone; Tom Gregan had run four flat indoors and was itching to run faster; and Brian McElroy, good for a 4:03 to 4:05 mile any day of the week simply on his pure talent. I knew I was capable of a 4:05 mile or better but I also knew how the decisions were made. Jumbo was the ultimate risk manager, and he would allocate his resources accordingly. So, the DMR team would be McElroy, Coghlan, Hartnett, and our freshman quarter miler Greg Eckman; the Four Mile Relay would be Gregan, McElroy, Coghlan, and Hartnett, four proven, experienced milers—how do you better that team? But I was given the opportunity to anchor the Sprint Medley. I finally got another chance to make my second Penn Relays' appearance.

The *Philadelphia Inquirer* said of the Penn Relays 1974 that it was "the oldest and largest track meet [facing] change, but Villanova goes on forever."[15] This time Team Villanova set another meet record with a time of 9:36.8, almost a full second faster than the mark set two years ago. Once again, the team looked unbeatable—McElroy with a 1:50.9, Eckman running a 47.9 quarter, Coghlan showing his ability with a 2:55.8, and Hartnett with a 4:02.2 mile. Little did the press know that one week earlier, John Hartnett struggled with a hip injury and could only manage a 4:15 mile at the Queen's Iona Relays. Jumbo referred to him as a walking corpse not three days earlier. But his courage prevailed. And win number one—the ninth consecutive DMR. Things were starting to look good.

That Friday afternoon there was still one more race, albeit a qualifier—the Sprint Medley Relay. Here's how the *Philadelphia Bulletin* reported it. "Now for the irony of all this. While the heart of Elliott's great distance corps braces to tough-out another triple, the possibility of a fourth championship suddenly surfaced. Villanova's sprint medley anchored by Jerry Bouma, had the fastest qualifying time, and appears to make a run at that title."[16] Indeed, I was flying that day. Handed the stick in third, I ran a controlled first lap and then moved easily into second. The Georgetown runner ahead of me was starting to labor. As we entered the homestretch, I moved passed him and won our heat running a 1:50.2 to anchor. Now my views of what tomorrow might bring changed considerably.

The 1974 version of the "Early Beatles" for the Four Mile Relay was the same except for the fifth Beatle: Gregan replacing the injured Schappert. Gregan led off with a 4:05.4 mile with a small lead. Manhattan, led by Mike Keogh, was matching every move step for step, then McElroy took over and followed with another similar paced mile—a 4:04.2 chased by Matt Centrowitz. Then it was Eamonn Coghlan's turn. Full of vigor and with his indefatigable father Bill visiting for the first time and standing by the rail, Coghlan put on a show—a 4:00.9—only a skip away from a sub four-minute mile. Joe Savage was not far behind. Finally, to the trusty Hartnett. In John's own words, "every race I anchored at Penn I was given the lead—this was no different. I knew Tony Colon could run four minutes and he was only a few yards behind. All I remember is that with a quarter to go, Tony brushed my heel ever so gently. I took off." John upped Eamonn's time ever so slightly with a 4:00.1 final mile. The overall time—16:10.6—a new Penn Relays record, and the second fastest time ever run in the United States. Never had a team run this fast and made it look so easy. Manhattan was only four seconds behind. Interestingly, this record stood for 31 years until 2005 when a team from Michigan, which included two upcoming Olympians, the Kiwi Nick Willis and Canadian Nathan Brennan ran a 16:04. Meanwhile, Ken Schappert in the stands was delighted to see the win, once again over Manhattan College and Freddie Dwyer.

The afternoon was still young, but the wins were over. The Sprint Medley came next. This time, I received the stick in fifth place and, in my enthusiasm and determination to win, ran the first quarter in 52 seconds, taking the lead with 350 yards to go. But the price paid was too high and I could not fight the fatigue as I watched the back sides of four team anchors pass by. I had felt full of running the day before. But today, I was dying, and it was a long slow death. On reflection, I now quote Oscar Wilde, who among his many witticisms once said: "His optimism exceeded his capability." All I can now say is that I had given it my best shot.

The Two Mile Relay met a similar fate, albeit this time in another head-to-head battle with the University of Tennessee. This time, recalling Ken Schappert's astute diagnosis from the previous year, Willie Thomas's head was still leaning left but Brian McElroy could not get past him. Both teams were given identical times—7:23.6. But the Volunteers were given the win much to the disappointment of freshman Phil Kane, as well as Eamonn Coghlan and Tom Gregan, who were bringing a full weekend's work to a close. While disappointed, both had two earlier wins and in possession of those prized Penn Relays watches to assuage that feeling.

Thus, the end of Penn Relays 1974. Two meet records and two near wins. Villanova track was far from a spent force despite the prognostications of some, and the wishes of others. Nevertheless, the Hartnett-Schappert era was coming to an end. Jumbo described John Hartnett as the greatest distance runner he had ever coached. And for good reason. Consider this: during his Villanova career, John won six individual IC4A titles—in six different events: cross-country, the indoor mile, the outdoor mile, the steeplechase, the three-mile, and the six-mile—a record that will never be matched. But his time was up, and he was heading back home to County Cork. McElroy had also met his academic requirements to graduate with his five-year college career (1.5 years at the University of Kansas; 3.5 years at Villanova University); it was also the end of the line for myself—the four years had flashed by. Just as I thought, I did run a couple of 4:05 mile times within the following two weeks, but it was too little too late to be part of one of those great Villanova DMRs or that Four Mile Relay Team in 1974.

It was a sad departure from Villanova—first John (or the "Duke" as most of us affectionately called him) set out for the West Coast to run a 1500 meters in Los Angeles, where he ran a 3:38 just behind Rod Dixon, before his return trip to Ireland. As he bid adieu, the remaining team members knew that John was one-of-a-kind. His quiet, steady leadership combined with his incredible performances left a deep impression on those who trained with him as well as those who were influenced by him.

While John headed west, it was also time for me to say farewell and head north—for good—back home to Canada. That June day when I stepped onto the Delta flight to travel from Philadelphia to Toronto remains one of the saddest days of my life. The intensity of four years, the dreams, the many miles run, the intervals, the deep friendships, being part of such a fabled group of athletes, yet spending two years on the sidelines was for me a case of lost opportunity. I felt I had not only failed myself; I had also failed to contribute my full potential to the legacy of my teammates and the history of Villanova Track. The Villanova "world" was now behind me; it could never be brought back. And I was returning to a world that knew nothing of what I had just experienced or a single person that I had spent four years with. Nor did I have any idea what was in store for me either professionally, academically, or personally. I had never felt so lost in my entire life as I did that June of 1974.

Meanwhile the "Duke", after his successful outing to California had one more stop to make as he continued his trip back home to Ireland. That was Toronto, where I picked him up and drove to Owen Sound to spend a few days at my stomping grounds. That previous summer, I had spent three weeks in Ireland, much of it on the Hartnett farm (Gurteen). During that visit I witnessed the full beauty of the Irish countryside as well as experiencing the Hartnett dairy operation firsthand. This time it was John's turn to see our dairy operation and compare notes after we had had so many conversations over the years. During John's visit, we stopped by my old high school track to do a set of repeat quarters (of course). A couple of my high school friends still talk about the smooth striding seemingly effortless stride of John Hartnett as he exhibited his trademark steady style. Finally, the last leg of his journey: Toronto to Shannon Airport, County Claire—which lay about two hours north of the Hartnett farm.

Four weeks later in early July, John ran the mile at the Cork City Sports Track Meet, held in Cork City about 30 minutes south of the farm. What had been a sheep pasture several days before, was clipped, levelled, and turned into a grass track. Determined to make an impression on the home crowd, John led from start to finish, running a 3:56.4 mile on "grass," the third fastest time ever run on such a surface. Two Olympic Champions had run faster and on much better tracks to be sure: Peter Snell and Kip Keino.

Despite the departures of the three seniors (Hartnett, McElroy and Bouma), the Villanova Track Team had much to look forward to. Schappert, who John Hartnett described as "the ideal teammate who loved Villanova and wanted everyone to do well," was back for another year. So was Tom Gregan. The cocky Dubliner, Eamonn Coghlan, was clearly coming into his own—showing great promise and just getting started. Plus, in the background and unknown to most, Ken Schappert had turned into Jumbo's most effective recruitment "closer." With his record of performance, his energy, and his most effective style, Villanova Track was about to see a new crop of performers and performances that would outshine everything that had happened so far. Hard to believe, but the best was yet to come.

7

A Day in the Life

"You do the running. I'll do the thinking!"

Jumbo Elliott

Live like a clock!" Without question, this was Jumbo's strongest and most memorable saying. No one asked what it meant. No one needed to. No need to split hairs. No need to stage philosophical arguments. No debate on what was right or wrong. Or some smart aleck statement as "even a stopped clock is right two times a day." We did not talk about it. We all intuitively knew what Jumbo was telling us.

We all lived on campus. There was no time lost commuting to and from a residence off-campus. Everything was close at hand. Proximity was one thing, but preferred proximity was another. There was a hierarchy. The best dorms to live in had to meet two essential criteria: first, be a single room (no roommates); and second, be close to the cafeteria. That meant one place and one place only: first it had been St. Rita's; then it became Austin Hall. The latter was without question the best dorm on campus. Once a tired and overpopulated residence, it had been completely refurbished and converted to single rooms. And it stood only 30 steps from the entrance to Dougherty Hall, which contained the cafeteria. You could literally roll out of bed and be in the food line within two minutes. That was where all the seniors would live. That was where we all wanted to be.

Live like a clock. Jumbo's famous adage needed no explanation—do the same things at the same time day in, day out. No phrase could better describe our life as track athletes on the Villanova campus. He also said, "While in college, you can do three things: your studies, your training, and your social life (aka chasing women). And you only have time for two." We knew that these better be the first two on the list and that they best be done like clockwork.

Tick Tock: 7:30 a.m. Time to get up. A quick trip to the washroom, a washing of the face, the brushing of teeth, a shave? That was more of a dream than a necessity for many of us. Quick dress, and off to the cafeteria.

Tick Tock: 7:50 a.m. Breakfast time. Usually the same thing each day—two eggs sunny side up, a couple of strips of bacon or a piece of ham, two pieces of toast, and a bowl of cereal. Stop and pick up two empty glasses: one for orange juice; the other—milk for the cereal. Then to the "table." The track table(s) were of course conveniently situated, just a few steps from the exit of the serving line as you entered the cafeteria. Two tables. Everyone knew that these tables were reserved. At breakfast time especially early, there were usually only one or two teammates sitting there. And quietly. Not much being said at this time of day. A tired "hello," a "howya doing?" Not much more. Missing breakfast would be a travesty. We were always on the edge of starvation. The track athletes generally came alone, a steady stream, a quick breakfast, 15 minutes at the table, and then off to class.

Weekends allowed for greater lingering. A time to relax and enjoy a leisurely breakfast. More extended conversations and the opportunity to hear about or regale what had happened the night before. That would be when the ever-feisty Donal Walsh would interrogate some unsuspecting freshman about any noteworthy party antics that may have occurred (or did not occur), all the while embellishing his own accomplishments (which we collectively knew were far from the truth).

One Saturday breakfast in January 1974, we read the morning paper in a state of disbelief: the world record for the 1500 meters had just been broken—3:32.2 by Filbert Bayi. Back then, the newspaper delivered the news first. And equally impressive were second and third place—Walker in 3:32.6 and Dixon in 3:33.4—who saw this coming.? The world had changed, and Jim Ryun was no longer in his own, unapproachable stratosphere. Not much was said. John Hartnett was especially quiet—that previous summer he had run a 3:54.7 mile—a second behind Wottle and a whisper behind Prefontaine. And John was a distance runner—a two miler. What might be possible if he concentrated on the mile?

A week later, John headed to Toronto to face a world class field including John Walker, the second fastest 1500-meter runner in history, and Pekka Vasala, the 1972 Olympic 1500-meter champion (see Chapter 6). Also reading the paper that morning with intense concentration was Eamonn Coghlan, lost in his own calculus, yet to break four minutes for the mile. His goals would soon become very clear.

Tick Tock: 8:30 a.m. First class of the day. Villanova University had two types of courses. First the Monday/Wednesday/Friday courses—50 minutes a class, three times a week, with 10 minutes between classes. Then the Tuesday/Thursday courses—80 minutes a class, two times a week. These started at precisely 8:10 a.m. We did not like this time slot; it forced us to get up 30 minutes earlier, something that we hated to do. Of course, to organize the ideal class schedule took some planning, and a bit of influence. You had to know who oversaw scheduling and if possible, get an advance access to the selection room on the day courses were being picked. This was back in the day when a system of cards was in place. Each course allowed a set number of students. If the class limit were 30 students, that class would have 30 cards in a file box. It was a simple case of being first in and securing one of those cards. That was easy when we knew the administrative staff, who looked the other way when we "stumbled" by before official course selection began.

Tick Tock: 9:30 a.m. Second class of the day. The ideal schedule would include five courses, with three hours of class per course for a total of 15 hours per week. If you could organize three classes on MWF and two for T/Th, that was academic sweet spot. Jumbo wanted his athletes to be good students, get a good education. But let's not go overboard. Engineering proved to be a special challenge—first 15 to 18 hours of classes per week; then another 12 to 15 hours in labs. This made it tough to put in the miles the same way a 15-hour a week student could do. But amazingly, the occasional athlete did just that. The Business School in Bartley Hall was ideal—never more than 15 hours a week. And conveniently located just across the street from the Field House.

Tick Tock: 10:20 a.m. Second class over. Time to head for the Field House and the morning run. But first, the necessity of stopping by the mail room. This was truly a place of unexpressed highs and lows. Would there be a letter? An update from family? A friend? A girlfriend? Or perhaps a reply from some romantic pursuit usually more rooted in fantasy than reality? The crowded mail room embodied the full range of emotion. Happiness, relief, despair, emptiness. Every time you entered, you would first peer through the tiny bit of glass in the door of your post box. Immediately you would know whether or not a letter awaited you. If you had one, you started reading as you walked out across the grass on your way to the Field House.

Tick Tock: 10:30 a.m. The Field House is before you. Always the same routine. In the side door, across the end of the basketball court and down the stairs to the hallway that served as our locker room. But first, stop by the cage and pick up your gear for the workout: T-shirt, socks, jock, and a towel. Charlie was the gatekeeper. He was like a man in a cage and most days, a grumpy, angry man in a cage. Try and be as polite as you can be. No point in agitating a grumpy man. The routine was always the same. Keep the socks you are wearing on—for the workout. Save the clean ones for wearing later. Less laundry that way. There may be two or three other teammates there. Some had come earlier after the 9:30 class; others came slightly later—closer to 11:00 a.m. Some would not come at all. Often you would come, change, and leave alone. The morning runs were supposed to be relaxed and easy. Most of the time, they were.

Tick Tock: 10:40 a.m. Exit the Fieldhouse and onto the roads. It is either the Radnor five or the Minga (another five-mile loop). Sometimes the Radnor five became the 6 ½ but that meant going up Triple F**k, and you had to be motivated for that. We usually left that to John Hartnett, who seemed to relish that hill. And it never seemed to beat him. The Radnor five had a long slow climb between the two- and three-mile mark—also the prettiest part of the loop. Quiet, past the stream, the many trees, mailboxes, and stately mansions. Then it was under the P & W tracks, past the TV Guide offices and a bit further to Lancaster Avenue. A sharp left and one mile later with the main campus to our left, it was back to the Field House. That loop never got boring.

Tick Tock: 11:30 a.m. The run would be over and there was time for a quick shower. Clean socks on and the old ones—now damp from the run, the T-shirt, jock, and towel, rolled up and back to Charlie in the cage on your way out. His mood had not improved.

Tick tock: 11:45 a.m. Lunch time. This time, as you came down the ramp to enter the food line, you would see the track tables to your left. Now there would be anywhere from six to10 teammates spread across the two tables. Conversation would be spirited. But job one was to put that food away. We were hungry. And whatever was being served, there was an added serving station set up in the eating area that supplied hamburgers. We would always be in that line after we inhaled what we had been served. There was a constant badgering—an exchange of viewpoints. Nothing is decided or resolved. Rather it is an act of exchange—the hierarchy has already been decided. It is done without words. The bantam roosters are tolerated but the head rooster does not lose ground. Everyone understands the pecking order. The best miler has the last word—sometimes no words need to be spoken. It may just be a look, a shrug, or a slight scowl of disapproval. But the team is everything when it comes to social reference. This is our group. This is our family. While we all had our separate class schedules, few of us did little with our respective classmates other than spend time in the same classroom. We had no association beyond that. We knew a few of them by first name but that was it. Ours was go to class and keep moving as fast as possible. No lingering, no loitering after class. We had miles to run.

On nice days when the weather was warm and the winds calm, we would eat and head outside. In front of Dougherty lay Kennedy Mall. Along the edge stood a series of metal poles with a chain hanging from one pole to the next. About 18 inches off the ground, these chains hung in the shape of gentle parabolas. Perfect to sit against and hold your back—you could grab the chain on either side and swing gently back and forth. This was the ritual of "chain hanging" and no one did it better than the Villanova Track Team. Accompanied with laughter and banter—an easy rhythm of coming and going. Some off to class; others with time on their hands; others for a bit longer and then to a later class. And the laughter and the banter never stopped. Nor the "ball-busting." You could not get away with anything in this group.

My first and only Penn Relays watch. Still keeping time.

Tick tock: 12:30 p.m. Third class of the day. Some of us would have a 1:30 p.m. class but the 12:30 p.m. time slot was ideal. Another 50 minutes of instruction and then you had an hour to rest up before the afternoon workout. This was usually the time when I started to get sleepy. So, as soon as class was over, it was straight out the door and back to the dorm as quickly as possible. Sitting near the back of the classroom, I was usually the first one out.

Tick Tock: 1:30 p.m. Into the room and nap time. This became a most critical time of day. The coveted nap—not too long; not too short. Usually about 20 minutes. Call it the Goldilocks nap—just right. If too long, you would start to feel groggy. If too short, you did not feel refreshed. But the afternoon nap—as essential as three (or should I say four) meals a day.

Tick Tock: 2:30 p.m. Up and off to the Field House. Usually, you would take your time as you leisurely strolled through campus. Check with one of your teammates living in your dorm. Head off together. A walk through Kennedy Mall—if it was a nice day, lots of people sitting around. Check out the scenery. Or through the quad, which became a lot more interesting the year the one dorm (Sheehan) became a women's dorm. Plan to be at the Field House by 3:00 p.m. Charlie seems a little less grumpy but certainly not ready for any lengthy discourse on any topic. Pick up the roll from the cage. T-shirt, socks, jock, and towel. Quick change and ready to go one more time. The hallway (aka locker room) is now considerably livelier. Most of the team is there. The bantering continues. The mood is usually light. On the heavy workout days, a bit quieter. Time to get to work.

Tick Tock: 3:15 p.m. The workout begins. In the fall, we would head out onto the roads, usually in groups of three or four. The choice was usually between the Frolic or the Tennis Court loop. Generally, the runs were steady, with lots of conversation. We would run two or three abreast; sometime single file depending on the traffic. Occasionally, the pace became a bit more intense. Like the time when a freshman got especially annoying on the Frolic. After a couple of miles of mindless and most uninteresting chatter, we picked up the pace and the banter quickly stopped. From that point on, we went flat out. That day John Hartnett and I hammered the next seven miles—we soon separated ourselves from the rest of the group. I stayed with John until Mt F**k—the dreaded hill at the nine-mile mark only to see John finally pull away. That day we ran the Frolic in under 53 minutes. Then we took a quick break, a drink of water and decided to do another easy five miles.

Another time, John and I were on the Frolic and saw a fellow washing his driveway. We both looked at each other and laughed. The two farm boys had never seen such fastidiousness. Or the time in early November when Donal Walsh and I engaged in a vigorous debate during the entire 10 miles as the cloud cover was precipitating: is this rain or is this snow? As the resident Canadian, I favored the latter. Walsh the consummate Irishman from the Emerald Isle argued vigorously for rain. We finally agreed "It's a dry rain."

Come January, it was straight from the Field House to the boards—a 15-minute warm-up. Jumbo would arrive and the three lappers would begin. The beginning of April would see us on the cinder track. Warmed up and ready to go. Then the repeat quarters would begin.

Meanwhile, as we were pounding out those miles on the roads or the track, campus life had its own rhythm and events. Villanova boasted one of the largest ROTC Naval Corps to be found on any American campus.[1] Every Tuesday was parade day and while we were training, more than 1,000 ROTC students in full uniform marched through campus for drills and inspection. This made for several interesting confrontations as the anti-war movement to no surprise, picked Tuesday afternoons to express their war protestations. That created for some interesting convergences—the juxtaposition of military order, neatness, and decorum carrying banners and flags set against a parallel formation of disorganized protesters in a semblance of a poorly formed platoon carrying a blood-stained (red paint) sheepskin rug. Tensions between the two groups were extremely high. You could feel it. Fortunately, no physical confrontations broke out.

One fall day in 1972 I decided to take the train to central Philly to take in a presidential election political rally. This was my chance to see American political royalty—Ted Kennedy and Sargent Shriver firsthand.[2] Walking toward Rittenhouse Square, I was astonished by the security—the multitudes of police and the visual presence of sharpshooters strategically positioned on the tops of the surrounding buildings. This was also my first exposure to bona fide hate literature, which was thrust into my hand while I strode toward the Square. I did not read it in full but literally jolted in surprise when I noted that it had been printed by some obscure Canadian publisher located in a small town less than 40 miles from where I grew up. You could feel the tension between the pro-war and anti-war groups—separated but circling each other like iron filings between the opposing poles of a magnet.

It was a strange era. We were all fully aware of the war in Vietnam—the casualties, the seeming lack of progress, the politics, the protests, the college exemptions, the draft. Yet we never really talked about it. It was a no-win conversation. One of the track guys lived next door to a veteran who had served as a chopper pilot in 'Nam and now back in school. He was about eight years our senior, a quiet kind of guy who liked to hang out with us. We enjoyed his company—of course he had our full respect. But we asked no questions and he told us no stories.

Tick Tock: 4:45 p.m. Workout is over. Another shower is behind us. Towels, T-shirts, jock, and used socks turned in. Clean socks are on. We dress and saunter up to the cafeteria past the Security Gate House. Most of the security officers were friendly toward us, but the sergeant in charge hated us. He would stare at us with great disdain—like we had just gotten away with something and he was out to get us—a look that we tried our best to ignore. We were never quite sure why he hated us. Did he feel we were an overprivileged lot? Did he feel we had it too easy? Perhaps he was a failed track athlete that never made it. Were our attempts to sneak in the concerts through the back door too much for him? We did not ask. He did not tell. One day, Ken Schappert started chatting with one of the older security guards who wore a revolver but buried deep within a leather case. Schapp said somewhat sarcastically, pointing to the fellow's gun, "By the time you pull out that baby, you would have been shot six times." That infuriated the old fellow—as his face reddened and he fumbled with his leather case ensuring that his gun was still there. We knew immediately that a quick exit was in order and we never lingered in his presence again.

Ken Schappert and Jerry Bouma—First Villanova Freshmen to run Penn Relays for Villanova, 1971

Tick Tock: 5:15 p.m. Dinner time. This would be a more spirited affair—again the two tables at the bottom of the ramp would be full. No one but the track team would dare sit there. An entire cafeteria would be full and bustling, but these tables remained empty. When we arrived, they filled quickly, and they were never quiet. This happened every day. The action never stopped. Now the characters were in full display: the aggressive, ready to take anyone on at any time of the New Yorkers and the Jersey boys; the wit of the Irish; the humor of the Brits; the more reserved comments of the Canadians; the silence of the Africans. It all came together—every day; the attempt to "hoop" the unsuspecting tea drinker three seats over or at the next table, with an arched morsel of bread. And every day it was different. Yesterday it was a spirited discussion about the next Ali-Frazier fight. Or the Wannamaker Mile. Today it is about Penn Relays; tomorrow—it might be about someone's new girlfriend. Occasionally, it got serious—about the "Troubles" in Ireland. Or the Vietnam war. But mostly, politics and religion were avoided. Or perhaps we were so locked into our own worlds of self-importance of miles and intervals that we did not know enough to bring forward a well-formulated point of view. But there was always lots of talking. That never stopped.

Tick Tock: 6:30 p.m. Study time. This was probably the quietest time of the day. Some stayed in their rooms; others went to the library. A few even had special places in the library such as the "Reserve Room" or a hidden corner in the stacks. But mostly, we would find a clear table or a study carol and put our heads down to address the academic challenges before us. Sometimes you would see one of the Irish runners reading the *Irish Times*—it was a week old before it arrived at the library. But this was as current as it got. Most of us did not have access to television. Some read the local newspapers to search out any articles pertaining to track. Most did not. For the most part we had little notion of current affairs, politics, or the issues of the day. We had miles to run.

Tick Tock: 8:30 p.m. Pie Shoppe Time. This was the fourth meal of the day. Jumbo knew that we were a hungry and relatively impoverished lot with limited resources. Thus, every week we each received an envelope with 15 "pie-shoppes"—a set of tickets, each worth 30 cents. It was enough in those days to buy a hamburger and a shake each evening. Or at least on three or four nights of the week. That became the ritual. Every evening, at precisely 8:30 p.m., the boys would come from all directions: some from the library, some from the quad to the east, some from the array of dorms to the west. In a matter of two minutes, the normally dead quiet Pie Shoppe transformed from a place of tranquility to an unhinged symphony of the superlative. Now the conversation rose to a new level of jocularity and verbal fabrication. The workouts for the day were behind us, and the studies. Everyone seemed more relaxed. This was when old stories were amplified, and new stories created, the feats of former two mile relay splits became faster on each retelling, past times relived, and new challenges presented—who was going to be on the DMR this year? Who would lead off the Two Mile Relay? Who did you say is going to run a marathon? How fast will he run? Want to bet on that? Who has got an extra pie-shoppe? Then, at 9:15 p.m., as suddenly as they came, they left. And the Pie Shoppe assumed its usual quiet demeanor.

This is where the interactions and the interpersonal challenges would reach new peaks. One memorable example took place in February 1974 when Frank Watkins, a quiet non-scholarship athlete announced that he planned to run the Penn Relays marathon in late April. I immediately responded and posed this challenge: "One dollar for every minute under three hours for you; one dollar for every minute over three hours for me." Amid the howls of the now totally-engaged team members, Frank accepted the challenge. Then he quietly disappeared for weeks on end. All we knew was that he was putting in the miles, mostly by himself. That earned him the nickname "Phantom." Where's Frank? Where is the Phantom? Must be running the Frolic.

Race day finally came, and the entire track team eagerly awaited the results. Soon the news came back: Frank (now firmly wearing the Phantom label) had run a 2.41. This of course meant the big payout of $19. I pretended to regret this "great financial loss" but was secretly delighted to honor my wager. I knew full well that this very modest bet gave Frank the motivation to put in those necessary miles essential to run a good marathon, which was exactly what he had done. From that date on, I responded to any jests by simply responding with this comment: "The best money I have ever spent." To this day, that marathon is the highlight of Frank Watkins's Villanova career. More importantly, Frank earned the abiding respect of his fellow teammates.

From time to time there would be other attractions. The occasional speaker came to campus—like Jane Fonda (better known at the time as Hanoi Jane) and her then husband, Tom Hayden, member of the Chicago Seven. Uri Geller came to demonstrate his mind- (and spoon-) bending techniques. On weekends, perhaps once a month, there would be a concert at the Field House. Sometimes we snuck in. Most times not. But a memorable array of big names paraded through including Bruce Springsteen, Jackson Browne, Steppenwolf, Rare Earth, and José Feliciano. We were looking forward to hearing Jim Croce, a Villanova 1970 graduate for the Homecoming Concert in 1973. Unfortunately, he was killed in a plane crash just two weeks before his much-anticipated concert. This was sad news and a reminder of the great fragility of life that we all shared, and how we were all connected.

On occasion, we might receive a dinner invitation from a friend who lived in the Philly area or some friend of a friend. It would always come down to one question: Do we stop at McDonald's before the dinner or after? One thing we knew for sure, that whatever we were fed, we would be starving.

Tick Tock: 9:30 p.m. Back to the room. Time to wrap up a few things. Write a letter home or to a friend, or to that girl you knew would never write back. Or time to stop by a friend's room to watch a half-hour of TV—never much more. Then to get back to your room and update your running diary. *Looks like a good week shaping up, or I missed a couple of workouts—need to pick it up the next few days. Getting tired.*

Tick Tock: 10:00 p.m. Bedtime. Tomorrow is another day. Sleep would come almost immediately.

Tick Tock: Live like a clock.

8

Coghlan Continues

"What made Villanova so successful? It was us! It was the guys! We were all equal and we looked out for each other."

Eamonn Coghlan

Fyodor Dostoyevsky, named by some literary critics as the best novelist ever, had an unconventional style. He ignored the standard format of the day and did it his own way. His approach was all about characters and how these characters responded to the "big ideas" within the milieu of social and political challenges of the day. Plot was almost secondary. For example, there is no mystery in *Crime and Punishment*—just the unfolding and the redemption—in effect the ultimate in thought experiments.

Eamonn Coghlan's Villanova career was no thought experiment. Rather, it can be described as the transformation of will into performance—the unfolding of a prodigious athlete who through determination, hard work, and a sense of destiny, moved from relative obscurity to the world stage in three short years. A prime example of converting "thought" into "action."

Perhaps now Villanova's best-known and most celebrated track athlete, Eamonn Coghlan's story is truly one of a kind. His accomplishments, which extended a full 15 years after he graduated, are both legend and legion: World record holder, World Champion, European Champion, NCAA Champion four times over, four-time Olympian, 100 plus sub four-minute miles and/or 1500-meter equivalents, the first Master (over 40 years of age) to break four minutes for the mile ... the list goes on and on. No one electrified the crowds on the indoor circuit like Eamonn

Coghlan. No one displayed such consistency and won races with such style and drama. No one won more races like the famous Wanamaker Mile-Millrose Games—a seven-time winner. No one would win a world-championship 5,000 meters with such joy and sheer relief. Eamonn would dazzle crowds in New York, Washington, DC, Philadelphia, Boston, Cleveland, Toronto, Edmonton, Los Angeles, San Diego, and the Meadowlands. The nomenclature "Chairman of the Boards" drew thousands of fans and resonated with the athletic, business, and entertainment worlds alike. Never had we seen such athletic prowess combined with wit, insight, a glint in the eye, those unmistakable dimples, and the rhythmic cadence of his Dublin accent.

But how did this all start? How was this character of characters formed? How did the milieu of the Villanova experience and the conditions in which he was embedded for four formulative years shape this individual to become one of the most venerated and accomplished middle-distance runners in the history of track and field?

To be sure, it began in Dublin, Ireland. Eamonn Coghlan, a hyperactive child, set out to be a football (soccer) player. Eamonn grew up in Drimnagh, on Cooley Road, an area of Dublin about two miles west of the famed Guinness Brewery, a neighborhood replete with modest row houses. Fortunately, it came with a nearby small park with the most fortuitous of names: Field of Dreams. On this patch of green, Eamonn and his friends would play for hours. He never stopped moving and arguably never stopped running. When asked, "Was it a tough neighbourhood?" To quote Eamonn, "There were areas in North Dublin that were tougher, but ours was tough enough." Tough enough to produce the world's best indoor miler. And years later, tough enough to produce the world's best and most ferocious UFC fighter Conor McGregor, who grew up about two blocks from the Coghlan home.

Although Eamonn did not realize it at the time, his life was already immersed in politics. His Granny's house in the center of Dublin, where his father Bill grew up, had been used as an IRA safe house during the sacrificial and ill-fated 1916 Easter Rising. He and his sister Mary would root through the basement seeking out artifacts and treasures that would testify to this. Little did he realize that in 2016, on the 100th anniversary of this pivotal event, he would be standing as a senator with the leading Irish politicians and dignitaries paying solemn tribute to the fallen leaders of the Rising.[1]

Eamonn excelled at sports that involved running. Soccer was a perfect training ground and even though his teams were not very proficient, his speed and his ability to accelerate made him noticeable. The odd street incursion tested both his wit and speed and led to running races; soon his cross-country abilities began to shine. As an 11-year-old, he beat a group of runners that were 12 and 13 years of age. Winning the cross-country league that year and being presented a medal, fueled his ambitions. And it caught the attention of Gerry Farnham, coach with the Metropolitan Harriers AC, an athletic club that trained in the Phoenix Park, some two kilometers to the north.

Eamonn Coghlan at 11 years of age

From the age of 14, it was all about running and the success he enjoyed. School life however brought a different set of challenges. Grammar school went fine but secondary school was another matter where he came face to face with a brutal Christian Brother who excelled at terrorizing and demeaning students. Eamonn had trouble with math and became a regular victim. Little did he know until much later in life that he suffered from a form of dyslexia. The confrontations went from bad to worse, to the point that one brutal beating resulted in blows so bad that stitches were required. Eamonn refused to return to that school. Fortunately, his father Bill, who heard the real story from his two older brothers, intervened and arranged a transfer to another class and ultimately to another school.

By the time Eamonn reached 18 years of age, he established himself as a top cross-country runner as well as a track athlete, which included a 4:09 mile. Coach Gerry Farnham introduced him to Fartlek, intervals, hills, the Munich Lap (an undulating 1200-meter loop in Phoenix Park) and most importantly, "shifting gears." Gerry had studied races and saw the importance of the decisive move. He introduced Eamonn to a speed drill that focused on a sudden lifting of the knees and rapid change in cadence, but with little noticeable change in arm action. While clearly physical in motion, it required a clear mental focus. It was a technique that Eamonn mastered to perfection.

Like every young Irish runner, Eamonn set his sights on Villanova University, influenced by the legendary Ron Delany, who after his 1956 Olympic triumph was second in popularity only to the Pope himself. But there was a problem.

Another young Dubliner (from Howth to be more precise) had just established himself as the second fastest all-time 18-year-old ever to run 1500 meters. That was Tom Gregan, who ran 3:43.5 for the 1500 meters and a 4:01.6 mile. By comparison, Eamonn's mile time seemed almost modest. Jumbo had his eyes on Gregan. But the wily Frank Murphy, who graduated in 1970, kept telling him, "I think you might be better off getting this Coghlan kid too." Jumbo relented and took them both. Coghlan was for all intents and purposes an unknown. But Murphy, like Jumbo, knew talent when he saw it. And in his view, there was plenty to see.

September 1971: unbeknownst to most, 1971 marked the beginning of Eamonn's first freshman year. I remember clearly when we first met. There he was standing somewhat uncomfortably on the steps of the Villanova Field House. He had arrived the day before wearing a modish blue turtleneck sweater, jeans and sporting a fresh haircut. The newly arrived and shorn Eamonn Coghlan was certain of two things: this was the place where Ron Delany became a legend; and that Jumbo Elliott despised long hair. In fact, the last thing he did before stepping on that flight from Dublin, albeit with great reluctance in saying goodbye to his girlfriend, was visit a barber. Then he saw both John Hartnett and me, wearing hairstyles not dissimilar to his pre-barber visit and he knew he had been had—by Donal Walsh no less. Later that same day, I took him on his first ever Frolic. Running sockless in his new blue Pumas he started to experience blister problems about seven miles in. As for myself, I was just coming off a series of 90–100-mile weeks that summer and was running with ease. I gave him directions on where to turn for home and carried on. That was probably one of the very few times I ran faster than Eamonn Coghlan.

Eamonn's introduction to Villanova proved most difficult. First, he was alone in a busy dorm and a stranger to everyone. Tom Gregan did not arrive until two weeks later—his father had passed away unexpectedly and there were funeral arrangements to attend to. Tom and Eamonn were roommates that first year—both were terribly homesick and completely unsettled. Tom worried about his mother; Eamonn had met Yvonne Murphy, the love of his life that previous year and missed her terribly. Neither Tom nor Eamonn were part of the team rhythm: because of his late arrival, Tom had to take night courses. Meanwhile Eamonn immediately experienced serious shin splints which limited his ability to train. Neither competed in cross-country that fall. The only eventful occurrence was a time trial between the two of them on the freshman cross-country course at Belmont Plateau. This occurred on a week-day afternoon under the watchful eye of Jack Pyrah while the rest of us were putting in the miles. Most of us thought that Gregan would win hands down. Then the word came back: Coghlan had outkicked Gregan and won. How prescient of an outcome that would become.

That entire fall and early winter was completely unremarkable. The increased weekly mileage continued to leave Eamonn with a series of injuries. His ability to train was limited—we did not see a lot of him—he was either nursing an injury or seeking solace elsewhere. We now know that the injuries, his limited ability to be part of the team, and his deep homesickness left him in a state of depression. But that was a condition that went unrecognized and unaddressed in those times. Then we heard that he had been named to the Irish Junior Team to compete at the European Cross-Country Championships to be held in Wales. It was early March, and the Villanova Track Team were in Detroit for the NCAA Indoor Championships. Quietly and without notice to any of us, Eamonn slipped away, and he did not return. So much for that Irish freshman. None of us ever thought we would see or hear about Eamonn Coghlan again.

However, in September of 1972 Eamonn Coghlan, to our astonishment, was back on campus. We were all very surprised because with Jumbo's no-nonsense, "take it or leave it" attitude, second chances were as rare as a snowstorm in July. Jumbo obviously saw something in Eamonn, his father Bill offered guidance, and together with the love of his life Yvonne, told him without any reservation: "Go back to Villanova or you have no future here."

Now came Eamonn's second freshmen year. This time, he seemed more settled and determined. John Hartnett and I both knew that Eamonn had experienced a tough initial entry to Villanova and when he we did not see him at meals or the Field House, we kept an eye on him to make sure he did not disappear. Fortunately, we lived in a dorm only 30 meters distant: our domicile stood directly opposite his dorm, and we could yell across the walkway to see if he was about. Together, we hung out a lot with Eamonn and his new north Dublin roommate—another Frank Murphy (or young Frank, as we would call him).

Eamonn's training became more consistent, and you could see him getting stronger every month. Injuries were still a bit of a problem. He had nagging shins, a slight muscle pull here, a twinge there, the typical afflictions of a maturing runner. However, his ability to run good workouts became increasingly evident. On occasion during warm-up strides, Eamonn would demonstrate his soon-to-be famous shifting of gears. It was quite amazing—we would be moving nicely together and suddenly he would shift and be two strides in front. His progress was such that I clearly recall the day when I said to John on a morning run, "If Eamonn doesn't get injured, he's going to run some serious times."

This freshman year it was Frank Murphy's time to question his future at Villanova. We could see that he was not doing well: he began to withdraw, his complexion was drawn and pasty-white, his confidence had completely dissipated. One exceptionally grey and dreary March day, Frank left—first to Toronto to visit relatives and then back to Dublin. In retrospect, he was struggling and not physically, but there was no recognition or support for such a condition back then.

Meanwhile, Eamonn was hitting his stride. His steady improvement and positive attitude caught Jumbo's attention. That gave Jumbo enough confidence to select Eamonn as the leadoff man for the 1973 Penn Relays Four Mile Relay Team, the classic first year apprentice role. He fit the part of an "early Beatle" perfectly. In fact, best of all since he really was a true Beatles fan. He'd told us before about his sister Mary seeing the Beatles at a Dublin concert in their early days in the mid 60s.

Then in 1974, he really started to roll: a neck-and-neck battle with Dave Wottle in Cleveland, two four-flat miles at Penn Relays, and then, only two months later, winning a double that had never been done before—the indoor IC4A 880 yards and the outdoor three-mile. In the summer of '74 he competed internationally for Ireland for the first time against Portugal running a 3:41.9—1500 meters, technically a sub-four-minute mile. He was also selected to run the 5,000 meters at the European Championships in Rome. He failed to make the final, but it gave him a taste of what was to come.

On his return to Villanova in September 1974, Eamonn arrived full of confidence. He had two successful school years behind him, and his athletic successes were starting to build. A sub-four-minute mile was clearly looming; and with the departure of John Hartnett, Ken Schappert and himself were now the clear leaders of the Villanova Track Team.

Eamonn Coghlan, John Hartnett, and Jerry Bouma reunite at the IAAF World Championships, in Edmonton, 2001

In response to the question, what contributed to his success at Villanova, Eamonn voiced a clear unequivocal response: "Us!! It was Us!! It was the guys! We looked out for each other!!" He went on to say: "Villanova grounded me. It gave me a foundation. It taught me how to work hard, how to deal with success and failure. And most importantly, how to deal with people."

So, who were those "Us"—those guys who played a part in the shaping of Eamonn Coghlan, the greatest middle-distance runner of his time? The "Us" would be first John Hartnett and myself—we spent a lot of time with Eamonn during his first two years. We knew when he was up; and we knew when he was down. When we could, we helped with his classes (remember his difficulties with math). I made sure he would have no trouble with the Statistics for Business course that he dreaded and took the course with him at an adjacent desk.

John of course set the tone for training—Eamonn's consistency and appetite for hard work did not go unnoticed. We had a lot of fun together both training and "playing." Once in the fall of 1973, the three of us went to the "Meet and Greet" function on Parents' Weekend at the Field House. Of course, we would be the last people to have parents in attendance, unlike the hundreds that were milling about. So, we registered as the "Nogood Family" bearing name tags to that effect—Eamonn Nogood, John Nogood, and Jerry Nogood. It did not take long before we attracted some female interest. With some "Irish Charm" and "Canadian bravado," we convinced three young ladies that we were brothers, and our parents were not able to attend because they lived too far away. That drew a measure of sympathy and even greater interest. Eamonn's dimples and Dublin lilt were in full display. We had some good laughs about the evening for some time after that.

Eamonn and I also shared a birth year and were only four days apart in actual age. Both Scorpions, we were November babies—I was born on the 17th; he on the 21st. Aside from easily remembering the other's special day, we would organize a gathering of sorts, usually around the 19th or 20th. To no one's surprise, the better-looking co-eds on campus were a target of our invitations—one year we were regaled by the attention of a bubbly young lady named Rosie. She made a cake for the occasion which we all thoroughly enjoyed. But I knew I was no match to the dazzling Dubliner.

Then the "Us" followed with Ken Schappert. It soon became evident that Ken and Eamonn were two characters poured from the same mold—both city kids—one from New York City; one from Dublin; both street-wise; and both without fear. They loved to mix it up with other so-called tough guys, but most of all, they loved to compete. It was a dynamic combination that served as the centrum for the team that 1974/75 year.

Eamonn Coghlan cruises to a win

The mix included a cast of colorful characters including Phil "Tiny" Kane—a 1:52—800-meter runner from Rhode Island. The smallest of four brothers, Tiny was the ultimate extrovert, a super Type A character. Together with Eamonn and Schappert, this threesome had more energy than a mid-sized power plant. Then came Ed Takacs, a 1:51 800-meter man, and the second Canadian to receive a track scholarship to Villanova. Ed was deceptively quiet but would not miss a thing when suddenly he would dish out a zinger that would have the whole team in stitches. The mix also included Steve Dorsey, a tough cross-country runner who could handle the verbal challenges with the best of them. Add George MacKay, another 1:53 800-meter high-school runner from New Jersey who would brandish Jersey toughness when required. Enter Russ Ebbets[2], a non-scholarship runner who kept a close eye on everyone and everything. On more than one occasion, Eamonn would find solace with Russ, bemoaning the days when he was struggling to be the 5th man on the cross-country team. Russ was the one to give him the moniker "Steamin' Eamonn" that seemed to fit the aspiring track star to a T.

Add to "Us" one Kevin Leonard, who served as the de-facto "team entertainer." No one could speak more loudly or genuflect more wildly than Kevin, who was quickly labelled as "Wildman," a label he wore proudly. His antics were a source of continuous bemusement as he found new ways to leave his mark on campus. Nevertheless, the colorful Kevin was an important part of the group and we missed him when he was not around. In due time, Kevin provided an important leadership role that was manifested years later when he organized and coordinated many track alumni events. Simply, without Kevin, the abiding Villanova track fraternity would not be the same.

But there was one more new addition to this group—a freshman who started his Villanova career in September 1974—Mark Belger, the freshman from Long Island who himself would leave a legacy that may remain unequalled. No one exhibited more "cool" or more talent than this new recruit. More about Mark in the next chapter.

Penn Relays 1975

The year 1975 can be summarized by the ascendancy of Eamonn Coghlan from a promising US college runner to the man who became a world-class miler and Olympic gold contender. This became the year when Eamonn expressed his ability both definitively, and in astonishingly short order.

It began early in the indoor season, first, with an easy win at the IC4A indoor mile, followed by his first NCAA indoor mile win in Detroit, with a 4:02.2. It seemed that every time he stepped on the track, his confidence grew. He began to solidify his track legacy as a one-man winning machine—no college competitor seemed to be a challenge.

That last week of April, on Thursday April 24th, a most interesting discussion took place in Bartley Hall on the Villanova campus. Three business students in Professor Willkie's public speaking course gathered for a brief post-class conference—Ken Schappert, Tom Gregan, and Eamonn Coghlan—to discuss the following day's Distance Medley Relay. All of them were running well—the workouts that week were "blistering." Everything pointed to a great performance and the talk turned from winning, to asking how fast we could run. They decided that they would not only go for the Penn Relays record. Why not the world record? Greg Eckman, the quarter miler and a science student who was elsewhere on campus at the time, was subsequently informed of the plan. Professor Wilkie listened with great interest. He was very familiar with this threesome—for years the portly professor would take his ample form and jog ever so slowly around the track during our workouts—mostly in vain, it seemed to us. He knew these students, but he also knew them as athletes and offered rounds of beer at his expense, should this record-setting enterprise be successful.

Friday April 25th unfolded as one of those nasty Philadelphia spring days, but the rain and the cool weather did not deter the determined Wildcats. Schappert, happy to return after a two-year hiatus, led off and quickly found himself in 5th place. He got mad and said, "Enough of that." He hammered, took the lead and handed off in 1.49.5. Eckman, now with a year's experience behind him, cranked out his best 400 meters ever (46.7) and passed to an eager Gregan. Tom's first lap in 56 seconds assured him that world record pace was still on and with his 2:56 ¾ mile, it was now up to Coghlan. Eamonn spared nothing. He ran like a man possessed, with his three teammates strategically placed at 100-meter intervals to cheer him on, each time he circled Franklin Field. On the last lap, he decisively dropped the Arizona anchor and finished with a 3:56.3 mile—his best time yet. The crowd was going crazy as they witnessed history in the making. The team time of 9:28.2 smashed the Penn Relays record (9:36.8, also held by Villanova).

It also broke the world record held by Kansas State by a full three seconds. Only Jim Ryun, with 3:55.6 anchor leg in the distance medley at the 1967 Drake Relays, had ever run a faster relay mile. Wilkie's beer offering now loomed large but would have to wait for a day. There was more business to attend to. Win number one. And Villanova's DMR streak now at 10.

The Sunday *Philadelphia Inquirer* said it all: "Villanova wins 4 and 2-Mile Relays."[3] This time, the apprentice Mark Belger led off the four mile event. The freshman displayed hints of future greatness as he easily romped his four laps in 4:08.6 and with a lead over Fordham. From there, it was just another regular working day for Team Villanova—Schappert followed with a leisurely 4:12, Gregan contributed a 4:07, and Coghlan had room to spare after Schappert and Gregan had built up a 50-yard lead. The crowd expected Coghlan to take time for tea, he was so far ahead. But he showed no signs of letting up. When he finished, and Jack O'Reilly announced the time of 3:59.6, the crowd responded wildly, knowing that they had just witnessed an exceptional run by a gifted runner. Final team time—16:27.4. Win number two.

Tiny Kane debuted his first Penn Relays' win with the Two Mile Relay. Leading off with a 1:53.5 he handed off to a tired Coghlan who dug deep to run a 1:51.9. As he passed the baton to Schappert, everyone knew this was Ken's last race. Eamonn wanted to give Ken as big a lead as possible. Ken wanted to leave Franklin Field a winner, no matter how tired. Having clocked a 1:51.6, it was over to the now more experienced apprentice Mark Belger, who finished the job with a good 30-yard win over Tennessee. Mark's time—1:51.4. Win number three.

Being named the Penn Relay's Most Valuable Athlete proved to be the appetizer for Eamonn Coghlan. The main course remained to be served. Technically, he was still not a sub four-minute miler. His two Penn Relay mile times did not qualify, but he was about to change that. The Invitational Mile in Pittsburgh, two weeks later lay ahead.

A critical thing about Eamonn was this: he needed his space. While he loved the limelight, he needed a place where he could quietly re-gather his energies and his thoughts. His father Bill had arrived on campus for the second year in row to witness the Penn Relays and take in all the ancillary activities, including life on campus. With his ebullient personality and youthful aura, Bill soon gained as much attention as Eamonn. Bill stayed with Eamonn in his single dormitory room. Finally, Eamonn had enough. Having Bill around was one thing; having your father hang around like "one of the boys" was another. Eamonn disappeared for a while and considered not going to Pittsburgh at all. That did not go over well with Bill, or Jumbo for that matter. The team had already left for what is typically a six-hour drive. Quick flight arrangements were made and later that afternoon, Eamonn ran his first official sub four-minute mile—3:56.4—precisely the same time as the DMR mile time he had run two weeks earlier. It was also the fastest college mile of the year.

On May 17th, everything changed. The 1975 version of the Martin Luther King Games were hosted in Kingston, Jamaica. Bert Lancaster, who had put together the famous Dream Mile featuring Liquori and Ryun in 1971, set his "dream" even higher. The plan: beat the world record of 3:51.1—now eight years old. Filbert Bayi, the 21-year-old Tanzanian who broke the world record for the 1500 meters in 1974 with a time of 3:32.2—in effect a sub 3:50 mile, was coming to town.

Lancaster assembled a top-class field including Filbert Bayi, Marty Liquori, Rick Wolhuter, and Tony Waldrop (the latter, both 3:53 milers), and Reggie McAfee from North Carolina, Walter Wilkson of England, and Eamonn Coghlan. Everyone knew that it would be fast and Bayi would take it out. Only one question remained: how fast would the first two laps be?

Kingston, Jamaica in mid-May is not the paragon of sanguine cool summer evenings. To no one's surprise, it was hot and steamy. All these years later Marty Liquori surmised, "If this race had been run in California or some place with lower humidity, everyone would have run 2 to 3 seconds faster." But the weather conditions did not slow Bayi. He stormed through the first quarter mile in 56.9—a stiff pace. In second place followed Eamonn Coghlan about 15 yards back. The half was reached in 1:56.6—still on world record pace. Then Bayi began to slow. And by the end of the third lap, to the astonishment of Bayi and the crowd, the pesky Coghlan started pressing him for the lead, both passing the ¾ mile mark in 2.55. Bayi jolted ahead with both Coghlan and Liquori in hot pursuit. Coghlan continued to hold off Liquori but coming off the last turn, Liquori passed. They touched elbows, which caused a slight momentum loss. The race was coming to a close in spectacular fashion: Bayi in 3:51.0—a new world record by 1/10th of a second; Liquori in 3:52.2—his best time ever. And Eamonn Coghlan in 3:53.3. All three times were astonishing.

Eamonn's 3:53.3 mile, a seven-second personal improvement within a two-week period, became the fastest mile ever run by a European, an Irishman, and a Villanovan. In less than four minutes, Coghlan had firmly seized center stage. The sporting world from near and far witnessed or heard about this race. The new world record for the mile caught global attention and made headline news in every major paper. To top it off, *Sports Illustrated* featured the event on the coveted cover—a full color shot of Bayi leading; Coghlan with his Villanova singlet in second; and Liquori with his red USA running vest, in third.[4]

That day and with that cover issue, Villanova track reached a new apogee. Because of the already-proven Marty Liquori, and the rise of a new star—Eamonn Coghlan— Villanova was now seen as the indisputable producer of world-class milers. That was the day Coghlan knew that there would be no race before him in which he could not be a contender. He could run with anyone. And the 1976 Olympics were exactly 14 months away.

Penn Relays 1976

The first six months of 1976, Coghlan looked unbeatable. Races on the US college circuit seemed like child's play. He would win every race he ran, deploy any tactics he chose, and take on whatever competitors threw at him. It was if he were saying, "Want to go out hard, go ahead. I'll just outkick you. Want to wait and kick? Well, I'll just outkick you! Want to run fast? Well, let's go. And good luck. You're not going to beat me anyway." He was like a kid again in the streets of Drimnagh or on the Field of Dreams where he knew when in doubt, he could outrun everyone.

Eamonn Coghlan was in a class of his own easily winning both the indoor IC4A and the NCAA mile (4:01.5). No matter what race he was running, however, he was looking ahead to one race and one race only—the Olympic 1500-meter final in Montréal. Shortly after Jamaica, John Walker did indeed break the 3:50 barrier running 3:49:4 for the mile—shocking the world and putting himself in the position as the favorite for the Olympic 1500-meter final. Eamonn began to study his every move. His confidence never faltered. He did not fear Walker. Or Bayi. Or anyone. All he needed to do was keep building his strength. He knew that if he was with the leaders with 200 meters or less to go, he could move with the best of them. Actually, slightly better than the best of them, with that famed "change of gear" in reserve.

You would think that after 10 consecutive DMR wins, and with a strong experienced team, getting ready for the 1976 Penn Relays would be routine. But every year is different, and every year brought new challenges. This year, Mark Belger, who was developing into a top class 800-meter runner, ran like a sack of potatoes that week before Penn. Earlier that week, Belger checked into the Bryn Mawr Hospital like a "body stuffed with asbestos"—congestion so bad, he could hardly breathe. And Tiny Kane was having heel problems; "like running on cardboard filled with tacks," is how he described the pain. But both quarter miler Greg Eckman and Eamonn Coghlan were fine.

Another win for Eamonn Coghlan

No matter, the usual Friday 3:00 p.m. start of the DMR saw Belger return to competitive form with a slim lead running 1:48.4. Eckman cranked his usual 47.4. Tiny brushed off the tacks and "tackled" the 1300 meters (the DMR went metric in 1976 and chose this unusual distance). That was completed in 3.14. Now to Eamonn. Full of confidence, he ran like a man without a worry in the world. Only Princeton stayed close, anchored by Craig Masbach, another emerging world-class miler. But with 300 meters to go, the cocky Coghlan waved to the crowd (which included Yvonne, his Dublin girlfriend visiting Philadelphia) and headed for home. It was an easy and a convincing win, leaving Masbach a good 40 meters in his wake. Eamonn Coghlan, a runner without equal on the US college scene had not only displayed his superior athletic skills, with his wave of supreme confidence like Babe Ruth, he had now ventured into the entertainment business. The crowd loved it. Win number one. And the 11th DMR in a row.

The 1976 version of the Four Mile Relay became a 4x1500 meters. Once again, Jumbo waved his magic wand and made his choices. Who would fill the apprentice spot this time? Usually, it would be a promising freshman because it was a great way to introduce the novice who would be required only to keep the team in the race by being in the top three or four. Then Jumbo would rely on the next three runners, particularly the star anchor, to bring the team home. Stars would be runners like a Patrick, Liquori, or Hartnett, and now Coghlan. This year Jumbo made a choice that is still the subject of conversation among Villanova track alumni 45 years later. He chose Gary Trojanowski.

Gary arrived at Villanova in the fall of 1972—a promising 1:51 800-meter runner from North Jersey. But he had two major limitations. He was often injured; and he was a pure introvert who was prone to worry. Gary would never say a word. He would sit quietly with the team during lunches or dinners or just as soon slip away. Gary kept to himself and worried. We called him "O.J. Tro Jay," tried to keep it light, but his demeanour and comfort level never changed. Yet he hung in there faithfully and quietly showing up for workouts. Then, at the very last minute, during the warm-up before the race, Jumbo grabbed Gary and said: "You're leading off." Jumbo knew full well that if he had told Gary even a day earlier or that morning, he would have worried himself sick.

Without having any time to worry, Gary was standing on the starting line (meanwhile the entire Villanova team was holding its breath and wishing out loud for Gary's best effort). And 3:48 later, he handed off to George Mackay. It was as if a cloud lifted from Franklin Field. Gary had finished and the baton was in good standing. George, now in his junior year, ran a 3:45.8; Phil Kane took over and added another 3:46.5 effort; then over to Eamonn to finish the job, which he did easily with a 3:42.5 (another sub-four-minute mile equivalent). This time Eamonn turned a five-yard lead into 50 over Dave Merrick from Penn. But this victory was dedicated to OJ Tro Jay's four tough years at Villanova coming to an end, and now with a Penn Relays watch. Win number two.

One more race, two hours and 40 minutes later, and the 4 x 800 meter team went to work. Again, if you thought each race was easy, think again. This time George MacKay, the leadoff man, was boxed and found himself in last place. But he went wide and with his 1:50.8 effort worked through the field and handed off in the lead to Tiny Kane who followed with a near duplicate time of 1:50.9; Eamonn as third man, wheeled off a 1:49.3 and by this time, the transformed "bag of potatoes" from the week before, Mark Belger, ran a magnificent 1:47.0 to seal the win.

Win number three, and wristwatch number nine for Eamonn Coghlan. His win record at Penn Relays now matched Liquori's. The outdoor track season was only starting.

In mid-June, Eamonn easily won the NCAA 1500-meter race in a record time of 3:37.0—the equivalent of a 3:54 mile. Again, he made it look easy. No US college runner posed even the slightest threat.

The Montréal Olympics were only six weeks away. During those final weeks, Eamonn returned to the Villanova campus to prepare for the games. Fortunately, he had company and was joined by Ken Schappert, Phil Kane, and Mark Belger. All three had competed at the US Olympic Trials but no one successfully made the team. Belger finished a narrow 4th and came within a hair's breadth of third position of making the US Olympic Team. Still full of running, they returned to work with Eamonn. The training went well—everything was moving in the right direction.

Now for my Dostoyevsky unconventional style and the telling of the outcome up front. Coghlan finished 4th in the Olympic final, and he was bitterly disappointed. Leading up to the final, he had moved easily through the heats and semi-finals with no more difficulty than with the US college scene. Now, only the final lay before him, which included the best milers in the world: John Walker, Rick Wolhuter, Ivo Van Damme, Frank Clement, Graham Crouch, Paul Wellmann, and Dave Moorcroft.

I will not comment about the race or how it unfolded. I will comment only on what I describe to be Eamonn running the Olympic final while carrying two voices in his head. First, it was the voice of Gerry Farnham. Gerry knew what Eamonn could do, his ability to shift gears at that critical point in a race. And he knew that while Walker was fast, he was "one speed" fast. Eamonn could take him no matter the pace.

The other voice was Jumbo Elliott—Jumbo who had coached both Dave Patrick and Marty Liquori to beat the fastest half-miler and miler in the world with a strong and early finishing kick. Jumbo had called that day before the race and said, "There are some fast guys in there! Don't let the pace be too slow." Eamonn clearly remembers that conversation. The inference of course, was to run the sting out of those speedsters early in the race.

That day of the final, Eamonn stood on the start line with the voice of Gerry Farnham in his head. When he heard the first split—62.8 seconds—slower than a high school mile, Eamonn suddenly heard the voice of Jumbo. He reacted immediately, moved through the field, and took the lead. And there he stayed for the next 800 meters and with 300 meters to go, Walker moved swiftly past him, and the race was on. Eamonn bravely fought Walker for the next 100 meters but the stress of leading had been too much as Van Damme and Wellmann also passed. Eamonn could not reel them in. The result is history.

Could there have been a different outcome? Again, I will not comment on which voice echoed the right strategy. All I can say is this: had Eamonn committed to only one of the two strategies from the very outset and stuck with it, he would have been on the podium. Had he chosen to run the sting out of Walker, that first lap would have been much faster. Had he chosen to wait and kick, let Walker make the first move, he could have met him stride for stride. Interestingly, over the ensuing years, Eamonn and John Walker had many duels and over the course of these head-to-head encounters, Eamonn won more than he lost. To this day, Eamonn regrets the move he made in that instant—upon hearing the 400-meter split time.

Here comes the end of the "Villanova Coghlan Era." To summarize, it was a magnificent college career. The Eamonn Coghlan story is a composite of many factors, but let's focus on the following four.

First, talent. Eamonn was a prodigious talent—there is no question of that. He had speed, endurance, and a deep desire to win no matter what. The harder he worked, the more his talent shone through. Once he overcame a series of nagging injuries that are not unusual for a developing runner and able to train regularly, his performances went from strength to strength.

Second, Jumbo Elliott. Eamonn Coghlan had been just one phone call away from obscurity—from being just another Dubliner working nine to five in some unknown capacity in some unknown place of work. Jumbo peered through the distractions, saw his talent, and gave him a second chance.

Third, the "Us" factor. In his own words, Eamonn acknowledges that he was a product of "Us"—that core group of caring and engaged teammates who supported and challenged him as he settled and developed during those early and vulnerable days at Villanova.

Fourth, the competitive environment. The US college system, despite the criticisms directed toward it, especially by Europeans, provided him with a full and diverse range of challenges with both individual races and relays, where he learned his skills and learned that he could win no matter what tactic was being thrown at him. Eamonn loved to race and loved the stage that racing provided. There was no better place than Villanova University.

Finally, the full story of Eamonn Coghlan is an almost unbelievable narrative of a promising high-school miler with good but not outstanding times who became a world-class miler in three short years. He did not arrive at Villanova as a high school superstar. He had not run a sub four-minute mile, nor like his Dublin counterpart was he the second fastest 18-year-old 1500-meter runner of all time. He came as a promising talent who was yet to develop. It is a remarkable story of hope, redemption (thanks to Jumbo), and accomplishment that occurred within the milieu of a team environment that would continue to inspire the next generations of Villanova runners for years to come. Eamonn Coghlan went on to become one of the most accomplished middle-distance runners in the history of track and field.

The full story of Eamonn Coghlan among track fans is well-known—his unparalleled indoor prowess; the world-record holder for the indoor mile—three times—and a record he held for 20 years! The first person to break 3:50 for the mile indoors; the 5,000-meter World Champion in 1983 at the inaugural

IAAF World Championships in Helsinki that featured athletes from all countries around the world unlike the African boycott at the 1976 Montréal Olympics, and the Western boycott of the 1980 Moscow Olympic. He was the four-time Olympian, held two fourth place Olympic finishes, and was a competitor in every major mile race from 1975 to 1985. He was the very first Master (40 years of age or older) to break the four-minute mile, at the age of 41.

Postscript 1

There is one addendum to this story specific to Eamonn's experiences at the Olympics. It can be argued that if he had committed to one race plan in Montréal and if drug testing had been fully adhered to in Moscow, Eamonn would have been the recipient of two medals. In the latter race, a finisher ahead of him either admitted to or was found to be using performance-enhancing drugs. I endeavored to set the record straight and find a way to award Eamonn the medal he justly deserved.

The plan was to request the CEO and President of the London Olympics, Sir Sebastian Coe on behalf of the IOC, to award Eamonn the bronze medal for the 5000 meters in 1980 (the silver medalist had openly admitted to taking drugs). But the request had to be initiated by the Irish Olympic Committee and subsequently supported by the Finnish Olympic Committee. We even went as far as having the support of the Irish Minister of Culture and Sport. However, the perennial head of the Irish Olympic Committee—a certain Pat Hickey—would not comply. There was no love lost between them. He disliked Eamonn and Eamonn disliked him. That is the same Pat Hickey who was ignominiously caught in the act of scalping 2016 Olympic tickets in Rio de Janeiro meant for members of the Olympic Council of Ireland, including families and friends of Irish Olympians.[5] This sordid affair placed Hickey's morality, small mindedness, and paucity of leadership skills in full display—Eamonn had conflicted with this so-called leader years earlier. Thus, the lack of required support, and the failed endeavor to secure the medal that is rightly and deservedly Eamonn's.

But in the end, does this matter? Not having an Olympic medal in his medal collection does nothing to diminish the accomplishments and legacy of Eamonn Coghlan. His record of achievement, his personality, and the excitement he brought to the sport, far outlives the asterisk in a book of records, that an Olympic medal might have added.

Indeed, Eamonn Coghlan was truly one of a kind—a precocious Irish street kid who took his natural talents and made the absolute most of the opportunity that Jumbo Elliott and Villanova University offered him.

9

New York's Finest: The Belger-Paige Era

"You can't do it alone. The team made me what I became."

Don Paige

Now for perhaps the most astonishing and unexpected period of the Villanova track dynasty.

The year was 1977, and Villanova was absent a world-class miler. The formula for winning relays, particularly the DMR, no longer applied. Patrick, Liquori, and Hartnett were distant memories. The dominant Coghlan had recently graduated and was now back in Ireland. The press sounded the alarm bells early with such headlines as, "It's No Longer Villanova's Party."[1] Gordon Forbes, with the *Philadelphia Inquirer,* went on to say, "On the eve of the 83rd Penn Relays, Jumbo remembered when his great relay teams were built around a world class miler, remarkable depth and Irish-style spirit. This year would have none of those!"[2]

No one was happier than Jim Tuppeny, Director of the Penn Relays and Head Coach of the University of Pennsylvania Track Program. While he focused on building the most prestigious track meet and relay carnival in the world, he had become a victim of his own success. Or should we say, a victim of Villanova's success. Not only was he stymied again and again in failing to win a major championship for his own team—University of Pennsylvania—he was also having difficulty attracting the best schools from across the country to participate in the Penn Relays only to be defeated by those damn Wildcats. Penn Relays had become known as the "Villanova Relays"—the annual bust-out for none other than Villanova University Track. Other venues, such as the Drake Relays, Kansas Relays, and Texas Relays became the preferred choice.

This year, Tuppeny boasted that the Penn Relays would be bigger and better than ever. He lauded that he had been able to attract new schools such as Arizona State, New Mexico, and Auburn; also, UTEP was back, and Tennessee and Rice would again bring competitive teams. Plus, he added a field of world-class sprinters (Don Quarrie, Olympic 200-meter champion; Steve Riddick, a top 100 meter specialist) as well as a world-class mile featuring Wilson Waigwa and Paul Cummings to add to the excitement. Tuppeny went on to predict that several relay and world records would fall—the 4 x 100 meters; the 4 x 200 meters; the 4 x 400 meters. He went so far as to predict new records for both the Sprint and Distance Medleys, although he would name no favorites. No mention of Villanova.

Meanwhile Jumbo pleaded poverty. He offered no forecasts. He let Tuppeny glow in his own self-stirred stew. Little did Elliott know that the stew had been further agitated the previous year when Gregan and Coghlan called Tuppeny over and ripped his coveted red Penn Relays Director hat (the only one) right off his head. Tuppeny screamed but was no match in pursuit as the two Irish scamps disappeared into the crowd at great haste. To this day, that same hat sits in Tom Gregan's trophy case. But Jumbo knew that despite Tuppeny's dismissive attitude, a new generation of Villanova stars was about to enter the world stage.

Who were these stars? The track world was about to be introduced to two of the most prodigious high school middle distance runners ever to emerge from New York State: Mark Belger and Don Paige. Their stories and accomplishments are remarkable. But before we explore these details, first meet some additional members of the Villanova cast:

Phil "Tiny" Kane. Now in his senior year, Tiny (an inherited nickname as the youngest of four brothers), showed steady improvement year after year. Arriving the fall of 1973, Tiny was a 1:52—880-yard runner in high school from Rhode Island. With the experience of the past three years (1974, 1975, and 1976), he had run the Two Mile Relay leading off twice and running in second position in 1976. A ferocious competitor, he had been thoroughly mentored by Ken Schappert and Eamonn Coghlan. No one could laugh louder or dish out sharper verbal attacks than Tiny. At 6 feet and 150 pounds, he was also very strong—he could bench press 260 pounds, substantially more than the next strongest member of the team. A four-minute mile was only a few races away and for Penn Relays 1977, he was ready for more. (Note: Tiny ran a 3:41.6—1500 meters at the NCAA Outdoor Championships, mid-June 1976).

Ed Takacs. Also a senior and the second Canadian to be awarded a track scholarship to Villanova, Ed became affectionately known as "Big Ed," not because of his size (5'10"—140 pounds), but because of his heart.[3] Freshman year, Jumbo put Tiny and Takacs up for an 880-yard time trial to compete for the last position on the Two Mile Relay Team (joining Coghlan, Gregan, and Bouma). In late January, on the boards, in the wind and in full sweats, they went head-to-head, with Ed leading the whole way. The time: 1:54—the fastest ever run on the boards in those conditions. In 1975, after stumbling with 330 yards to go, Ed blew by the entire field winning the IC4A outdoor 880 yards in 1:47.6. Ed had talent to spare but fought a continued series of injuries. He also bestowed an endearing innocence. When he arrived at Villanova in September 1973, he told John Hartnett and me the story of winning the Ontario high school 800-meter championships in a pair of borrowed spikes—two sizes too big. John and I burst out laughing and still laugh about that encounter to this day.

John Burns. A Philadelphia boy, John was the product of Coach Tom Donnelly who had graduated from Villanova in 1969. One could not find a better facsimile and duplication of the model coach-athlete relationship than John and Tom. Both were quiet, both were thoughtful and extremely courteous, both made for the most supportive teammates you could possibly find, and both were very tough runners. John ran a 4:13 mile as a junior and despite injuries his senior year, never considered going anywhere else but becoming part of the legendary Villanova coached by Jumbo Elliott. As a LaSalle high school graduate, John was fully schooled on the importance of Penn Relays—he competed both on relay teams and the high school mile finishing fifth in that event his junior year. Specific to Villanova, Coach Donnelly had taken John's high school cross-country team to the campus several times for training purposes. John had never seen a college campus prior to that and was in awe by the number and size of the buildings. More significantly, the reputation and quality of the track team left a deep impression.

Glen Bogue. The third Canadian on scholarship and a 400-meter runner, Glen ran one of the fastest times in the country for that distance at the age of 18. Highly intelligent, the only thing that moved faster than his feet, were his lips. From Toronto's Michael Power High School, a perennial track power, Glen could talk a blue streak on any subject and would often end up arguing with himself. He was always looking for that special edge, that inside viewpoint or advantage. It began on his recruiting trip—instead of entering campus past the Security Gate (which was usually a non-starter to the casual visitor), he slipped into a back parking lot, not seeing the reverse entry prevention teeth. Four flat tires later and sheepish grin, he found his way to the cafeteria, located the track table, and announced his arrival. His muted entry drew a good laugh and a modicum of sympathy. But he could deliver a great one lap any day of the week. And by 1977, Glen brought Olympic experience to the Villanova team having represented Canada in the 4 x 400 meter sprint event at the Montréal Olympics, 1976.

Mark Belger making it look easy

Now to New York's finest. Villanova had the incredible fortune to attract not one but two of the very best high-school half-milers/milers that the state had ever produced. First came Mark Belger, from Wellington C. Mepham High School, Long Island who arrived in September of 1974; second was Don Paige from upstate Baldwinsville, New York, a small town just west of Syracuse, who arrived one year later in 1975. Both finalized their decisions to come to Villanova (as did Ed Takacs) thanks to the ultimate salesmanship of Ken Schappert. Ken who by now had established himself as a top national-caliber half-miler, served the role as Jumbo's final pitch man and closer. The recruit would receive the tour of campus, the Field House, a walk around the track, and possibly a visit to Jumbo's house about a 15-minute drive away, and then be delivered to Schapp. He would quietly settle down with the recruit and then deliver his famous and most effective pitch: "If you go to another school, you are likely to be the top dog. If you come to Villanova, there are four or five guys who are going to push you every day. "If you train with the best, you become one of the best." It worked every time. Add to that mix was Jumbo's practice to never talk about track. Instead, he would inquire about family, school, interests—all probes that would help him understand the character of the recruit in front of him. After the Schappert pep talk, Ed could not wait to sign the letter of intent; Mark liked the idea that as an athlete at Villanova, "I was going to be one of a dozen middle distance runners and not a loner."

Don recalls after visiting Tennessee, Kansas, Fordham, and Georgetown, that the Villanova recruiting trip was quite frankly not very impressive, until the conversation with Ken. He spoke in his usual blunt style: "Don, we are total opposites. If you go somewhere else, you are going to be top dog right off the bat. Here you can become the best in the world." That comment really got Don's attention and his mind was made up—he was coming to Villanova.

Mark Belger had shown his incredible capability already as a junior in high school when he clocked a 1:50.4 – 880 yards at the New York State Intersectional Track Meet. That time was the second fastest time ever recorded by a 16-year-old, the fastest being Jim Ryun who went on to set world records in both the 880 yards and the mile run. Needless to say, the entire US college world was interested in this prodigiously talented kid. A year later, he set a record in the indoor 1,000-yard run, ran a 4:11.7 mile, and another 1:49.7 – 800 meters at the Junior AAU Championships in June. To top those times, he produced a demonstration of speed with a 48.8 – 440 yards.

Running fast was one thing. But the remarkable quality about Mark was his incredibly relaxed attitude toward racing. He may have been the coolest cat ever—his good looks, full head of blonde hair and his almost "aw shucks" attitude, which disguised his relentless will to win. The first time I saw Mark was in February 1973, the Millrose Games High School mile. There he was bouncing along near the back of the pack seemingly in his own world enjoying the ambience of the "Gawdens." Then, with three laps to go, he woke up and quickly passed the entire field to win easily. He never seemed to worry about races or racing. Once he said, "Winning is easy. Make your move, go to the front, and don't let anyone pass. What's hard about that?" His relaxed approach to life extended to his early Villanova days. On weekends, he would regularly hitchhike back home to Long Island. That is, until Jumbo heard about these peregrinations. He quickly intercepted Mark on a subsequent weekday and slipped him twenty bucks and some advice: "Take the train. And get a job to support your travel costs."

Don Paige embodied an entirely different personality. For Don, running was serious business. If there was ever a prototype miler to be designed from scratch, it would be Don Paige. Standing just over six feet, he represented the perfect cross between Jim Ryun and Marty Liquori. With his neatly cropped dark hair; broad square shoulders; distinctly sculpted jaw line; perfect posture; carefully selected sweaters, casual trousers, and shoes; and his sartorial style, Paige was every inch the All-American. He adored Jumbo, a man who represented everything that Don admired and sought to emulate. But more than anything, he hated to lose. Which meant he would win, win, and win again.

A youthful Don Paige

Don's Baldwinsville high school was far from a paragon for the development of track and field. In fact, it did not even have a track. Don would be doing his "track" training in the form of laps around the parking lot. Clearly, that limitation did not thwart Don's abilities or his ambitions. By his senior year, he did something never done before in New York State—he won both the 880 yards and the one mile run in times of 1:52.9 and 4:11.2 respectively.

Both Mark and Don established themselves as strong finishers and known for having "devastating kicks."[4] With the running of the State 880 yards Championship, spectators aware of Don's strong finishing style were waiting and waiting wondering, is he going to move? Finally he did, and flew by the field and the leading runner on the homestretch.[5] Mark would also wait, wait, and then make his big move, inevitably to be in full control by race end. If there was any difference between the two and how they could finish, it was perhaps this: Don Paige had this uncanny capacity to find yet another gear, even when he was kicking. It seemed that no matter how fatigued he might be, he could still find that extra dose of speed. That capability put the icing on Don's winning cake, first in high school and many times in future races.

Finishing the full workout for Mark almost became the exception. Some of his teammates would chuckle and ask: Does Mark even train? He was famous for doing strides. No matter how much time he took off, or whatever break necessary because of injury, within a couple of weeks of light training and some strides on the grass, Mark was ready to run sub 1:50 for the half-mile. In contrast, Don took every workout, every road mile and every lap on the track seriously. Ed Takacs recalls one morning six-mile run—it was flat out from the moment they stepped outside the Field House. No room for idle chatter—it was push, push, push the whole way. After the run, which led the somewhat bewildered Canadian to say "Don!! This is a training run, not a race!" Don just looked at him, shrugged, and walked away. Whatever the differences and whatever the situation, Jumbo knew one thing: keep these two boys apart. While at Villanova, Mark and Don never raced each other.

The lead up to the 1977 Penn Relays saw Belger as a junior and Don as a sophomore. Despite what appears to be Jim Tuppeny's deliberate oversight of Villanova's potential, Mark had already established himself as a bona fide big-time

American indoor Four Mile relay record holders:
George MacKay, Don Paige, Mark Belger, and Tiny Kane

performer. The previous year he finished fourth at the Olympic Trials. Leading the race, coming into the homestretch, he was outdistanced for third place by .08 seconds running 1:46.36 for 800 meters. Furthermore, he was the 1977 NCAA 880-meter Indoor Champion with a 1:49.17 time, second fastest only to Dave Patrick's world-record 880-yards, a full 10 years earlier on that same Cobo Hall track.

Don meanwhile has gone from one injury to the next. His freshman year was close to a complete write-off although early in the season he ran a 4.01 mile as part of the Four Mile Relay as the Villanova Team set a new world and US national indoor record at Dartmouth College in New Hampshire. This team included Mark Belger, Tiny Kane, and George MacKay. Significantly, Jumbo had left Eamonn Coghlan off the team to allow the four American-born athletes to achieve this record. Shortly thereafter, a hairline fracture had Jumbo scrambling and making the decision to have Don redshirt the year and spend the necessary time to recover. A quick phone call to Marty Liquori and Don was on the next flight to Gainesville, Florida. Under Marty's watchful tutelage, Don regained his running capability and gained further insight into the routine and mind of the number one miler in the world, now a top 5,000-meter runner. Don could not have been placed with a better mentor than Marty. The 1977 year showed promise, but once again injuries prevailed and by the time Penn Relays came around, he was on the sidelines.

Penn Relays 1977

One of Jumbo's favorite phrases when talking about his relay teams a week or so before the Penn Relays would be referring to the "walking wounded." Sometimes he applied the term in jest to keep the press guessing or to take the stress off the team. But in 1977, this was no joke. There were "wounded" everywhere.

Mark Belger wins another

Don Paige had a stress fracture in his fibula; George Mackay had been in a nasty auto accident that damaged his lower leg resulting in phlebitis; Greg Eckman pulled a leg muscle while running at the Dogwood Relays in Knoxville, Tennessee; and Ed Takacs had an infected hip. With respect to the latter, Jumbo shrugged and muttered with obvious frustration, "Don't ask me how you get an infected hip. Check with the doctor." What's more, the teams were not looking good. Two weeks earlier at the Dogwood Relays, Villanova lost the DMR and the Four Mile Relays to the University of Tennessee. In both those races, Phil Kane had been outkicked by Dave Lapp, Tennessee's top miler.

Friday, April 29th rolled in as one of those nasty spring days. While not raining, the winds were cold and gusty. At the last minute, Jumbo named his team: Takacs seemed to be OK (or 85 percent according to the increasingly worried head coach) and would lead off with the opening 800 meters; Bogue would run the 400 meters replacing Greg Eckman who had run this event the previous three years; then it would be Mark Belger on the 1200-meter leg followed by Tiny Kane as anchor.

But the final DMR team selection was not without considerable mystery and drama. John Burns, who had shown increased progress both as miler and a half miler, was hoping to be named to this team. With Takacs still complaining about his injury and Tiny being outkicked twice which undermined his confidence, things were very much in the air. The day before, Jumbo sent for John to come to the office. He told him, "Ed may not be able to run, so be prepared to run the 800 leg in the event that Ed can't go." Before the race, John warmed up with the team and Ed was clearly struggling. John recounts the moment: "I was nervous knowing the continuation of the streak may ride on me stepping in. But Ed decided he could run, and I had to wait my turn."

Running with doubled determination, Ed Takacs struggled from the sound of the gun. By the end of lap two, he was well back of the leaders, in seventh place. The *Philadelphia Inquirer* already predicted an upset in the making: "Villanova could not have got the lead in the DMR by tossing the baton, much less carrying it."[6] So dire was the outlook, but then Canadian number two, Glen Bogue, cranked the 400 meters of his life. Passing all but three runners, he unleashed a 45.8 time for the single circuit—his best ever. Wait a minute—this race may not be over yet. Now Belger receiving the baton a good 15 meters back of the leaders, went to work. Flowing with ease but with evident speed, the crowd soon realized that they were witnessing one of the greatest runs of all time—two minutes and 50 seconds later, Mark handed a 15-meter lead to an eager Phil Kane, ahead of Tennessee's Dave Lapp. This time it would be different. Tiny went out strong and on the second lap allowed Lapp to catch up. But as soon as that happened, Tiny picked up the pace again and made Lapp work all the harder. But this time, Tiny was in control and closed with a 3:59.7 mile to win by 10 yards.

Win number one. And the 12th DMR win in a row. The streak had held and afterwards the headlines read: "Villanova Wins With A Fast ¾ Leg."[7] Thanks to Mark Belger.

The time of 9:28.5 now stood as a new record. Jumbo as always was ecstatic, having expected that this might be the year at long last that the Villanova luck might have run out. But Tiny Kane was slightly more reflective: "Sure we won but Villanova is so strong. If we had Mackay, Eckman, Paige, and any half-miler you wanted, we would have finished one, two in this race."

John Burns's chance came less than 22 hours later, along with more drama. He recounts the lead up: "We were going to try for three more Championship of America titles (4 x 1500, the Sprint Medley, and 4 x 800), but Jumbo changed things up as the Dogwood Relays were still on his mind. He pulled Tiny off the 4 x 1500 to save his strength for the 4 x 800. Tiny was not pleased that he was replaced by Carey Pinkowski, and we lost at least 10 seconds due to that change. Without Tiny, Jumbo put me on to anchor that 4 x 1500 team. By the time I got the baton from Jimmy Flynn, we were well behind Tennessee and Penn State, and we finished third." Indeed, the hard-working, dedicated team member John Burns received his first chance to represent Villanova at the event he grew up watching. But he would have to wait another year before he would be able to place a coveted Penn Relays watch on his wrist.

Meanwhile Mark Belger's weekend of "fun and frolic" had just begun. There was nothing he loved more than relay races—"it's like playing tag as a kid." That Saturday, he would display his enormous capabilities by anchoring two more winning relays: first the Spring Medley, which had eluded Villanova's winning domain since 1970. The team of Tim Dale, Keith Brown, Derek Harbour—all top-quality sprinters plus Mark Belger—this time with a 1:46.2 anchor leg to take that event. Again, Jumbo was over-the-moon delighted. This was not expected. Win number two.

Two hours later, the Two Mile Relay was on deck. Mark Fallow (1:51.3), a recovered Ed Takacs (1:49.7), Phil Kane (1:47.7), and Mark Belger (1:47.6). Win number three. Belger ran another brilliant anchor and continued his undefeated streak at Penn Relays—this was win number seven and he still had a year ahead of him. Jumbo had mixed his magic brew once again and looked like a genius. And Jim Tuppeny could not believe his eyes. Not again! That was supposed to be Arizona State's grand debut. What happened to Tennessee? They had the Wildcats eating out of their hands two weeks ago. But this? This is supposed to be the year of the Villanova shut-out. He tried to hide his frustration as he twisted his newly replaced Meet Director's hat back into position. "Those damn Wildcats," he was heard to say.

Penn Relays 1978

Jerry Bouma and Carl Lewis, 2015

The absence of a world-class miler and the lack of Irish charm did little to stop the Villanova Wildcat train in 1978. It seemed that a whole new assembly of incomparable track stars emerged from all fronts. Villanova rolled over its competitors at the IC4A Indoor Championship with Belger winning the 880 yards, Paige winning the 1000 yards, and Glen Bogue winning the 600 yards. Then, at the ensuing NCAA Indoor Championships, the Belger-Paige duo continued that one, two punch as they redefined the term "dominance" in the shorter middle distances: first Mark Belger won the 880 yards in 1:49.3; literally minutes later Don Paige stepped up to win the 1000 yards in 2:07.88 in what would become classic Paige style, winning by 1/100 of a second, out-leaning Randy Wilson from Oklahoma with a 2:07.89.

And two freshman sprinters emerged to leave their marks on the national college scene: Derek Harbour—a fourth in the 440 yards (48.93) and Anthony Tufariello with a sixth in the 600 yards (1.10.4). Unbeknownst to most, Jumbo had been quietly recruiting several top-quality sprinters including Tim Dale to join the speedy Glen Bogue. One of these recruits, a promising long-jumper with some speed, Carl Lewis, accepted an invitation to visit Villanova in February of that year. In 2015, Carl was a personal guest when we hosted the Pan-American Junior Championships in Edmonton when he told me the story. I said, "Let me guess. You walked out to the boards and met with Jumbo in his little hut to shield yourself from that cold winter wind." Carl burst out laughing and said, "Man! That was too much for me. I'm going to Houston where it's hot!"

The Villanova Track Team approached the '78 Penn Relays with eager anticipation. They knew they were strong, but how strong? Don Paige at last was healthy. And after nearly two years at Villanova, would you believe that this would be his first outdoor track meet as a Wildcat? Of course, Belger was ready—it did not matter what kind of shape he was in, or what injury he might be enduring, or even if he had a bad cold. Everyone knew that Mark Belger would be ready. In his words, "There's no excuses. Once a year you pull out all the stops—don't even think about it—just go. All you have to do is run for two minutes (or three). Who cares? Go nuts for those two minutes." The sprinters were looking good and the middle-distance group with John Burns, another Canadian—Dean Childs from Calgary, and Jim Flynn being both deep and strong.

Don Paige in full flight

The ultimate teammate, John Burns described the lead-up to the Penn Relays this way: "We were again battling with Tennessee, but this time we had a healthy Don Paige on the squad. Again, reporters came to the track a few days before the races, and we heard that New Mexico was bringing their 4 x 800 team to Penn to beat Villanova. New Mexico won the NCAA Championship indoor Two Mile Relay (we were second), and they featured a Kenyan national champion named Sam Kipkurgat. New Mexico was only going to run the 4 x 800. We were eyeing the possibility of winning five Championship of America races, something that had only been accomplished three times before ... by Villanova, in 1968, '69 and '70, so a number of us would be doubling. It was going to be interesting!"

The DMR went as planned on Friday. Don Paige would anchor and openly mused: "We have so many good guys on the team, it's almost impossible for us to lose!"[8] Freshman Tony Tufariello led off with the usual pre-ordered 1:51.5, followed by Bogue with a slight slower 400 meters than the previous year with a 46.9 putting Belger who was to run three laps (1200 meters) in a position most unfamiliar to him: in the lead. So, Belger thought it was time to put on a front running clinic. Running like a "wild eyed freshman" the experienced Belger cranked out the first quarter in 52 seconds; one lap later he passed on 1:52 almost as fast as Tufariello had run his two laps. By this time, he had built up such a lead he could almost walk the last lap. Which he did. But not quite. One more time, after a pedestrian pace of around 65 seconds, he handed off to Don Paige, who was still in the lead. Don ran comfortably, gave the Northeastern anchor Bruce Bickford the temporary illusion that he might have a chance by letting him lead the second and third laps, but blew him away in the last lap to win easily. Win number one. And the 13th DMR win in a row. And as Paige said: "impossible to lose." And of course, the all-important start to Penn Relays 1978.

Frank Dolson, seasoned reporter for the *Philadelphia Inquirer* summed up the following Saturday's proceedings with this headline in the Sunday paper: "Villanova Gets 5 for 5 Sweep."[9] Unbelievably, this relatively unknown group of athletes dominated the Penn Relays. Yes, Villanova had done it three times before (1968, 1969, and 1970) but Jumbo confessed that this display of relay power was the strongest he had ever seen. First, on Saturday, came the 4 x 1500 meters. This time John Burns was in command. Here's how he describes his first opportunity to claim that coveted Penn Relays watch: "The 4 x 1500 would be a battle with Tennessee. Dean Childs led off, Jimmy Flynn ran second leg and handed the baton to me even with Tennessee and Penn State. As I took the stick, I heard a woman yell from the stands, 'You better not lose that lead, Villanova' (that has stuck with me all these years later). Tennessee's man clearly had a plan to drop me so that he could give a substantial lead to their anchor who would compete against Paige, so he took the pace out hard. After two laps, I dropped back a little bit and Penn State passed me, moving me to third position. After another lap, the Penn State man started fading, so I went around him and got on the shoulder of Tennessee. With 150 meters to go, I moved to lane two and passed Tennessee. As I passed him, a huge roar came from the crowd, and I felt super energized. I sprinted to the exchange and handed the baton to Don with the lead. Both Tennessee and Penn State anchors eventually caught up and passed Don, just what he wanted before he blew them away with a finishing kick." Win number two.

Now to the Sprint Medley—a clinic in execution with Jumbo's new trove of sprinters plus the unflappable Mark Belger. Tim Dale led off in a sizzling 45.9

400 meters; two 200's later, one 20.9 and one in 20.7 by Keith Brown and Al Graves respectively put Belger in his preferred "office." Everyone knew what was about to happen—he kicked home in 1:47.4, smiling down the homestretch. Win number three.

Once again Jumbo stirred his magic brew. John Burns was only scheduled to run that one race, so his day was done … or so he thought. He gathered his gear and got a Coke and made his way up to the stands with his relay-mates. All the boys were congratulating him, and he felt a sense of relief and happiness that the prized Penn Relays watch was now his. In his own words, he described what happened next: "Mr. Pyrah came down from his seat next to Jumbo and told me 'to put down the Coke … Jumbo wants to see you.' So, I hustled up the steps and sat next to Jumbo who said, 'So how'ya feeling ch-ch-Champ?' I told him I felt great, and he said, 'Good, because you're going to lead off the 4 x 800.' Now my heart started pumping like crazy and I remembered New Mexico had come to get us."

It was 4 x 800-meter time. John Burns, the newly conscripted leadoff man kept his eye on the New Mexico runner throughout the leadoff leg of the race. He handed off to Tony Tufariello in a crowd of five, including New Mexico. After rounding the first turn, Tony got tripped and stumbled, but managed to keep his feet although he lost about 20 meters to the leaders. By the time he passed off to Don Paige, Villanova was in fifth place. From there, Don passed everyone but New Mexico and handed off to Mark Belger a good five meters behind New Mexico. More fun and games for Mark. He recalls the race vividly: "I had a cold, my throat was scratchy, I felt lousy but when I got the baton, all was forgotten." Five hundred meters later, Mark caught up to Kipkurgat, looked back three times, and by the time he hit the homestretch he had a 10-yard lead. Win number four. And Mark Belger just became the winningest athlete in the history of the relays with his record 10th watch. "This one's mine," he said. He had given all nine earlier watches away to family and friends.

The final race was the 4 x 400 team of Keith Brown, Derek Harbour, Glenn Bogue, and Tim Dale. Again, it was Villanova vs. Tennessee. At the Dogwood Relays, these two teams finished neck and neck with the nod going to Tennessee. This time both teams duplicated that performance and ran 3:04.5. But this time the nod went to the Villanova Wildcats. Win number five and the 1978 team now matched those Villanova teams of 1968, 1969, and 1970. Jumbo could not be prouder or more surprised. One superstar performance after the next. But in another corner of Franklin Field, Meet Director Jim Tuppeny kept checking his program. Who were these guys? Did this really happen?

That final weekend in April 1978, the still 21-year-old Mark Belger placed himself firmly and indelibly into the Penn Relays history books. Named Performer of the Meet for the second year in a row, Mark responded in his usual humble manner but waxed philosophically: "When you are senior, you are fully aware of the Villanova track history and the Penn Relays. And when they are over, it's like the Dave Patricks never left. It is really unique. Everyone takes it in stride. We know that we've got a job to do, and we just go out and do it."[10] And no one did it better, more often, and with more fun than Mark Belger.

The 1978 track season ended with another amazing occurrence. This time it came during the IC4A Outdoor Championships. The University of Maryland with its newest star hurdler Renaldo Nehemiah was well on its way to winning the Team Championship until the most amazing unfolding of finishes occurred. Two races were left: the 1500 meters and the 4 x 400-meter relay.

First came the 1500 meters. Finishing 1-2-3-4 came Don Paige, Sydney Maree, Dean Childs, and John Burns—a unprecedented show of middle-distance strength. In the final race of the day, the Villanova 4 x 400 meter team—the same foursome as Penn Relays, but anchored this time by Glen Bogue, won in 3:04.5, Villanova beating Maryland 99–98 for the title.

Afterwards, an exasperated Frank Costello, the University of Maryland coach was heard to say, "You can't tell me that from 107 schools, there's not another runner better than Villanova's fourth-best miler!" Never before had one school so dominated the mile/1500-meter event as Villanova did that day.

Penn Relays 1979

The 1979 track season was anything but quiet. Villanova's re-emergence as a national collegiate track powerhouse continued. That display of strength was clearly expressed at the NCAA Indoor Championships at Cobo Hall in Detroit. Again, the drama unfolded in true Jumbo style—day one of competition and the team stood in 25th place in the team standings with only two points. Then the train started to roll. Villanova began to make its move with six events to go on the second and final day. Tufariello won the 600 yards; the Villanova distance medley team placed third; Paige won the 1,000 yards. In the mile, Maree and Korir finished second and third behind meet-leading UTEP's Suleiman Nyambui. Their combined 14 points were five more than UTEP got for Suleiman's first. With only the Mile Relay to go, Jumbo's "not so secret" sprinters took command and won that event. The Wildcats would win by a point.

Penn Relays were just around the corner and the Paige prophecy that "it's almost impossible for us to lose" was again being put to the test.[11] Once again, the

Wildcats had the pieces to take all five Championship Relays of America. Don would be central to at least three of those wins. But he knew it would not be easy—it never is—as the Friday's DMR approached, he looked for a way to spare himself for the two hard finals he would be anchoring on the Saturday. En route to Franklin Field, Mike McDonnell III, a member of the cross-country team and close friend of Don Paige, recalls hearing about a vigorous conversation that took place in Mr. Pryah's car: "Coach Pyrah, Don Paige and Sydney Maree were having quite the discussion. Don did not want to anchor since he would be running the Sprint Medley heat shortly thereafter. Nor was Sydney up for the responsibility given some recent injuries that impeded his training. There was quite the argument. And finally, Sydney agreed."

Shortly thereafter, at 3:00 p.m., the gun went and this time Mike England, Jumbo's latest apprentice and the Pennsylvania State high-school 880-yard champion led off. No two races are ever the same. And this time Mike had to literally wrestle his way through the hand-off area "to blast through one of the wildest body bumping scenes in the 85-year history of the relays" to pass to Al Graves, the 400-meter runner.[12] Even so Mike ran a very respectable 1:50.7 while Graves ran a 47.4. Then Don Paige set off to "save" himself as he ran a scorching 2:52.5 - 1200 meters. Sydney Maree, now fully clear of the field, wheeled off a 3:59.3 - 1600 meters, well clear of Arizona State and Georgetown, both a good 40 meters back. Win number one. And the 14th DMR win in a row.

Later that afternoon, Don anchored the Sprint Medley to win the heat running a 1:48.4 - 800 meters and a team qualifying time of 3.18.0. After the race, Don reminded the press, "People think we come here and coast. You can't coast in anything. They think Villanova is monkeying around. This is serious business!"[13]

The serious business continued on Saturday. First up, the 4 x 1500 meters. Up stepped Dean Childs, John Burns, Amos Korir, and Sydney Maree to take care of business and win the event in a total time of 14:59.3. This time Maree ran a 3:40.7 -1500 meters to anchor—a 3.58 mile equivalent. The time—both a national and new Penn Relays record. Win number two.

Next up: the Sprint Medley. Keith Brown, Al Graves, and Tim Dale handed the baton to the speedy Don Paige who needed a 1:47.0 - 800 meters to take this race. Win number three.

Then the 4 x 800—the team of Mike England, Amos Korir, Anthony Tufariello, and Don Paige took care of business like the afternoon clean-up crew. No fooling around, no questions; just get it done. By the time Tufariello handed off, Paige had a 35-meter lead and could literally enjoy the ambience of the adoring crowd as he cruised to the finish line. Win number four.

As always, the final race of the day came down to the 4 x 400. Was another five-repeat win possible? That's how it looked as the first three Villanova runners (Brown, Graves, and Tufareillo) handed Tim Dale a five-meter lead. But Dale was tired, his legs were sore, and he was not running with the usual smoothness that he had shown many times before. With one of the finest runs ever by a new star Renaldo Nehemiah from the University of Maryland, it took a 44.3 split (second fastest only to Larry James's 43.9 in 1968) to defeat the tiring Dale. The drive for five had fallen short. There was no question that these relays remained very much the Villanova Relays as the tired team celebrated yet another successful Penn Relays.

Postscript 1

The much-anticipated race between Mark Belger and Don Paige finally took place on February 4, 1979. Fittingly, the two New York State prodigies met on the world's biggest stage: New York City and Madison Square Garden. While politely attentive to the races being run, the crowd was eagerly waiting for this battle. Coming into the Millrose, both had extraordinary streaks on the line. Belger had won 20 consecutive races at distances from 800 meters to 1,000 yards. Paige was undefeated indoors both this season and last.

Belger, with his Villanova career behind him, now lived in Boston and was learning the ropes as a full-time econometrician at an investment firm. Needless to say, life for Mark had changed dramatically. No more rolling out of bed late in the morning and planning his class schedule to suit his relaxed college lifestyle. But after work he kept up his training as best he could. Don of course, was now a Villanova senior and rapidly realizing his full potential. The night before, at an officials' dinner, when asked who was going to win, Belger had said with confidence, "It won't take a world record to beat Don Paige, but it will take a world record to beat me."[14] Little did he know, the full prescience of that forecast.

At last, the gun went off and for three laps (the 1,000 yards is a six-lap race plus 40 yards), they jogged behind the field. Then suddenly the dam burst. With 3½ laps remaining, the race leader, Marcel Philippe of the New York Athletic Club and Olympian on the 1972 French team, strayed wide, allowing Belger to burst to the fore unchallenged. Paige, forced to go outside, moved quickly to cover Belger's move. The crowd, now all on their feet, were going wild. It was a flat-out, two-man race. Using up a lap and a half, Paige gradually closed the gap, then moved past Belger just before the gun sounded for the final lap. Belger could not work his way back to the lead and finally conceded defeat with 20 yards remaining and simply jogged to his second-place finish. Paige's time—2.05.3 - a new world indoor record, exactly as Belger had predicted the night before. Even with his shut down finish, Belger's time was 2:06.5, a personal best, and under the old Millrose record of 2:07.1.

Paige graciously handled the win as if this was another day of business. His view of track remained extremely focused: "If you run, you run to win." When Belger was told his time, he just waved a forefinger as if to say, "Big deal."[15] He had reason to be discouraged and added, "To this day, I wish the race was 1,010 yards."[16]

Postscript 2

The Don Paige story would not be complete without the inclusion of what happened at the NCAA Outdoor Championships in Champaign, Illinois from May 31 to June 2, 1979. That meet saw the most dominant exhibition of middle distance running ever displayed in US collegiate history. Don Paige won both the 800 and the 1500-meter championships. Yes, it had been done before by none other than Villanova alumnus, Ron Delany in 1958. But Ron had three races in total—a semi and final in the 880 yards, and a final in the mile. Don faced five races: a qualifying round and a semi-final in the 800 meters on the Thursday; plus, a semi-final for the 1500 meters; and two finals on the Saturday. What's more, the time interval between the two finals was a mere 35 minutes.

Jumbo had taken Don by surprise just a few days before the meet and uttered his famous last words "Ch, Ch, Champ, I think you can do it! Just keep waiting and kick when you need to." And it came to pass. That Thursday, Don finished second in his 1500-meter heat (3:43.3) to qualify; specific to the 800 meters, he ran a 1:48.2 heat (second) and a 1:50.1 to win his semi.

Two days later, and all eyes were on Don Paige. First up: the 1500 meters. Don waited and waited, running near the back of the pack until the last lap. Then he started to move, and with 60 meters remaining, he exploded, winning in 3:39.2, a mere 7/100th of a second ahead of Todd Harbour, himself a 3.50 miler. Now to rest up for the 800 meters.

Don recounts the day. "I found a bench and was lying there with my eyes closed and my feet up. Suddenly I feel someone banging my foot! I opened my eyes and there stood Jumbo. And he starts talking about golf.... Ch, Ch, Champ, did you bring your sticks? There's a really nice course close by we should play tomorrow." Don was astounded at the subject matter not to mention the timing. But all these years later, he now understands what Jumbo was doing—taking his mind off the race to come. And it was a race for the ages.

Once again, Don let the field fight it out, settling in near the back of the pack. At the end of the first lap, he passed the bell in 54.3 seconds. Then the leaders picked up the pace. Paige moved steadily faster and as they entered the homestretch six abreast, Don put on the most amazing finish yet to be seen. He ran his second 400 in 51.9 seconds, finding yet again that special gear that so few have. But there it was. With his time of 1:46.2, Don had just clinched his second NCAA Championship in less than 37 minutes. That day, five runners broke 1:47 for the 800 meters but none could match the blistering finishing speed of Don Paige, this being his fifth race.

Postscript 3

The astonishing collegiate careers of Mark Belger and Don Paige beg the question: How fast could these guys have run? Mark set off to build a career in the high-technology industry (before the term had even emerged) and ended up moving to San Diego. While he continued to train and even broke the four-minute mile (3:57.4 in 1980), he never regained that competitive edge he so masterfully displayed at Villanova. Don Paige went on to win the 1980 Olympic Trials 800-meter trial in 1:44.6—a personal best, but geopolitics prevailed, and his Olympic dreams were shattered because of the US boycott of the Soviet Union's actions in Afghanistan. Shorty after the Games, Paige ran a match race against world record holder and 1500-meter Olympic champion Sebastian Coe, winning by a mere 100th of a second. That year *Track & Field News* ranked Paige as the top 800-meter runner in the world. But Don continued to face injury problems. It seemed that his lower legs and feet could not withstand the force and torque of his speed. He finally retired from racing shortly thereafter.

How fast could Mark and Don have run? Sammy Kipkurgat, the New Mexican anchor on that 4 x 800 meters at Penn Relays 1978, having experienced Mark power by him on the homestretch, said after that race, "If he worked on his stamina, he could be a good 1500 meter runner."[17] Others have said that they have never seen the talent and the unmatched competitive spirit that these two fine athletes brought to Villanova and to the sport of track and field. Jumbo would agree. They both came with much promise, as relative unknowns and developed to become top of class. What more could a coach ask for? To this day, Mark and Don are revered and respected by their teammates who talk about them with a sense of awe. They were indeed two of a very special kind—a kind that very infrequently comes around. And they both came to Villanova at the same time.

During this very same period, Jumbo now had another runner on his mind. A most unexpected prodigy from South Africa had shown up in Philadelphia and literally knocked on his door. A young Sydney Maree had come to town. How fast would he run?

10

Never Faster: The Sydney Maree Era

"If you want to be the best, you better train with the best."

Ken Schappert

One fine day in the summer of 1977, a young man literally came knocking on Jumbo's door. "You ran what?" Jumbo nearly dropped when he heard that this young high-school graduate standing before him had run a 3:57 mile seven months earlier. Quickly summoning Jack Pyrah to undertake a modicum of due diligence, Jumbo had just "recruited" Villanova's first black athlete from South Africa—Sydney Maree.

To understand Sydney Maree or even come close to understanding him, requires at least a modest knowledge of South African history, sociology, and politics. The United States venerates Independence Day—July 4, 1776; France celebrates Bastille Day—July 14, 1789; South Africa—more specifically, the Afrikaners (or Boers), celebrate the Battle of Blood River, December 16, 1838. This is the day on which the "Covenant" that defines the relationship between the Afrikaners and the indigenous African peoples was consecrated. Of course that day, known as the National Day of Celebration, dissipated with the end of Apartheid in 1994.

Sydney Maree, born on September 9th, 1956, entered a firmly entrenched apartheid state. That state was not just a nice idea or a benign "separate but equal" concept—a "we'll help you and you'll help us" neighborly pact. No, it flowed from a deeply embedded ideological position fused and sanctified at Blood River, a remote rural area approximately 30 miles to the northeast of Ladysmith, in eastern South Africa (formerly Natal Region).

On December 16th, 1838, the two opposing forces met. This "meeting" had been several years in the making. On one side, stood the Zulu nation, under the leadership of Dingane—an expanding tribe stemming originally from areas to the north and what is now Zimbabwe. On the other side, stood the Afrikaners—a people of Dutch origin, now 200-year inhabitants in Africa living in the southern tip of the continent. They were now moving north into the interior to advance their own freedom—a freedom they had lost when the English took over the Dutch settlement during the Napoleonic Wars in 1812. They chafed at the new regime and made the decision to move into open and unknown country and establish their very own new society.

Both were "cattle" people. Both needed pastures and wide-open spaces. And both were now stepping on each other's toes, resulting in a series of small but deadly conflicts. The matter needed to be settled, once and for all. As the inevitable conflict drew closer, the deeply religious Afrikaners established a strategic position adjacent to a winding river and a hippopotamus pool that made for a natural barrier on their western flank. Then they waited, prayed, and made a "covenant" with God that if He would protect them, they would be forever faithful and dedicate their lives and nation to Him.

That morning in 1838, an estimated 12,000 supremely fit Zulus, who were able to move 40 miles in a single day, came armed with spears and attacked the "laager[1]" of 64 Boer wagons encircling 464 men equipped with rifles and four gatling guns. The Boers, under the leadership of an extremely calm and experienced Andris Pretorius, withstood wave after wave of attacks. Two hours later, the score looked like this: thousands of dead Zulus and three slightly wounded Afrikaners. The rout was simply unbelievable. To the Boers, it was an unquestionable act of God—a divine intervention and clear evidence that God himself had ordained the Afrikaners to be lords of this land—a chosen people directly synonymous with the Biblical precedence that had led the Old Testament Israelites out of Egypt into the Promised Land some 3,000 years earlier.

In 1948, at long last, the Afrikaners gained political power over their British victors who had defeated them during the Boer War, and apartheid ("apartness") began. This was no casual restructuring of society. It was a complete overhaul that drew on the 1838 "covenant" that was based on the Afrikaner experience and belief in indisputable religious principles. The "chosen ones" were totally and absolutely in charge. And the black "infidels" were destined to serve. These "servants" were not even allowed to be citizens within their own lands. Instead, a series of areas called homelands or reserves, usually located in remote northern regions and on extremely poor soils, were designated as "countries" for the "kaffirs." The latter term was freely used and is as equally insulting and demeaning as the "n-word" in America. For the native Africans, if you wanted to be a citizen, no problem, you have your homeland to go to. If you want to stay or work in South Africa, you are now a guest worker. And by the way, you have no rights. But always carry your "passbook." because without it, you are subject to deportation to your homeland.

This was the society that Sydney Maree was born into. A society into which black South Africans were structurally relegated to an inferior class. A black South African would never speak to a white South African unless spoken to. And when that occurred, there would be no eye contact—just one party taking instruction or insult from the other. He was born as one of eight children and lived in a brick box house with a tin roof that had only one bedroom. And he was always on the run—running to pick up some essentials at the store nearly two miles away; running as he played soccer non-stop when he could; and running on occasion from the State Security Police who would at any time brutalize the black residents at will. He turned to soccer, but he lacked agility, and anyway, soccer saw him leaving toenails on the rock-strewn vacant lots. He obtained his first pair of shoes at the age of eight. On weekends, he did garden work for a white man, lowering his eyes and calling him Baas (Boss), as all white men were referred to. He would sit outside the man's house in the morning, terrified even to lay knuckles on a white man's door, until the man came outside[2].

By the 1970s, tensions were building steadily. To no surprise the black community increasingly protested the unjust laws and persistent inhumane treatment.

In 1976, thousands of black children in Soweto, a black township outside Johannesburg, not far from where Sydney and his family lived, demonstrated against the Afrikaans language requirement for black African students. The police opened fire with tear gas and bullets. Over 700 young students were killed but the exact count will never be known.

That same year, Sydney started attending a school in Pretoria (so named after the victorious general in 1838). A white schoolteacher by the name of Naudë Klopper, encouraged him to run track and begin training. He showed steady improvement and started winning races. And now for the great irony: on the evening of December 15th, 1976, the night before the annual Blood River commemoration, the National Day of Celebration which had now become the most important national holiday in South Africa, Sydney was invited to run the "Dream Mile." Not having any idea of pace, splits, or what a "dream mile" even was, Sydney, the only black athlete in the field, blew past them all in the last lap and ran 3.57.9. Suddenly, he was in the national limelight as one of the most promising athletes in all South Africa, and the most promising black athlete over that distance.[3]

That led to an opportunity to visit the United States as part of a public relations exercise by the South African government to showcase the country's "enlightened" athletic policies. And who should Sydney meet upon his arrival in New York City? None other than Mr. Bert Lancaster, the architect of the original Dream Mile, that great showdown between the two best milers in the world, namely Marty Liquori and Jim Ryun, six years earlier. The plan was to spend two months in America and then return home. During that period, Sydney lived with Bert in Philadelphia. That led to a side trip to Villanova University and meeting Assistant Coach Jack Pyrah. In short order, a subsequent meeting was arranged with Jumbo Elliott and the offer of an athletic scholarship. Sydney Maree was not going back to South Africa.

Adjusting to life in the United States proved challenging for Sydney. "I hated apartheid," he says. "I never felt like a human being until I left South Africa." In actual fact, he never felt he belonged anywhere, and Villanova was not much different. To quote the in-depth *Sports Illustrated* article, "His sense of not belonging was almost too much to bear. He didn't belong to a father, and his family was split and scattered. He didn't belong to any group of friends. He didn't belong to a tribe, which at least lent some stunted version of pride to the Zulus on South Africa's East Coast. And already, at age 12, a dim awareness was growing that he didn't even belong to his own country."[4] Now he was in the United States, and he had no idea how to behave, where he might fit, or if he belonged.

Assistant Coach Jack Pyrah, Sydney Maree, and Head Coach Jumbo Elliot

Sydney Maree

Word soon got out that a new sub four-minute miler was on board. This was the second time Jumbo had landed such a big fish—the first being Marty Liquori exactly 10 years earlier. Everyone assumed that in a short while, this new sensation would become the next leader, join the current star Don Paige, and follow the tradition set by Dave Patrick, Marty Liquori, John Hartnett, and Eamonn Coghlan to lead as the top miler, but also step up as a team leader off the track. That was how it worked. There was a natural team hierarchy, albeit unwritten or even unspoken—the best miler got the last word, set the tone, Patrick, Liquori, Hartnett, Schappert, Coghlan, Belger, Paige….

But it was not working out that way. Sydney seemed overly shy; he seemed to want to keep to himself; he would often run on his own; he neither sought company nor invited it. Little did anyone really know or understand the society from which Sydney had just come from and how foreign it was to him to deal with white people as equals. Meanwhile, he was viewed by his teammates as another fast black athlete like other American milers such as Bryon Dyce, Dennis Fikes, and Reggie McAfee. He was anything but.

Sports Illustrated described this situation best: "On his return to Villanova after Christmas for the second semester of his freshman year and the outdoor track season, his teammates could not understand why he ate and stretched and ran alone. When they tried to joke with him, he grew yet quieter. The regular banter so characteristic of the Villanova team culture eluded him. He didn't smoke or drink or go to parties. He didn't throw Frisbees or shoot baskets. He would not study in the library, only in his room. Togetherness was an adhesive he had never known. All his energy was poured into proving himself."[5] And keeping himself together.

The Villanova team atmosphere began to change. The comradery and the constant togetherness that was characteristic of the early and mid-70s was no longer so evident. New residences had been built with new cafeterias. Team members lived across campus and the three-times daily gathering at mealtime became more of an exception than the rule.

There also seemed to be a divide between the two stars on the team. Don Paige, the senior and now a world leader in both the 800 meters and the mile, represented the all-American athlete. He was all business when it came to track.

Sydney Maree, the emerging star on the other hand, was a mystery. He would run by himself—his hard Frolics became legend as his teammates learned that he regularly cranked out this 10-mile loop in just over 50 minutes. Often Sydney would be experiencing leg problems and would bicycle down to a nearby golf course to run on the grass, again on his own. The competitiveness between Paige and Maree would at times spill out during track workouts. One day, while doing the legendary repeat 440 yards (the Jumbo classic), each quarter mile would be run faster than the last one. Alternating the leads but not speaking to each other, it became an open contest. Paige remembers: "Each quarter became a half-second faster. By the 10th one we were both exhausted, and still we were flying. Neither of us looked at each other. We got to 16, and Jumbo came out. He stood there with his hands on his hips and shouted, 'What the hell are you guys doing?' If Jumbo hadn't come out, we'd still be out there today."[6]

Life began to settle down, but for the most part, Sydney kept to himself. But it was not easy. On one occasion, an incredibly insensitive teammate expressed offense toward Sydney's standoffishness and barked, "Hey Sydney, you better take those spears and go back to Africa!!" The offhand comment shocked Sydney and other listeners alike. It took considerable effort on the part of John Burns to restore some measure of calm within the team as he tried his best to assure Sydney that this form of "busting" meant no harm. And by the way, upon seeing Sydney's bicycle parked in the bushes near the golf course, that same teammate chose to hide it elsewhere. That made for another tense encounter with a bewildered Maree.

Freshman year was a time to settle in. The Villanova team was replete with middle distance running talent led by Mark Belger, Don Paige, John Burns, Tony Tufariello, and Dean Childs. By the end of year two, Sydney was making his mark—he finished second in the NCAA indoor mile to Suleiman Nyambui, the UTEP runner from Tanzania with a time of 3:59.9; he anchored two Penn Relays team: the Distance Medley and the 4 x 1500 meters and once again broke four minutes (or the equivalent each time). A few weeks later, he had set an NCAA 5,000-meter meet record of 13:20.63 in the outdoor championships with a scorching last lap of 52.2 seconds—that same season he set an IC4A indoor record in the three miles and an IC4A outdoor record for the 5,000 meters as well as setting the South African record for the mile at 3:53.7.

But the pernicious nature of the complex array of forces working against Sydney Maree cannot be understated. He was truly in a political and social purgatory—one of a kind in every way. First, he had been systematically marginalized thanks to apartheid; then as a high performing black athlete he was regarded by South African whites more as a curious phenomenon; they were more prone to say, "that Kaffir sure can run,"[7] than afford him the respect he deserved. Then the absurdity of geopolitical politics delivered a vicious irony. First, the sporting world boycotted South Africa because New Zealand chose to play rugby— a non-Olympic sport—against the Springboks[8]. This gave cause for all African nations to boycott the 1976 Olympics. Then, Sydney, a black South African, the target of his country's discrimination but now in the United States, became the reason why other athletes would not compete against him. So here he was discriminated against for being discriminated against. Did that make any sense at all?

The full absurdity of the situation came to a head in the New Jersey Track Classic at Rutgers University in 1979. For the first time, Sydney was scheduled to run against John Walker, Olympic 1500-meter champion. Then he received word that he would have to withdraw since he was South African. Then he was told that if he ran for Villanova, that would be okay. Finally, as he warmed up just minutes before the race, he was told "No! No! You can't run." It is no wonder that Sydney, in total frustration, would pound out those blistering 10-mile Frolic solo runs—no one could possibly understand what he was going through.

Penn Relays 1980

Internal team dynamics aside, the winning DMR formula was back: a world-class miler plus three top runners. The 1980 Villanova team looked even stronger: this time the formula had two world-class milers in the persons of Don Paige and Sydney Maree. Sophomore Mike England describes: "We had such a strong team. The difference between good runners and great runners was that the great runners believed that they were unbeatable. What made Don and Sydney so great was their strong belief in themselves. I saw this in both of them." Then add to that mix Tony Tufariello, the 1979 NCAA indoor 600 yards champion—thus three world-class runners. The team was rounded out by Mike, who was also knocking on the world class 800-meter door. The Villanova DMR team looked invincible. If the Paige prophecy, "It's almost impossible for us to lose," were to ever hold true, this would be the year.

But 1980 was no ordinary year. There was talk about an Olympic boycott by the West against the Soviets for invading Afghanistan. Consequently, the Olympics seemed very much in doubt, leaving major questions on what the competitive scene for the year ahead would look like. At the same time, major league baseball players were talking about an all-out strike. And Rosey Ruiz, the unexpected winner of the Boston Marathon earlier that same week of April as the Penn Relays, had just been exposed for cheating. The sports world seemed upside down. However, the perennial and venerable Penn Relays, now more important than ever, brought a dose of sanity to a world seemingly gone mad. In Philadelphia, the last Friday in April, you could count on one thing: Penn Relays and the Championship of American Distance Medley Relay. And again, Villanova would be the team to beat.[9]

Fourteen straight wins and you would think that by now the Jumbo DMR winning formula would be locked in and permanently set in "Villanova track stone." But there is always something new. This year, in mid-April, Sydney Maree made the decision to travel to South Africa where he was honored as one of the country's top 10 athletes of the decade. And he was determined to bring his mother back to the United States with him. All great, but the arrival back to Philadelphia was scheduled for Thursday, just one day before the DMR. To be clear, travelling from South Africa is no small side trip—it is about as far as you can go since it is almost halfway round the world. First, 13 hours flying from Johannesburg to London—an overnight changeover—then another seven hours to Philadelphia. Plus, he was nursing a hamstring injury and could not do any speed work. Come Friday and enter a jet-lagged Sydney Maree to Franklin Field in much less than top condition. But Jumbo had no choice. He had to split up his two stars and put Maree on the anchor. Paige was anchoring the Sprint Medley, which meant another qualifying race on Friday followed by two races on Saturday—the Sprint Medley final and the Two Mile Relay final.

Sydney Maree takes the lead

Paige led off. The DMR now had the 1200 meters as the first leg. The team knew that Sydney was tired and would need a lead. A big lead if possible. Don's contribution began with a sizzling 2:51.6 which produced a five-meter advantage—with Georgetown in hot pursuit. Tufariello circled the track in 46.8, handing off to Mike England who went all out with a 1:48.4 - 800 meters, a personal best. By this time, the Wildcats built a 10-yard lead over Georgetown. Despite Sydney's first lap in 55 seconds and a lead that increased to 18 yards, a fiercely determined John Gregorek started closing the gap, opening up with a 1:54 - 800-meter split. Third time around and Gregorek was now only a stride behind. Things were starting to look serious. Would Sydney be able to hold off this rising star? Would the jet lag overcome him and put an end to the DMR streak?

Sydney did the one thing that he knew how to do and had done often—put his head down and run for his life. All those 50-minute Frolics were still there. He may not have built speed over the past few weeks, but he still had strength. This was not going to be easy. Gregorek stayed on his shoulder every step of the way and it took a total effort approaching the finish line to hold him off. Maree ran a 3:57.4 metric mile (1600 meters) just two steps ahead of Gregorek, who had run the race of a lifetime—a 3:54.7.

Villanova had done it one more time, and with a new world record time of 9:24.4. First win of the 1980 Penn Relays. And the 15th consecutive DMR. To be sure, the win took every fibre of Sydney's being to bring home. Of all the previous wins, this one may have been the toughest, even though it was supposedly a sure-win for the Wildcats. Against numerous odds, the lack of speed work, the fear of reinjuring his hamstring, the fatigue of a long trip, and the anxieties he would have felt worrying about his mother who had just arrived to visit him, Sydney had arguably displayed as much courage and grit as any Villanovan before him.

It became clear that next day that Georgetown had firmly focused on building a relay team to beat Villanova. Their DMR defeat on Friday resulted in a change in strategy. This time, their star miler, John Gregorek, was deployed not to go head-to-head with Sydney Maree. Instead, his job would be to open things up in the third leg and provide the Georgetown anchor a lead that Maree would not be able to make up. Such was the plan for the running of the 4 x 1500 meters or the de-facto classic Four Mile Relay.

The Villanova apprentice for 1980 was Carey Pinkowski, a Chicago-based miler/two-miler from Hammond, Illinois, about 25 miles southeast of Chicago. Carey caught national attention in 1976 when he was one of three two-milers from the same high school to run under nine minutes. But he had also run a 4:12 mile in high school and on this day, he led the pack with a lead off 3:49.1 – 1500 meters (or a 4:07 mile). Dean Childs, another top miler from Calgary, Alberta, increased the lead another few yards with his 3:46.5 effort (4:03 mile). Then he passed the stick to Amos Korir, who hailed from El Doret, Kenya. Amos, who came from the same area as the legendary Kip Keino, could also run a four-minute mile any day of the week. But today was not one of those days and John Gregorek soon closed the gap and ran a 3:41.2 (sub four-minute mile pace) to open a five-yard lead for Jim DeReinzo, the newly assigned Georgetown anchor. This left the less than rested Sydney Maree in hot pursuit. For 3½ laps Sydney remained content to sit on DeReinzo's shoulder, waiting, waiting. Then with 250 meters to go,

Sydney made his move. DeReinzo bravely fought off the surging Maree stride for stride but by the time they entered the homestretch, the battle was over. Maree surged once again and with his 3.39.4 anchor leg, he opened up a 2.5 second gap in just the last 100 meters. Win number two.

Like every year, Jim Tuppeny had been busy recruiting more schools to compete at the Penn Relays. This year he convinced Florida Agricultural and Mechanical University that the Sprint Medley was there for the taking. And for three legs of this race (the 400 meters and 2 x 200 meters), that appeared to be the case. Florida had established a commanding lead of 10 meters, especially since Tony Tufareillo, who came down with bronchitis, could only manage a 49 second, 400 meters, about three seconds slower than normal. Two excellent 200-meter legs by Rodney Wilson and Carlton Young put the team back somewhat into contention. But Don Paige, now one of the best 800-meter runners in the world, made quick work of narrowing that gap and breezing home, winning by nearly two seconds. His sizzling 1:46.2 was no match for the dispirited Florida team. Win number three. Once again, Tuppeny just shook his head in dismay. All that effort to recruit new teams to win championship races but the results never seem to change.

However, there would be no Villanova 4 x 400 meter team because of injuries and the inability to field a team. That left one final Championship of America race—the 4 x 800 meters. This time, the team of Mike England, Sydney Maree, John Hunter, and anchor Don Paige left no doubt whatsoever which school had the best selection of 800 meter runners. Both England and Hunter ran 1:50 legs. The now tired Maree held his own with a 1:52.1. But Don Paige, running his last race as a Villanova Wildcat, saved his afterburners for this final race of his storied career. With his 1:45.8, he scorched the field, winning the race by a full 2.5 seconds over second place Rutgers, who were followed closely by Virginia. Win number four for Villanova. It was like the old times were back and the *Philadelphia Inquirer*[10] ran this headline in the Sunday paper: "Another Clinic On Relays: Villanova Wins 3 More!"[11]

Don Paige's Penn Relays career was over. Nine races; nine wins and named the Penn Relays Performer of the Meet. He now joined several of his alumni teammates who had never experienced a loss, including Liquori, Hartnett, Coghlan, and Belger. Meanwhile, Sydney Maree also remained undefeated and now carried the banner as the world-class miler who would lead the Villanova track team to more future victories.

Penn Relays 1981

The 1980/81 season came with a new set of highs and lows. It started with a low. The summer of 1980 came with the full disappointment of many countries, including the United States, of not competing in the Olympics. What could Don Paige or Mark Belger have done in the 800 meters? Or Don in the 1500 meters? Or Marty Liquori and Dick Buerkle in the 5,000 meters? Or Sydney Maree, regardless of which country that would let him run in the 1500 meters or the 5,000 meters? There will never be answers to these questions, but one thing is certain. This group of outstanding runners would have made their presence felt. And possibly returned with medals that will never be awarded. Ah, the speculations about what could have been.

Then came September, which started with a memorable high. After all those years of sub-standard track facilities, Villanova University finally completed the construction of an all-weather Tartan track. Gone were the cinders or what was left of them. The third Saturday, Homecoming Weekend, witnessed the dedication of the new Jumbo Elliott Track. That day Jumbo's boys returned like lemmings to the sea: they came from all directions—Ron Delany, Noel Carrol, Frank Murphy, Donal Walsh, John Hartnett, Eamonn Coghlan all from Ireland; Chris Mason from England (although he now resided in the Philadelphia area); the Canadians, led by Ed Takacs and Glen Bogue; and of course the Americans—Marty Liquori from Florida; Dick Buerkle living in Atlanta; Dave Patrick from Baltimore and posted in Texas, Paul Drayton, Frank Budd, Erv Hall, Larry James, Don Bragg, Vic Zwolak, Browning Ross.... The list went on like a who's who of the sport. And of course, the current track team led by Sydney Maree, John Hunter, Carleton Young, and a new Irish recruit, a sprightly Marcus O'Sullivan from Cork City.

Jumbo Elliott was over the moon, happy. There was nothing he revelled in more than being in the midst of his "boys." Especially those "boys" who had graduated, emanating success, class, and pride. Those qualities meant more to him that all the individual and team wins. It was a day of speeches, happy reunions, telling old stories, telling a few new ones, cherishing memories, of standing amid the awe of sheer accomplishment. And it all centred around Jumbo Elliott and his jaw-dropping success as a coach. That day he took it all in accompanied by his wife Kay and their four children: James Jr., Tommy, Jeff, and Joy.

But a new low was not far off. Everyone could see that Kay was not well. It took all her strength just to walk to her seat and take in the ceremonies. We all wanted to see her. While we all stood in awe of Jumbo, we had all experienced the warmth and hospitality that Kay discharged to us. We had all been to their house on various occasions and it was Kay who really made us feel at home. We all knew that she had been fighting cancer for years, a battle that she was clearly losing. Jumbo was more distracted than usual and his visits to the track became even less frequent. Mr. Pyrah filled in as best he could. Then a few months later, on February 21st, 1981, she passed away.

The NCAA Indoors, held three weeks later, brought little for the Villanova Wildcats to celebrate. The only win came in the DMR, anchored by none other than Sydney Maree. But injuries left him not fit enough to run either the mile or the two-mile.

Then just one week later came the biggest and most unexpected low. On Sunday, March 22nd, 1981, Jumbo now in Florida for a brief vacation, took a nap. He never woke up. Instead, he passed to that other world to join the love of his life. The great James Frances Jumbo Elliott was dead at the age of 66. We would never know whether he died for reasons of poor health or simply from a broken heart. Underneath that prickly exterior beat the heart of a very sensitive man who was mourning the loss of his life partner. That heart was now stilled. Note: the details of his funeral, another gathering that brought his boys together from far and near, is dealt with in the following chapter.

Despite the physical passing of Jumbo, his spirit continued to linger as if it was held in a giant balloon. But the balloon was getting smaller, albeit still present four weeks later for the Penn Relays. The team prepared with great determination to carry on the legend and the tradition. And there was no one more nervous than Jack Pyrah. Year after year of championship victories topped with that 15-year DMR streak were at stake. He did not want to go down into the history books as the coach who lost the very first race after Jumbo's passing.

Friday April 24th was one of those nasty April spring days. The sky was grey, the winds were gusty, and the conditions were simply miserable. It seemed that the universe was in mourning with the loss of its most accomplished track coach. Standing around without multiple layers of clothing was a guaranteed formula for misery. As always, rain or shine, the DMR was up at 3:00 p.m. But where was Maree? That entire week he had complained about a groin injury. Shots of cortisone and novocaine had been administered, anything to ease the discomfort and enable him to run. Then Mr. Pyrah pulled a classic Jumbo—he would make the final decision on whether Maree would run after the warm-up. So, the wait. Especially the agonizing waits of two Villanova teammates, John Borghese and Ken Lucks, who warmed up just in case. Then, just 20 minutes before the race, Maree nodded, "It's a go!" Pyrah let out a huge sigh of relief.

Maree digs deep to honor Jumbo with a win

The pressure was on like never before. With the memories of Jumbo and his recent funeral on everyone's mind, Gail Shister with the *Philadelphia Inquirer* wrote this: "This was no ordinary race, and everyone knew it. This was Jumbo's race, the one he wanted to win more than any other."[12] Not only was the 15-year streak on the line, this race, the DMR would be the true test of Villanova resilience and spirit.

The DMR team, all wearing black ribbons, would be comprised of John Hunter, another Corkman, now running close to four minutes for the mile, to leadoff the 1200 meters; Carlton Young, a dead ringer for Greg Govan 10 years earlier, running the 400 meters; an "impish looking freshman[13] " by the name of Marcus O'Sullivan on the 800-meter leg; and the "crippled" Sydney as anchor. Marcus recalls, "It was all nerves that entire week. No one wanted to lose. There was a lot of pressure—we were all thinking about Jumbo. You could feel it."[14]

Leadoff man John Hunter decided that the best view of the field would be from the back of the pack. That is exactly where he situated himself after the first lap. Deciding that he had seen enough of backsides and numbers, he rapidly worked his way to the front over the course of the next two laps. With his spectacular 2:54.4 - 1200-meter leg, he handed off in second place, a yard behind Arkansas who under their Irish coach, John McDonnell, had come to Penn for one reason, and that was to beat Villanova. Indeed, it was an impressive Arkansas team with an ensemble of top-end American sprinters and a new cohort of Irish milers now being recruited to that institution.

Next came the 400 meters and while Carleton Young ran an impressive 46.5, he still lost ground to Arkansas' Stanley Redwine who gained another five yards with an even faster 46.0. Now to the fresh-faced Irishman, Marcus O'Sullivan in his first Penn Relays appearance, producing a 1:51.5 - 800 meters to put Villanova within five yards of the Arkansas leader. Taking the baton in second place it became clear that Sydney had other designs than just to follow. Running against the Arkansas anchor Frank O'Mara—a sub four-minute miler, Sydney set out to control the race starting with a quick first lap to take the lead. Then Maree slowed down, reaching the 800-meter mark in a pedestrian 2.06. And who should suddenly emerge? None other than Georgetown's John Gregorek, who used the slow pace to catch up and then carried on taking the lead in lap three.

Now the race was on. Running with his "antelope stride and indefatigable spirit,"[15] Maree calmly followed and then started to blast that final lap. Twice Gregorek held him off, but entering the final straight, Maree's speed was too much. Sydney's final 400 meters in 53.5 seconds had burned whatever fires that Gregorek could muster. Villanova's final team time stood at 9:36.39. Gregorek, despite his bold moves, finished with a team time of 9:38.9 followed by Arkansas just .5 seconds back. Villanova had done it yet again. First win of the Relays and the 16th DMR in a row!

Mr. Pyrah breathed his second huge sigh of relief. He looked like a man who had just had a mountain lifted from his shoulders. He could not stop smiling. There was nothing he dreaded more than a DMR loss first time out as head coach of this storied Villanova Track Team. Asked to comment after watching Maree's spectacular finish, Pyrah simply uttered, "Not bad for a cripple!" Then he played another Jumbo card. No greeting of his runners after the race. Instead, he would stay in the northwest corner of Franklin Field—the Jumbo corner—now the Villanova corner. The runners would come to him.

Meanwhile the Villanova DMR quartet celebrated quietly and talked about the specialness of the race and winning it for Jumbo. "It means a lot," said a very emotional Marcus O'Sullivan. "To win this race and keep the streak going means everything."[16] Thanks to the performance of this foursome and especially to the unparalleled courage of Sydney Maree, this race proved to be a high point that served to break the series of lows that had ushered in the year of 1981.

Weather conditions on the following day showed little improvement. Once again, the winds swirled, and the temperatures remained in the mid-40s. The only comfortable position to be in was the act of running itself. But that was not the case for over 30,000 spectators as they awaited the start of the 4 x 1500 meters. This time, Ken Lucks, another Canadian, from British Columbia, did not have to warm up in vain. As the apprentice leadoff man, he ran a respectable 3:49.7—but was a good 30 meters back of the leaders in sixth place. Marcus O'Sullivan, now with his one-race Penn Relays experience, followed with a 3:48.3 but lost another 30 meters behind the impressive running of both Arkansas and Georgetown. Now Villanova was a good 60 meters back of the leaders. Enter Irishman number two: John Hunter with his "passing" experience from the day before, who wheeled a 3:43.8 to reel in all the runners but one. The Villanova vs. Arkansas duel was on—Maree vs. O'Mara. Sydney, who afterwards admitted that "I had given up,"[17] after seeing the deficit that had been built earlier, slowly closed the 20-meter gap. With one lap to go, he pulled up to O'Mara and finally edged by him just before the finish line. The narrowest of margins separated the two teams: a time of 15:01.96 vs. a time of 15:02.02—or .06 of a second. But Maree had done it and come through for a second time. However, it took a 3.39.4, 1500 meters to do so (a 3:56 mile). Mr. Pyrah breathed yet another huge sigh of relief. Win number two. Maybe things were working out after all.

Villanova competed in two additional races that afternoon. First came the Sprint Medley won by Southern Methodist University from Dallas, Texas. Villanova finished third, competitive in the race but without a Don Paige or a Mark Belger to bring it home, a win was no longer assured. The same could be said for the 4 x 800 Meter Relay. This time Sydney ran his best 800 meters ever—a 1:48 third leg. But once again, it came down to a close finish—two seconds behind a winning (and jubilant) Georgetown team. Villanova finished fourth in this race behind teams from Rutgers and Richmond.

Penn Relays 1981 came to a close. Instead of the usual three, four, or even five Championship Relays of America, Villanova went home with two victories. Sydney Maree was selected as Performer of the Meet, a fitting way to end his Penn Relays legacy. But the most amazing winning streak in sports was still intact—16 consecutive DMR wins. That day Jumbo smiled from above. And Jack Pyrah continued to grin from ear to ear.

The Sydney Maree story is indeed a case of truth being stranger than fiction. Who could have made up such a story? Who could have imagined that a strange 1838 battle fought in one of the remotest regions on the planet would precipitate such a sequence of events? Who would have envisioned such a convergence of coincidence that would produce an athlete who would culminate a winning streak in the world of sports some 143 years later? And by an individual coming from the crucible of oppression to the cradle of freedom—from the embodiment of servitude—Pretoria, a symbol of extreme discrimination, to the citadel of freedom—Philadelphia, the very city where the Declaration of Independence had been signed. Could you find a greater juxtaposition? But that is what happened. That is the essence of the Sydney Maree story.

Perhaps, in the end, it was the universe conspiring to set things right. Sydney Maree had become the fastest miler ever to join the history of Villanova Track. In many respects, it was a most unexpected outcome. It took a talented outlier from a faraway land, together with the acute intuition of an accomplished coach, to make this happen. There is no question that Sydney had talent and an insatiable work ethic, both of which he applied to his athletics and his studies. But it took an experienced risk manager in the form of Jumbo Elliott to create this possibility. And it took the Villanova track heritage, that incredible lineage of middle-distance supremacy to inspire and guide the way forward. But all that said, there will never be another Sydney Maree. There will never be another story like his.

Postscript 1

After years of being prevented from running internationally, Sydney Maree, the man without a country, was free at last to run. On September 5th, 1981, when he stood at the starting line of the 1500 at the World Cup in Rome and saw the letters USA across his chest, something he did not think would happen: "It was like a beautiful butterfly coming out of a caterpillar," says Maree's former teammate, Mike England.[18] Sydney heard the Americans cheering him from the infield and had to hold back his tears to think of the race ahead of him. He finished fifth, and then four days later, on his 25th birthday, he raced in Rieti, Italy against Ovett, one of the runners who had been most adamant about not competing against him. With 400 meters to go, he left Ovett and won in 3:48.83, the fifth-best mile ever run and only 1.5 seconds behind Sebastian Coe's world record.

Sydney Maree with Coach Tom Donnelly

By standard measure (the stopwatch) Sydney Maree is the greatest male runner in the history of the Villanova program. His accomplishments are the stuff of legend: a world record over 1500 meters (3:31.24 in August 1983), American Records at 1500 meters (3:29.77 in 1985), 2,000 meters (4:54.20 in 1985), 3,000 meters (7:33.37 in 1984), and 5,000 meters (13:01.15 in 1985, at the time the third fastest time ever). He won the first Fifth Avenue Mile in 3:47.52—a record that still stands. His mile time (3:48.83) is the fastest mile ever run by a Villanovan including those run by Coghlan, Liquori, and O'Sullivan. Same for the 1500. He won multiple NCAA championships over 1500 and 5,000 meters. He was an All-American in cross-country. In 1981, he was the first Black to receive the South African Athlete of the Year award. Upon graduating, Sydney was coached by the ultimate Villanova teammate and fellow alumnus, Tom Donnelly, who provided invaluable technical and personal guidance on an ongoing basis. Needless to say, Tom, who continues to coach at Haverford College, was extremely well-qualified to extend the culture and zeitgeist of the Jumbo era.

Postscript 2

Maree graduated from Villanova University in the spring of 1981. One person who attended the ceremony was Naudë Klopper, Sydney's first coach, who had flown from South Africa. "He started to tell me how he could never thank me enough," Klopper recalls. "I stopped him and said, 'No, it is I who must thank you.' Before I'd met him, I'd only known blacks as people who did gardening for me. Now I know there are blacks who are 100 percent better than white people I know that they too have goals and aspirations and can be like a son in my home."[19] Yes, South Africa was changing. Sydney Maree proved to be an agent for that change. He proved to the world but most importantly to apartheid South Africa, that an individual from the most unlikely of places and backgrounds can rise to become the best in the world. However, as with many places in the world today, there remains a long road ahead before people of all races and creeds can truly be free.

11

The Streak Ends

"Sunrise doesn't last all morning.... all things must pass."

George Harrison

Is that Liquori?" "Isn't that Coghlan?" "I think that's Don Paige...." The handful of casually-dressed college students playing a round of pool stood up and began to recognize the faces. The whispering continued. "There's Buerkle. That's Patrick...." In just a short two minutes, the suddenly attentive students were subsumed by a group of well-dressed young men invading Kelly's Bar, transforming the usual low-key Wednesday evening to a new level of energy brought on by a new flight of unexpected patrons.

It was Tuesday, March 25th, 1981. Jumbo Elliott had passed away unexpectedly on Sunday, just two days earlier. Without delay, the funeral was scheduled for Wednesday. Word went out quickly. Plans to travel to Philadelphia were made in an instant. There was no time to dawdle. They all came: Ron Delany, Dave Patrick, Charlie Messenger, Larry James, Tom Donnelly, Marty Liquori, Dick Buerkle, Chris Mason, Billy McLaughlin, Ron Stanko, Warren Clark, Karl Kinscherf, Ken Schappert, Jerry Bouma, Tom Gregan, Brian McElroy, Eamonn Coghlan, Kevin Leonard, Steve Dorsey, Greg Eckman, Tiny Kane, Ed Takacs, Mark Belger, Don Paige, John Burns, Mike England—the "boys" who defined the essence of Villanova Track from that 60s and 70s period. The only ones missing were some of the Irish—Noel Carrol, Frank Murphy, Donal Walsh, and John Hartnett, who just could not make the trip with such short notice.

Earlier that evening the "boys" had arrived singly or in pairs at the Bryn Mawr funeral home where the wake took place. Greetings, salutations, and condolences were delivered with the greatest of respect. But it was a strange mixture of joy and sorrow. Joy in seeing each other so unexpectedly. But sorrow for the reason why. No one saw this coming. Jumbo was still a relatively young man—only 66 years of age. Given his slender physique and active lifestyle, there was no reason to think that he would not be around for another 20 years. But now, suddenly he was gone, and no one had really had the chance to say goodbye. Solemn respects were paid; sympathies offered to the members of the family—to Joy, Jimmy, Tommy, and Jeff. It was difficult not to feel immensely sorry for the Elliotts—the loss of both parents within four weeks. The deep sense of loss extended further—to his larger family, the "boys" who had come from far and wide to be here and to say farewell.

As the wake progressed, a suggestion was quietly passed among the "extended family" to meet at Kelly's afterwards. There was really no other place to consider. Kelly's was nearby and this was the place where most of us had spent many an hour and told many a tale. But rarely (if ever) had Kelly's witnessed the sartorial splendor of such a fine-looking cast of young men—all in their late twenties and early thirties, all fit and trim, all in dark suits, and stylish matching ties. A group that would fit well on any stage be that sports, business, or entertainment. Now playing pool and commiserating with jackets cast aside, sleeves rolled up, and amid the sounds of animated conversation rising higher and higher. The suds were flowing freely as many individuals bought rounds with no regard for precedence or request. Armed with two or three "Rolling Rocks" at a time, the pool games carried on until the evening drew to a close.

Kelly's Bar in Bryn Mawr

My wife and I stayed at Chris Mason's that night. The following morning Chris emerged from the bathroom looking like he had just survived the Battle of the Somme. I have never seen such a hatchet shave-job—blood and pieces of tissue everywhere. Whether it was the result of the late night or early morning sorrow, we will never know.

The funeral commenced at 11 a.m. It was a solemn affair that we all secretly dreaded. Most suitably, it took place at the chapel—St. Thomas of Villanova. The day itself refrained from raining but had a restless, uneasy somber feel about it. Walking up the path on the approach to the church, the yet bare branches of the trees seem to tremble in their own sorrow. Once inside, we moved to the front where Jumbo's casket had been placed. The immediate family members were seated in the front pew. The next few pews were appropriately assigned to seat the "boys"—Jumbo's extended family. They slowly filed in all looking especially pensive, lost in thought. The entire chapel was filled with friends, well-wishers as well as a good number of the press representing the *Philadelphia Inquirer, Washington Post, New York Times,* and local TV stations.

The ceremony itself was a blur for me. University President Father Driscoll presided over the funeral mass offering greetings, sympathies, and a message of hope. He lauded Jumbo as one of the greatest Villanovans ever. It included the singing of the "Battle Hymn of the Republic" and the "Villanova Alma Mater," which sounded especially sad. Each time I looked over to my teammates both left and right, I saw silent weeping. Nothing was being held back—tears of sorrow, tears of regret, tears of thankfulness, tears of memories, tears of victory, tears of loss mingled with tears for the guidance, inspiration, and the opportunity to be part of this great legacy, thanks to this one man, the man who was being buried that day.

Upon completion of the Mass, we followed the cortege to a nearby cemetery just outside of Conshohocken. It was located just beyond the Tennis Court loop, which you could see beyond the rise and through the trees to the east. Never did we imagine that we would be here for this reason, but here we were. The final blessings were given, prayers offered up, silent wishes made, and Jumbo Elliott was lowered into his final resting place. He was gone, left now to the domain of history and the abiding memories of those whose lives had been forever changed by him.

To no surprise, we found our way back to campus and to no other place but the Field House. That seemed to be the natural place to gather. The indoor season had just passed, and the outdoor season was only a few weeks away. Several within our midst were in full training, most notably Eamonn Coghlan, now 29 years of age and holder of the world record for the indoor mile with a 3:50.6 that he had set just one month prior. Also present was Tiny Kane, who had run in that world-record-setting race and served as Eamonn's pacemaker. He was supremely fit having run 3.55 for the mile. So, a run it would be. Entering the Field House and walking down the stairs into the old hallway or our familiar locker room felt like coming home. Nothing had changed. The trunks where we had always sat, awaited us. Charlie in the cage seemed less grumpy as he too appreciated the loss of Jumbo and expressed his sympathies with a slightly more empathetic mood.

That is when we met the new kid in town, Marcus O'Sullivan, the freshman. On first notice, we looked at him in surprise and muttered to each other, "That looks like a little Eamonn." Sure enough, the physical resemblance was there. The height, the body shape, the curious and mischievous look in the eye, that innate competitive instinct. For the first time I could truly see the difference between the men that we had become and the boys who formed the present Villanova Track Team. As we stripped down and changed into our running gear, there stood Eamonn Coghlan and Tiny Kane, both mature men, both in their late twenties and at their physical peak and full strength; in contrast stood the young Marcus O'Sullivan and his teammates—a full 10 years younger, literally in a state of boyish innocence—muscles still forming, body structure yet to fully mature, and in many cases, baby-faced and yet to experience the ravages of the daily razor; and all early stages of development when it came to experience and the ability to bear the emotional burdens of the stresses associated with high performance. At that moment it struck me deeply to recall how young we actually had been during our Villanova years—arriving at 17 or 18 years of age; not seeing our 22nd birthday until after we graduated. And fully convinced, thanks to Jim Ryun who had set the world record for the mile at 19 years of age, that if we did not achieve our peak before graduation, our athletic lives would be over. How wrong we were. Eamonn still had his best races ahead of him. Marcus was just beginning. And both would leave an extraordinary and extended list of achievements behind.

The loss of Jumbo clearly marked a change within the Villanova Track zeitgeist. While his spirit lingered for several weeks after the funeral, providing the necessary sustenance for the 1981 Penn Relays, and the 16th consecutive DMR win, 1982 was a different story. Charlie Jenkins, the former 400-meter Olympic champion from 1956 had been named head coach. Mr. Pyrah resumed his role as assistant coach (and COM—Chief Operating Mother) to nurture and look after the team. At first there was great enthusiasm—a gold medal Olympian and former Villanovan as head coach, a man who was fully versed and experienced with the nuances of the Penn Relays having won eight Championship of America races from 1955 to 1957. In addition, Don Paige, who continued to train and develop his astonishing career, joined the coaching squad as an assistant coach.

Soon it became evident that Charlie did not know much or seem to be even that curious about middle distance running. His focus not surprisingly was the sprints up to the 400 meters. The milers and the half-milers could sense the lack of knowledge and the disinterest, and it began to unsettle them.

Nevertheless, the team was running well. John Hunter ran a 2:22.27 – 1000 meters to win the indoor IC4A Championships. Marcus O'Sullivan was getting stronger every week as he approached the four-minute mile barrier. A new transfer by the name of Ross Donoghue was now eligible to compete for Villanova. Ross, who hailed from the small community of Oswego, upstate New York on the south shore of Lake Ontario, started his college career at St. John's University, located in Queen's, New York City. He came with strong credentials having broken four minutes for the mile in 1979 with a 3:58.0 effort. Furthermore, that same year he had finished fourth to Don Paige in the NCAA Outdoor final with a 3:39.8. But he had not been happy at St. John's and longed to be a part of team that had the depth of talent and the performances that were being achieved at Villanova. Seeing Don win that unbelievable double (the 800 meters and the 1500 meters) sealed that desire. With his strong NCAA showing, Jumbo had offered him a scholarship knowing full well that the most that could be returned would be two competitive seasons.

The first competitive season for Donoghue and the Wildcats was looking good. He anchored the DMR at the King Games in Palo Alto, California with a 4:04.2 mile and "coasted" to a win in early April.[1] Two weeks earlier, the team did well at the Dogwood Relays in Knoxville, Tennessee by winning both the 4 x 1500 meters and the Sprint Medley. The latter was anchored by one of the most promising 800-meter runners in the country, John Marshall, a freshman.

Penn Relays 1982

The two weeks leading up to the relays saw the tension steadily increase. Each day, the team became quieter. Words were not required to express what was at stake. Would Villanova be able to make it 17 DMRs in a row? Who was going to anchor? Would Georgetown and their star miler John Gregorek finally get the better of the Villanova team? Technically (on paper), Ross Donoghue had the fastest mile time, but John Hunter had the most experience. Ross had never run a relay leg for Villanova at the Penn Relays. Hunter had run on several winning teams during the past two years—the 4 x 800 meters in 1980; and the DMR as well as the 4 x 1500 meters in 1981.

There is something special about a Villanova runner, especially one of the stars. And especially when it was show time like the Penn Relays. There was a sense of supreme confidence, an ever-so-slight swagger that the likes of Patrick, Liquori, Hartnett, Schappert, Coghlan, Belger, Paige, and Maree would emanate. You could tell a Villanova runner when you saw one by the aura, the self-assurance, and the way each one carried himself. You would feel the gathering of energy and confidence building up for Penn. It did not seem to matter what ailments or injuries might have been at play, these seemed to fall by the wayside. The stars were the purest of the pure when it came to receiving the baton for that critical final leg. By then, the remaining team members knew that the certainty of winning was almost always 100 percent. Jumbo knew exactly what he was looking for—he could sense that critical inner courage and who was willing to pull it out in the last 100 yards.

The lead-up to the 1982 Penn Relays did not have this feeling of certainty. Without Jumbo, the energy seemed scattered, and confidence remained hidden like the contents of those mysterious trunks in the Field House. And when Ross Donoghue was selected to anchor the 1982 DMR, there was a growing sense of uneasiness. Was this the right choice given what was at stake? Simply put, would Ross be able to handle the pressure? As one teammate put it: "If you are a theater director putting on *Hamlet,* you want an actor with a lot of experience to play the part. We were not getting that feeling here."

Ross was described by his teammates as one of the nicest guys you could meet. But he was still new to Villanova and had never run a Penn Relays race as a Wildcat. He had not been tempered with that all important apprentice role borne by so many Villanova runners in the past—those who were introduced to Penn Relays by being the leadoff man in either the Two Mile or Four Mile relay. Being named as the anchor of the DMR, his very first race as a Villanovan at Penn, put Ross in a position of enormous responsibility. The anchor role is stressful in and of itself. But the DMR, that prestigious race which Villanova had won 16 consecutive times, increased that level of stress exponentially. Should a different choice have been made? No one will ever really be able to answer that question, but John Hunter was now a senior with four years of experience and getting stronger every year. He was clearly running well and capable of a four-minute mile, but Head Coach Charlie Jenkins decided that the fastest man on paper should be the anchor. And that was that.

The day of the race, Ross was all nerves. But as all runners know, there are two types of nerves: the positive ones where you can't wait to display your ability, like a Mark Belger; and the negative ones when racing is the last thing you want to do. Ross's nerves were far from the former and unfortunately, too much of the latter.

The night before, Ross had tried to distract himself by watching a funny movie but found nothing to laugh at. Then sleep eluded him as he tossed and turned all night. At one point a teammate heard him say that "the streak started when I began grade school—I don't want to be known as the one to end it." At times, he wished he could be anywhere but Franklin Field, but the die had been cast. His lot had been drawn and the burden of carrying forward the 16-year DMR streak now fell on his shoulders.

John Hunter led off the 1200-meter leg and the Wildcats were in immediate trouble. John found himself in the midst of a group of runners and could do nothing but simply keep himself upright. Trapped and not free to move either to his left or right, he looked for an opening that failed to appear. Finally, with a lap to go, he forced himself to go wide and quickly went to the front. Despite all that circumnavigation, he gained a seven-meter lead and ran a very respectable 2:54.6. Carlton Young was on fire and produced one of the fastest one lappers of the meet with a 45.2. Now the Villanova team was well clear of the field with a 15-meter lead. Then the freshman John Marshall demonstrated his enormous potential by cranking out a 1:46.8 – 800 meters. That translated into a clear gap of 35 meters (or a full 5-second lead) over the pursuers from Georgetown.

St. John's transfer Ross Donoghue in Villanova colors

Ross Donoghue received the baton in what should have been a free run for home. But he was in a psychological no-man's land. Consumed by stress, he lost all sense of pace and ran like a man without purpose. Meanwhile Gregorek, full of memory as to how Sydney Maree had dismantled him piece by piece for two years running, set out in a cool calculative style to close the gap. He knew he had three laps to make up that 35-meter deficit—that meant 58 seconds a lap assuming that the Villanova leader would run approximately 60 seconds per lap. His task was abundantly clear. After two laps the gap narrowed to 15 meters. Then at the end of the third lap, Ross's biggest nightmare came true—Gregorek was on his shoulder. There he stayed and while Ross tried to hold him off, he could no longer withstand the speed being applied. With 100 meters to go, Gregorek took the lead, and the race was over.

The press had a field day. The *New York Times* read "Georgetown Ends Villanova's Streak."[2] The *Philadelphia Inquirer* offered a similar report: "Georgetown Snaps Streak by Villanova," followed by the opening line, "It will be remembered as one of the great moments at Georgetown University, which has had few of them at Penn Relays."[3] The statement could just as well have read, "It will be remembered as one of the lowest points at Villanova University, which has had many high points at Penn Relays." The Villanova Track Team was stunned—it had finally happened. After the race, Donoghue stood for several agonizing minutes about 15 meters past the finish line. His head was bowed and when asked to comment he simply said, "not today" and disappeared.

Charlie Jenkins showed no emotion and put on a brave face. "I feel badly about Ross but it's not the end of the world,"[4] he said philosophically. "Ross has been running well. Today he lost but he did not lose because he wasn't trying."[5] Indeed, the final splits show that Gregorek ran a 3:55 – 1600 meters, as of that date, the fastest time ever run for this distance at Penn Relays, while Ross had run just over four minutes. That was the gap—the five seconds that Gregorek made up. The Georgetown team ran 9.26.16—the second fastest DMR ever run, second only to the world record set by Villanova in 1980 with Maree and Paige, who had run 9.24.20. Villanova's time today was 9:26.67—the third fastest time ever.

The next day, Donoghue could not be consoled. He quietly surmised his feelings by saying "losing the DMR is like losing a member of the family. Yesterday, was the lowest point of my life."[6]

Could there have been a different outcome? Clearly the Jumbo magic and his intimate knowledge of pressure and the inner spirit required to hold off all challengers in that final lap might have led to a different set of choices. To be sure, there was no clear superstar miler in the ranks. But Villanova teams had been in this position before—in 1966, with Dave Patrick as an unproven sophomore; in 1972 with John Hartnett, also a sophomore with little experience as a miler; and 1977 with Phil Kane, a senior but just coming into his own. But all these individuals exuded that positive stress vibe—they loved to compete and would do everything possible to win. This was the vibe that Jumbo could discern, and he had been right for 16 consecutive DMR wins.

It is my belief that in all likelihood, Jumbo would have gone with experience and selected John Hunter to anchor the DMR. John was quite capable of running a sub four-minute mile. His personality and his easygoing style imbued confidence. Most importantly, as a seasoned senior he had witnessed the preparation and lead-up to Penn Relays on three previous occasions. He had the experience to handle the pressure, but the opportunity was not presented to him.

Could Villanova have won a 17th DMR and possibly continued the streak for another few years? A strong team of runners were still in place as the next day's performances testify. But with respect to extending the DMR streak, no one will ever know. To be sure, the win by Georgetown over Villanova took a supreme effort. Not only was the anchor John Gregorek ranked at that time as the top miler in the US college system, but the winning time was also a new Penn Relays record. Could there be a more fitting loss for Villanova and the end of the DMR streak? Hard to imagine a better script.

Postscript 1

The following day, the Villanova Track Team was far from done. In fact, they rose from that Friday defeat to win every race they entered: the 4 x 1500 meters; the Sprint Medley, and the 4 x 800 meters. The wins were a clear demonstration that Villanova's depth was real, and the team was taking no back seat. The 4 x 1500 meter team was comprised of Mike England (3:44.7), Marcus O'Sullivan (3:46.1), Ross Donoghue (3.50.1), and anchored by John Hunter (3:41.9) or the equivalent of a 3:59 mile—the very time needed to have won the DMR the day before.

The Sprint Medley was another display of Villanova strength and speed. The team of Carlton Young, Rodney Wilson, Jim Adams, and freshman John Marshall outbattled both Tennessee and Michigan with his 1:48.5 – 800-meter anchor to win the event in 3.16.84.

Later that afternoon, the Villanova 4 x 800 meter team won that event in 7:12.29—a national collegiate record and of course, the fastest time ever run by a Villanova team. That team included Marcus O'Sullivan (1:50.2), Michael England (1:46.6), John Hunter (1:46.5); and John Marshall (1:49.0). Marshall received the baton in the lead but ran a leisurely first lap (56 seconds) and then fought off runners from Georgetown and Richmond to seal the win with a 53-second lap.

Postscript 2

The "impish" Irishman, Marcus O'Sullivan, became one of the greatest middle-distance runners of his time. Who we had seen as "little Eamonn" in 1981 fulfilled that prescient insight by running a 3:50.94 indoor mile in 1988, second only to the world record run by the Chairman of Boards, none other than Eamonn Coghlan. Eamonn became the first man to run sub 3:50 for the indoor mile with his 3:49.4 in 1983. Marcus O'Sullivan's record of performances is legion, including: 10 Big East Championships; winner of six Wanamaker Miles at the Millrose Games; six Penn Relays Championships of America; a four-times Olympian; three-times World Indoor 1500-meter champion; and a member of the 1985 Four Mile Irish Relay team that set the world record with a time of 15:49.08. The other members of that team were Eamonn Coghlan, Frank O'Mara, and Ray Flynn, representing an average of 3:57.3 per mile for each runner. Perhaps his most astonishing accomplishment is this: Marcus is one of three athletes[7] who have run more than 100 sub four-minute miles, an accomplishment that he achieved 101 times. Like Sydney Maree, Marcus was also coached by Tom Donnelly, former Villanova track star.

In 1997, Marcus O'Sullivan became Head Coach of Villanova University Track and Cross-Country Team, a position that he holds to this day. He has worked long and hard to build onto the rich Villanova track heritage which he has done with numerous championship teams and world leading middle-distance runners, both male and female. Interestingly, since he has become head coach, 17 more Villanova runners have broken four minutes for the mile.

Postscript 3

On February 27th, 1983, Eamonn Coghlan sought to improve his world indoor record for the mile for the third time. In 1979, he broke Dick Buerkle's record (3.54.9) with a 3:52.6 in San Diego; in 1981, he reduced this time to a 3:50.6 with the help of Phil (Tiny) Kane as a rabbit, again in San Diego. Then at the Meadowlands, East Rutherford, New Jersey on 10 laps to the mile track, Eamonn received the help of a now-graduated Villanovan, Ross Donoghue, to set up the race. Ross led the field with a 56.6 second first quarter; continuing through the half mile in 1:55.7—a perfect pace, leaving Eamonn to take over finishing with a 3.49.73 for a new world record and the first person to break 3:50 indoors. To this day, Eamonn remains thankful for the quiet steady pacing provided by Ross—one of the nicest guys to ever don a Villanova singlet, to make this monumental achievement in the sport of track and field possible.

12

Coach Jack "Mother" Pyrah

"We shall come to ALMA MATER In our dreams again"

Villanova Alma Mater

"Talk to Pyrah." This was without doubt the most common statement uttered by the members of the Villanova Track Team. No matter what the problem, no matter how big or how small, this utterance would inevitably arise. Almost daily. Pyrah was the man to fix all problems.

While Jumbo Elliott was rarely seen on campus, Jack Pyrah was omnipresent. He was everywhere, or so it seemed. We were never sure quite what his range of duties and obligations really were. But part of that duty involved security detail. Most days we would see him "guarding" the exit door to the cafeteria—there to discourage anyone from entering for a free meal through the back channels. While most security personnel wore uniforms, Jack remained plain-clothed. Other days, we would see him in the "tower" located in the main parking lot. If you looked carefully through the cafeteria windows and across Lancaster Avenue, you could see him in the distance attending to the task of ensuring that non-paying parkers would be appropriately discouraged.

The freshmen quickly caught on that Pyrah was never far away and could be summoned on short notice. One day as the hourly Corr Hall bell sounded its usual 12 gongs at noon, I told these wide-eyed freshmen that Pyrah was responsible for bell-ringing as well. That was why he was not at the side door as per usual and that every hour he had to "whip" over to the tower just to perform this important task. I passed this information with the most serious look I could convey. Slowly this fact sank in, until I grinned, and my intentional misdirection was taken with much amusement as fully intended.

Coach Jack "Mother" Pyrah

We knew of course that he was the Assistant Track Coach and the Head Cross-Country Coach. But he was really Jumbo's right-hand man—the man that looked after everything. We also knew that the school had a limited budget and Mr. Pyrah would be dispatched across a variety of functions that went beyond his coaching duties. He started as a supplies manager buried deep in the science department in the basement of Mendel Hall—one of those vital administrative managers to make certain that professors and their laboratories had the necessary chemicals to teach their classes and conduct research. But in 1966 when Jim Tuppeny, Jumbo's assistant took the head coaching job at the University of Pennsylvania, Jack Pyrah stepped to the fore as the new assistant coach. That's when he shifted out of the basement of Mendel Hall on the periphery of campus to assume a more prominent role based out of Dougherty Hall, the center of student life, where the cafeteria was located.

There could not have been two more opposites than Jumbo Elliott and Jack Pyrah. While Jumbo drove a shiny new Cadillac, Pyrah drove a beat-up Ford Galaxy that had seen far better days; while Jumbo lived just a few miles from campus, Pyrah lived in Gloucester, New Jersey—one of those communities across the Delaware River from Philadelphia. While Jumbo never arrived before 3.30 p.m., Pyrah would be there by 7:00 a.m.—God only knows how early he got up to make the busy one-hour commute to campus each day. While Jumbo presented himself in the best of business dress looking stylish and sleek, Pyrah wore the same tweed jacket or blue blazer that hung loosely over his ample frame, day in, day out. While Jumbo would freely roar and genuflect at will at the many things in life that would frustrate him, Pyrah would constantly seek to smooth and to sooth the issues at hand or accommodate anyone who needed attention.

That latter point describes the Pyrah "essence" and why he earned and deserved the name "Mother" Pyrah. No one cared more and did more for his athletes, than Mother Pyrah. If you had a problem, big or small, you would "talk to Pryah." If you needed a pair of running shoes to replace that overused set you were wearing, "talk to Pyrah."

If you were having persistent injury problems and you needed more medical attention such as a specialist or x-rays at the Bryn Mawr hospital, "talk to Pyrah." If you were having problems with school and needed help such as special tutoring, "talk to Pyrah." If you were just struggling with life and issues that were getting you down, "talk to Pyrah."

I recall one late April morning in 1974—it was the first Monday after Penn Relays. I had just sat down for breakfast at the table when I looked up and saw Mr. Pyrah and a distraught looking Ed Takacs coming toward me. Now at full attention, I knew something was wrong. Sure enough, Ed's mother, who had been ill with cancer during that year, had just passed away. Ed's first reaction—"talk to Pyrah," which he did as soon as possible early that morning garnered Pyrah's great sympathy. But Pyrah knew what to do next—bring Ed to a teammate—the other Canadian, and that was me. That morning we spent a few hours together. We talked, reminisced, shared family stories, walked to the track, ambled a slow lap or two, sat under a tree and talked some more. After that, Ed gathered his things, headed to the airport, and then for home. It was a time together we will never forget. But facilitated by Mr. Pyrah.

"Mother" Pyrah was the go-to guy for all matters other than the actual workouts or matters pertaining to races. He was probably the most selfless man you could ever meet. Marty Liquori put it best: "We all realize now that Jumbo had a real attention-deficit problem, and it was Jack who kept everything on an even keel. He was the detail guy to Jumbo's George Patton. Some coaches may have been able to do both, but I never had one. As Jumbo said, 'I kick them and Jack kisses them.' Without either of them, Villanova in the '70s would not have been as successful."[1]

This reflection on the Jumbo-Pyrah relationship shared by Liquori, summarized the views of many others. Ed Takacs reminisces: "Jumbo was a no-nonsense type of coach. He did not coddle his athletes. Empathy was limited; if one was seeking or needed this, his alter ego, Mr. Pyrah served this purpose—he provided the emotional support and caring for the team."

Tom Donnelly called Pyrah the "soul of the program" at Villanova for nearly one-third of a century. He had an enormous positive attitude on hundreds of athletes. John Hartnett ascribes the major reason why Villanova track members still maintain regular contact all these years later, to Mr. Pyrah "I very much appreciate this. Our getting together and keeping in contact is not common at other schools or programs—a lot of this is due to Mr. Pyrah. We did not call him Mother Pyrah for nothing."

Marcus O'Sullivan recalls how Jack was always positive, and always had an encouraging word for his runners no matter their performance on the track. "Jack was a huge inspiration to me as a runner and a coach." Marcus continues: "Jack's loyalty and dedication to Villanova were unmatched." As of 1997, Marcus has been the Villanova Head Track Coach and went on to say: "I saw Jack's great gift after I became coach at Villanova- his gentleness and positive outlook and limitless patience."

Each of us have our own "Mother" Pyrah stories. Interestingly, most of our stories took place in private. Simply, because when you went to see Pyrah, it was just you and him. And whatever was discussed stayed between you and him. For many of us, the first person you would meet upon arrival to Villanova would be Jack Pyrah. He would be the first person to greet you if you arrived on campus or to be waiting for you at the train station or the airport. In my case, he was there to pick me up from the Philadelphia airport when I stepped into what I hoped to be the most exciting chapter of my life, that sunny day in September of 1970. We climbed into that beat-up Ford Galaxy and drove from southwest Philly up the Schuylkill Expressway (better known locally as the Surekill Expressway) as it wound and weaved along the edge of the river with multiple lanes and a dense forest on the southwest side.

On arrival to campus, Pyrah suggested we stop at the local Howard Johnson's—it was a Wednesday evening featuring the popular "All You Can Eat Fish Fry." That appealed to me, given my usual state of starvation, but I soon discerned a more undisclosed motive on the part of my host. Pyrah loved to eat. And be on guard if you ever have a plate of French fries in front of you. Should that be the case, whether in the cafeteria or on the road, Pyrah would smoothly edge close to you, sit down, and start picking the fries off your plate.

One occasion some years later still brings a chuckle to John Hartnett and me. It was January of 1974—we had just competed at the Olympic Invitational Indoor Meet at the Nassau Coliseum on Long Island. Our team bus headed back to Philadelphia that night and we were joined by two Irishmen, Neil Cusack and Eddy Leddy, both friends of John, and heading back to East Tennessee. Neil had become nationally prominent having won the NCAA Cross-Country Championship in the fall of 1972 and finishing fourth in 1973. They decided to join us and fly out of Philly the next day. On route we stopped at a restaurant in North Jersey. The four of us were sitting at a table only to be joined by Pyrah just as the food was arriving. Neil had ordered a large plate of fries. John and I had long learned to "keep our eyes on our fries" and had positioned ourselves physically to do so. But Neil had no idea what was coming. He looked our way in a mild state of dismay not knowing what to do. But the process had begun, and Neil reluctantly shared his fries with Mr. Pyrah while John and I chuckled away.

Jack Pyrah was born in 1918 in Germantown—a working-class neighborhood on the north-western edge of Philadelphia just north of the Schuylkill River. Today it is considered one of Philadelphia's most historic neighborhoods and a sought-after place to live. But 100 years ago, it was a bustling, industrial, blue-collar area with a decided European feel. One of the most iconic businesses in Germantown is the Tasty Baking Company, makers of the famous and indeed "tasty" coffee cakes to be found anywhere. Known as TastyKake, it continues to be the cause for mouths of Philadelphians to water and can be readily found in vending machines including at Villanova University. As a hockey fan I learned early on that only in Philadelphia can you hear the loud exclamation of "He shoots! He Scores for a case of TastyKake!" each time the Flyers scored. No wonder Mr. Pyrah liked to eat—he developed his palate early on the best coffee cake I have ever tasted.

Germantown ended up being an unplanned detour on the one occasion when I had the "privilege" to drive the Pyrahmobile—that beat up Ford Galaxy. Several of us returned on a flight from Knoxville after our annual University of Tennessee-Villanova dual meet. For some reason, Pyrah stayed behind, and gave us the keys to drive his car, which was parked at the Philadelphia International Airport, back to campus. So, there I was the freshman member of the "foreign" contingent—Chris Mason, Davey Wright—the Brits; Donal Walsh, John Hartnett—the Micks; and myself the Canuck and the only one with North American "right-hand" side of the road driving experience. Not surprisingly, I was quickly enrolled into the position of designated driver. As soon as we gathered speed upon leaving the airport, I could tell that both hands were required on the steering wheel—the vehicle was pulling hard to the right. Shortly thereafter we entered the legendary Schuylkill Expressway (first time driving it for me) and approached a multiplicity of lane choices, I stayed to the right—not so much the result of my steering but more the desired direction of the vehicle itself. Well, at a critical juncture, that right lane veered off to Germantown, across the river, requiring a quick exit on a side street and a doubling back. Despite being admonished by the indecipherable exhortations of heavy Cork accents accompanied by the more polite-sounding Brits, I recovered quickly and soon returned to the proper route. After that experience, you can be assured that I avoided driving the Pyrahmobile thereafter.

Mr. Pyrah also loved to talk. Perhaps this was his real charm. He could talk and talk and talk. Mark Belger remembers those lengthy recruiting calls he would receive from Mr. Pyrah. As would Don Paige. Even John Hartnett would find his way to the one phone booth in the center of Ballyhooly, two miles from the farmhouse to talk to Mr. Pyrah. With a smile, Marcus recalled Jack's gift for gab. "Jack would call while you were making dinner to chat and the next thing you knew it seemed like it was time to get the kids ready for school."[2]

When Mr. Pyrah talked, there would be no end of stories about what Villanova runners were doing. And of course, long dissertations on the success of the team and the greatness of Jumbo as a coach. As Browning Ross put it, "Jack Pyrah never wanted the conversation to end." Marcus emphasized this quality: "I can recall getting calls from Jack right after dinner and my wife wishing me a good night, knowing I would be talking to Jack for a while. The most amazing part of the conversation—nothing was ever about Jack. It was about you, the team, and runners you were coaching, and the conversations always featured Jack's priceless stories told in his rich gentle voice."[3]

But it was Mr. Pyrah's easy style, his kindness, and his knowledge that worked so effectively as Jumbo's main recruiter. He attended his first Penn Relays in 1934 at the age of 16. From that time forward he attended every year until his passing in 2007—a total of 73 consecutive Penn Relays. To be sure, he was no casual spectator. As he became more involved as a track coach in the 1950s and '60s, he would focus carefully on the high school races. And no better place that Penn Relays. Every high school runner or team of renown in the eastern United States competed at Penn Relays, either in the High School DMR or the High School Invitational Mile. Consider the list of Villanova runners that would have been first identified and earmarked for further investigations at Penn Relays: Dave Patrick, Charlie Messenger, Larry James, Tom Donnelly, Marty Liquori, Andy O'Reilly, Greg Govan, Ken Schappert, John Burns, Mark Belger, Don Paige, Mike England.... the list goes on. They were all there exhibiting early demonstrations of their capabilities at Penn Relays all the while being observed carefully by Jack Pyrah. His memory and mind for statistics were prodigious. He knew times, splits, and placings like none other. Pyrah would often be seen writing, making notes, and adding to the multiple slips of paper he kept in his many pockets. How he kept track of all these details remains a mystery to all of us. Jumbo called Pyrah a walking computer.

Pyrah's keen eye, his knowledge of times, and his interest in individual runners initiated his recruiting process. A first contact at a track meet, followed by more conversations on the telephone, and finally the introduction to Jumbo. The top prospects would be invited to visit the campus. Again, Mr. Pyrah would serve as the lead host, make all the introductions, tour the athlete, and take the prospect for lunch or dinner. Then at long last, the final introduction to Jumbo would be made and in most cases the deal sealed. And the pièce de résistance, when the stakes were high and Jumbo really wanted a particular prospect, Ken Schappert would be deployed as the closer without equal. By then, the heavy groundwork would have been done by Mr. Pyrah.

Mark Belger reflects on his experience: "Jumbo was the ultimate recruiter, but Jack was the glue that kept us together. Sometimes I think that Jack was Jumbo's greatest recruiter. If it were not for Jack, Jumbo would have been successful, but maybe not as successful but for Jack's insight, love, and knowledge of the sport. They each had a role in the team's NCAA successes." When it came time for Jack to step back and let Jumbo take over, he did so invisibly. Mark remembers on one occasion after Jumbo and Jack strategized about who was going to be on which team at the Penn Relays, Jack stood quietly by letting Jumbo do the typical thing he did to pep us up. He'd smile a lot, squeeze your shoulders and say, "How you feeling? How you feeling?" Pyrah kept smiling and just let Jumbo ramble on.

The Jumbo-Pyrah duo was a miracle in itself. Had Pyrah been ego-driven or in need of the limelight, even in the slightest way, it would never have worked. But Pyrah needed neither and instead sacrificed himself for the sake of the team, and in pleasing Jumbo. If Jumbo was the "Ying," Pyrah was the "Yang." Jumbo cast the hard driving "Father" figure. Pyrah presented himself as the nurturing "Mother" figure. When Jumbo would hear about one of the runners being injured, he would get frustrated and want no details—he just wanted that runner back on his feet; Pyrah never stopped asking the runner how he was doing, wanted all the details, and attended in any manner he could.

There were times when Jumbo would rail at Pyrah and even express anger on matters that Pyrah had no influence on whatsoever. Pyrah knew that Jumbo was a mega personality and a big ego. He knew that Jumbo needed a place to vent. Pyrah did not compete in any way or steal any of the accolades that the Villanova Track Team and Jumbo would receive. He assumed the role of service and would never stop serving. At times it was almost embarrassing to see and hear what was going on between Jumbo and Pyrah particularly on the boards, when the winter winds were most bitter, the injuries among us were at their greatest, and the mood most grim. The relationship was an amazing dynamic to observe. No one knew why it worked. But we all knew that it worked.

In August of 2001, Jack and Jean Pyrah made a trip to Edmonton to take in the IAAF World Athletics Championships produced by my now home city[4] for the first time in North America. As one of the organizers, I had the opportunity to host the Pyrahs and show a measure of appreciation for all the attention and kindness both had shown me. Aside from the daily competitions, we were able to host them at two memorable events. The first was the Legends of Gold—an assembly of the top track stars featured at a gala banquet with 1,500 patrons and the Edmonton Symphony Orchestra providing the background ambience. The line-up included 25 of the world's best—winners of either an Olympic gold or World Championship gold, including Kip Keino, Peter Snell, Herb Elliott, Sebastian Coe, Frank Shorter, Joan Benoit, Dick Fosbury, Sergei Bubka, Ralph Boston, Perry O'Brien, Al Oerter, Wyoming Tyus, Irena Szewinska, Harrison Dillard, Donovan Bailey, and Mark McKoy among others, and of course our very own Eamonn Coghlan. The whole event came about after a conversation between Eamonn and myself in early 1999 when I asked him what he thought about the idea of such an event and inviting these stars and their families to come to Edmonton for a week. Eamonn was of course highly enthusiastic, and we went to work to make this happen. That evening, Jack and Jean joined us at the "Frank Shorter table." It was an evening of great celebration, fraternity, jocularity, and memories that we all thoroughly enjoyed, including a recollection of Frank's win of the 1970 AAU Cross Country Championships—a bitter cold November day at Penn State, when he was clad in pantyhose!

John Hartnett, Craig Masbach, Jerry Bouma, Frank Shorter, and Eamonn Coghlan, with Jean and Jack Pyrah celebrating Jack's birthday in Edmonton, 2001

Vi Becker and Jerry Bouma with Jean and Jack Pyrah in Edmonton, 2001

The second event was a smaller affair—something I called Villanova and Friends Night. It coincided with Mr. Pyrah's birthday, and we rented the top floor of Sherlock Holmes, a local watering hole. We invited several athletic friends who were attending the World Championships, as well as a group of Edmontonians, many of Irish descent. Again, it was a most memorable and enjoyable evening—we were joined by Eamonn Coghlan, John Hartnett, Frank Shorter, and Craig Masbach—all paying tribute to the Pyrahs, telling stories to the assembled attendees, and expressing their appreciation, especially for Mr. Pyrah's contribution to the world of track and field. It was a fitting tribute to a most deserving man.

Ed Takacs, Jerry Bouma, and John Hartnett at the 2001 IAAF World Championships

On July 19, 2007, Jack Pyrah passed away at the age of 88. The funeral was held three days later in Gloucester City. Once again, the "boys"—that core group from the '70s—were all there: Marty Liquori, John Hartnett, Ron Stanko, Ken Schappert, Kevin Leonard, Steve Dorsey, Ed Takacs, Tiny Kane, John Burns, Don Paige, Gerry O'Reilly, and me. This time, the mood was more celebratory in nature compared to the sadness of Jumbo's funeral when he had passed so unexpectedly. But it was clear that Mr. Pyrah was greatly missed.

It was even more clear that the appreciation for his contribution had grown over the years. As young men in our time on the track team, we stood in awe of Jumbo and his achievements. Pyrah, the "stay at home mom," was that non-threatening ever-present assistant who could easily be overlooked and even taken for granted. But now as we had matured and reflected on our experiences both at Villanova and what life's path had delivered to each of us, the blessing of "Mother" Pyrah was ever more apparent and valued. It was Mother Pyrah, our Villanova "Mater," who provided that critical stabilizing ingredient that made success possible. Without Mother Pyrah, the Villanova Track Story would have been a different tale.

Coach Marcus O'Sullivan and Mrs. Jean Pyrah after the funeral of Jack Pyrah

The service closed with the singing of the Villanova Alma Mater. But while the song honors the school itself, that day, 20 reflective middle-aged men sang ALMA MATER with someone else clearly in mind with these words:

When the last big game is over
And the last roll call is heard
When the oldest pedagogue
Has had his final word
We shall come to ALMA MATER
In our dreams again
With prayer for Villanova
And a sweet amen.

Sing a hymn of praise
To our dear old ALMA MATER
And our College days …
Villanova, Villanova
When we leave your sheltering walls
We shall leave an echo ringing
Through your treasured halls.[5]

Meanwhile, Mr. Pyrah, beyond the "pearly gates" in a place high above, had just been tapped on the shoulder for a new recruiting assignment.

The Boys after Mother Pyrah's funeral in the Pyrah Backyard, July 2007

Kneeling: Paul Regan, Mike McIntosh, Don Paige, Ed Takacs, Jerry Bouma

Standing: Marcus O'Sullivan, Cory Smith, Gerry O'Reilly, Ryan Payne, John Burns, John Hartnett, Frank Watkins, Phil Kane, Kevin Leonard, Ron Stanko, Ken Schappert, Marty Liquori, Steve Dorsey, Mike McDonnell III

13

Can It Happen Again?

"The most beautiful experience we can have is the mysterious."

Albert Einstein

It is often said that history repeats itself. But is that really true? Do the exact same set of social, economic, and political conditions ever reoccur in such a way as to produce the same outcome? Consider the all-important dimension of individual character—that special blend of personality that rises to the fore—and then consider the essential ingredients of critical leadership and vision, so necessary for exceptional athletic performance to happen.

History is not some inevitable deterministic process as some would argue. Instead, it is a much more mysterious process—the merger of individuals or groups of people responding to, and sometimes clashing with, the ideas and circumstances of the day. A cursory review illustrates this. What would the United States look like today without Abraham Lincoln? Or a Marxist revolution in Russia without Vladimir Lenin? Or the free world in the 1940s without Winston Churchill?

A similar historical lens can be applied to the 1966 to 1981 period, when the Villanova University Track and Field Team won 16 consecutive Distance Medley Relays (DMRs) at the Penn Relays. During that time span, it was arguably the most prolific middle distance running powerhouse on the planet. The results are simply astonishing: the DMR wins were really the icing; the cake during that 15-year period totaled 52 Championships of America Relay titles; 45 NCAA Champions, 16 World Records (three outdoor and 13 indoor); 14 Olympians two gold and one silver; and generated a steady stream of world-class milers—Patrick, Murphy, Liquori, Mason, Hartnett, Schappert, Gregan, Coghlan, Takacs, Kane, Belger, Childs, Burns, Paige, Maree, Korir, Hunter, Donoghue, and O'Sullivan.

In many respects, the components in producing this elixir of excellence can be classified as "one of a kind." Or simply a mystery. But starting with the uniqueness of the Villanova campus—the quiet inspirational serenity in juxtaposition to the bare, spartan athletic facilities that spoke loudly to the necessity of hard work and dedication—some lessons can be learned.

Jumbo Elliott himself represented a one-off individual both in terms of the social conditions that shaped him, and the business-like manner that he applied as a coach, imparting incomparable confidence and unquestioning self-belief.

Countering his sometimes harsh, hands-off, and clinical approach, stood the one and only Jack "Mother" Pyrah, who nurtured those same athletes with personal care, all the while paying great attention to detail and ensuring that the recruiting funnel was being filled with a new assembly of talent for future consideration and final selection.

Then the athletes themselves, each of them unique and from such differing backgrounds, arriving and subsequently shaping and supporting a new leader every three to four years. That leadership manifested by a diversity of effective styles, beginning with the tenacity and sheer courage of Dave Patrick, to the savvy confidence and intelligence of Marty Liquori, supported by the steady workman-style consistency of Chris Mason, to the quiet steely determination of John Hartnett, in concert with the unrestrained commitment to team above all by Ken Schappert, to the street smart and unassailable cockiness of Eamonn Coghlan, to the playful exuberance and incredible and unlimited talent of Mark Belger, to the deep-burning desire to be very best of Don Paige, and finally to the dogged determination to simply survive of Sydney Maree. One feature prevailed above all: each of these leaders shared that deep drive to win no matter what the circumstances. And complemented by the other side of that same card—they all shared an intense hatred of losing.

All these leaders exhibited that same deep hunger to succeed and to win. While the factors contributing to the formation of this essential quality differed from leader to leader and from personality to personality, it continued to be expressed the same way: "Give me the baton and I'll look after this." The result: win after win after win for 15 straight years. This "hunger," which itself is difficult to quantify, was accompanied by another dynamic—that of deep appreciation. Mike

McDonnell III, one of the more erudite and observant members of the Villanova Track Team during the early 1980s, described it this way: "All of those great runners particularly the anchormen, possessed a deep understanding of and appreciation for the opportunity to attend Villanova University. They all knew that without the scholarship offered by Jumbo Elliott, they would not be here. And when it was time to put on the Villanova singlet, you could see and feel that burning intensity and the ability to focus. Jumbo could see that inner courage and knew who was ready and who was capable of anchoring and winning."

McDonnell makes another interesting observation: "Those great Villanova runners also exhibited a strong element of compassion—they were able to connect with their teammates—you could tell that they deeply cared." More specifically and based on a long-standing friendship, Mike describes Don Paige as the purest of the pure when it came to the qualities that define the prototypical Villanova runner. In Mike's own words: "Don is one of the most committed and compassionate guys you could meet."

But there was another major factor that made this record of success possible. Simply, no world class runner does it alone. While Villanova had a steady pipeline of such high-quality performers, they were consistently surrounded and supported by an incredibly talented ensemble of team members. The results, particularly at the Penn Relays, speak to this loudly and clearly. Every relay race needs four runners. You may have a world-class finisher, but the baton must first be delivered to that finisher. And that is exactly what happened year and after year. Indeed, not only must there be three very willing, capable, and able team members, in many years there were several more teammates, ready to step in should one of the chosen four be unable to run.

In the end, that is perhaps the real secret behind Villanova's success—the team culture reinforced by the continued presence of an incredibly talented and motivated team. The team that did not just show up for practice. Rather the team operated and behaved like a close family—a team that lived together, ate together, went to class together, socialized together, watched TV together, looked after each other, and held each other to account. That inextricable glue was cemented further by compassion and genuine caring, and it bound the team together and served as an irreplaceable ingredient that contributed to the success of the Villanova track program. A glue that persists to this day.[1]

Back to the question: Could it happen again? A simple question that warrants thought and indeed a degree of speculation. The sport of track and field has changed dramatically over the past 50 years. The biggest change pertains to the motivations underlying the sport itself. The days of pure amateurism are long gone. Now the sport is heavily influenced by professionalism, sponsorships, and the opportunity to pursue a bona fide athletic career. While only a select few realize such a vocation, the drivers behind the sport are nevertheless markedly different than those more innocent or simpler days of the '60s and '70s when the sheer opportunity to excel as an amateur was sufficient. Of course, the novelty of breaking the four-minute mile led by Roger Bannister in 1954 with all the accompanying publicity, served as a major draw, not unlike the summiting of Mt. Everest. Today, such accomplishments barely receive mention.

Economic and social conditions have also changed dramatically. Overall income levels have risen and the "modest" backgrounds that characterized many of my cohorts on scholarship, are now more the exception than the rule. The motivation to achieve has changed. One might even argue that deep drive to make the most of a scholarship opportunity is no longer the same as it was in our day.

It almost seems strange to state this, but I can honestly say that during those simpler times of the '70s, the entire time I was at Villanova University, we never spoke about jobs, what we were going to do with our lives, or how much money we would or should be making. Somehow, we just assumed that all these things would come to pass. On such matters, we spent no time discussing or worrying. In retrospect, can any of us look back and say that our life post-graduation has been sub-optimal because of this lack of worry and career planning? Indeed, the answer is quite the opposite—most Villanova track graduates went on to become successful professionals (lawyers, doctors), independent business-people, investment specialists, sales representatives, hospital CEOs—Jumbo would have been so proud. While at Villanova, we focused on two things: making sure our grades were in order and of course, our running, which meant putting in the miles, doing the track workouts, and nursing or overcoming injuries. Indeed, we can now say that at the time, we were fully immersed in the present.

How different things are today. Many students arrive as freshmen with career paths fully defined. They know what they want, where they are going, and the academic path required to get there. Getting a good job or gaining entry to a professional program or graduate school is of paramount importance. Parents are leading or influencing every step of the way. In our case, our parents might have known where we were located geographically, but little more.

Track and field as a sport of interest in North America has also experienced a major demise. Since the early '80s, professional sports have applied highly-successful marketing and branding techniques. Meanwhile, track and field continued much as it always had, in its usual fragmented, disjointed manner, with no apparent season, circuit, or a coherent marketing strategy. In addition, the great rivalry between the two major political ideologies, namely the Free World vs. Centrally Planned Economies—the US vs. the USSR, peaked during the late 1960s, but were no longer at play. Consequently, interest in track and field generated by those great contests being televised on major networks, declined.

The once fabled indoor circuit, which drew so much attention, lost its appeal. Again, this was due to the lack of marketing and branding, the lack of clear contests, and the public's lack of awareness about what or who to cheer for. The 1988 Olympic Ben Johnson drug scandal seemed like the last straw as public confidence in the sport plummeted. In due course, every major indoor event in major locales (New York City, The Meadowlands, Boston, Philadelphia, Washington DC, Cleveland, Toronto, Saskatoon, Edmonton, San Francisco, Los Angeles, and San Diego) all shut down operations or moved to much smaller venues.

The science of training coupled with sports medicine has also advanced dramatically. During the decades from the '50s to the '70s, it was mostly trial and error. Today's athletes have the advantage of metrics and monitors that provide vital information specific to ascertaining optimal training loads. Interval training is much more nuanced than it was 40 years ago. Anaerobic thresholds are carefully measured. The athlete-coach relationship is now fused through technology and the constant interchange of information. By comparison, we just ran repeat quarters on the track. This might be under the supervision of a coach but just as easily done by ourselves. Mileage today is carefully managed—each workout has a specific purpose, and easy or active rest days are an important part of the program. We just ran hard miles, day after day, unsupervised.

Today's runners are also faster than 50 years ago and there are more of them. It took a period of 37 years for the United States to produce five high-school athletes to run a sub four-minute mile. The last six years have seen eight more added to that list. As well, many more US college runners break four minutes for the mile, which means training has improved and more coaches possess the knowledge that balances speed and endurance workouts to reach the once seemingly illusive objective.

Communications and associated technology are now more advanced and omnipresent. Today's athletes have ready access to information on all matters and every possible subject. Significantly, instant and ongoing communications between coaches and athletes are the norm. This has also impacted social structures, personal relationships, and how a team functions. Today's athletes are in some respects more self-sufficient when it comes to team interactions but more dependent when it comes to coaching.

When we were at Villanova, a phone call back home might take place once a month or perhaps only once a semester. There were virtually no calls between athletes and Jumbo. None of us, except for one or two individuals, had a television set or access to one. None of us had cars, all of us lived on campus, again with the odd exception. Our social life and reference group revolved around the team. And aside from relatively few running sessions on the track that were supervised by Jumbo, we were left on our own. It really was a case of "survival of the fittest"—a true Darwinian zeitgeist that made the strong even stronger while the weaker ones fell behind or simply disappeared. This process, however, did result in the development of those exceptionally strong leaders and fierce competitors, characteristic of that 1966 to 1981 era.

Recruiting has also changed. No one or two programs stand out as middle-distance islands of excellence such as the Villanova vs. Oregon rivalry. Now there are many schools[2] that provide excellent coaching and top-class results. Significantly, the Villanova DMR streak occurred prior to the full implementation of Title IX[3]—now programs offer equal support to both male and female athletic programs. Of course, this is a positive development and addresses a gender imbalance that had long been overlooked. But it becomes a limiting factor for a school once having five or six scholarships per year to recruit young men, to now having only two or three, making it more challenging to develop middle distance running depth for a men's program the way Villanova was able to establish, some 50 years ago.

So back to the question: Can it happen again? I would say no. The uniqueness of so many factors and the one-of-a-kind characters were such that during the 1966 to 1981 period, a duplication of results is almost unimaginable. Times and conditions have changed so much. The mix of ingredients that made the Villanova University Track and Field Team so successful will never come together in the same way.

So, aside from this interesting recounting of events, races, and personalities, is there anything to be learned? Are there deeper insights that are of relevance to today's athletes and coaches, to life in general, or perhaps to the world of business? Let me offer the following.

First the power of personality and the leadership associated with that personality. One cannot underestimate the incredible influence that one person can have over so many people for such an extended period of time. Jumbo Elliott embodied such a special combination of positivism, confidence, and self-belief that he impacted an array of diverse athletes from different places and backgrounds to achieve superior outcomes—the world-class athlete equipped to compete under any conditions. The importance of vision and leadership can never be overstated.

Second, the importance of simplicity and focus. Once again, Jumbo manifested his genius by identifying and boiling down the key ingredients for success: live like a clock, put in the miles, run repeat quarters, and make your choices—while in college you can only excel in two out of three (studies, athletics, and social pursuits)—valuable advice to any runner no matter the time or era. Interestingly, in the world of business, highly focused strategies are often stunningly simple. But the key always comes down to unfailing and relentless execution.

Third, the combination of talent and hard work will produce results every time. Finding that talent means recruiting the type of individual who displays the intellectual and physical qualities that are most likely to succeed. Jumbo knew what he was looking for. And he was almost always right. Then apply hard work consistently, patiently, and the results will almost always come. I noted earlier that today's runners are faster and there are more of them. But consider this: Jumbo produced five milers who all ran sub 3:55 mile times as undergraduates: Maree—3.48.8; Coghlan—3.53.3; Paige—3.54.2; Liquori—3.54.6; and Hartnett—3.54.7. Also, Patrick's 3.56 on a clay track would have made for six. Should these athletes be competing today on current track surfaces with the most advanced shoe technologies, all these runners would have run three to five seconds faster and still be at the top of world rankings. This speaks to the absolute necessity of selecting for talent but combining this with the aptitude to do the hard work.

Fourth, no one is unbeatable. Perhaps this was a byproduct of Jumbo's education in the streets of Shantytown, West Philadelphia, where he learned that no matter how strong or fast someone may be, there was always a way to beat that person. He imparted that confidence to his athletes. He intuitively knew the strengths and weaknesses of his runners, as well as their competitors. He knew what to apply and when. And when it came to relays, his intuition of who was ready and who could assure victory was unassailable. Said in another way, there is always a way to win—you just need to believe, go find it, and then execute.

Most importantly, excellence breeds excellence. Jumbo knew that. This is perhaps the most important lesson to be learned from the Villanova Track experience. Jumbo knew that great athletes produce more great athletes. He knew the importance of team, giving his athletes the time and space to work things out—letting them wrestle with commitment, priorities, re-enforcing their own motivation and the freedom to select their own leaders. Again, it came back to recruiting—choosing those athletes with talent but who exhibited humility, the willingness to listen, and the strong desire to do their very best. Put a small group of such like-minded athletes together and the only thing he had to do was "keep them hungry." That hunger was a case of "not too much, not too little" which led to the 16 consecutive DMR wins, and the 52 Championships of America at Penn Relays between 1966 and 1981. That was the hunger that kept Villanova runners at the top of the world for all those years. Again, this speaks to the imperative of sustaining a team culture rooted in commitment, self-motivation, and belief.

The Jumbo statue overseeing Marty Liquori, Dave Patrick, and Don Paige circa 1990

Another factor to consider and one that is perhaps the most intangible of all: intuition. All great leaders possess an elusive, hard to define "intuition"—that innate quality of knowing what to do, at the right time, with the right people. This can be observed in great businesspeople, politicians, or artists. And when it came to athletics, Jumbo had intuition in abundance. Whether this was inherent, the product of experience, or some combination of the two, it need not matter. Jumbo had that intuition, which he applied in an uncanny manner. When it came to Penn Relays, he exercised it time and time again. He knew who was ready; he knew who could carry the baton in crowded situations like the leadoff leg; he knew who could close the gap when necessary; he knew who was capable of doubling or tripling; and most importantly, he knew who was best suited to anchor—that unique athlete who could handle the pressure and fight to win no matter what. Had Jumbo Elliott been blessed with more time on this earth, that streak of 16 consecutive DMRs could well have continued for several more years.

There is another lesson for coaches to be gleaned from Jumbo Elliott's approach. I call this "the paradox of presence." Or simply, how involved or engaged should coaches be with their athletes?

Today, coaches are increasingly drawn into the daily lives of their athletes because of available technologies and social media. In effect, they are constantly "present" and expected to be so. Jumbo took quite the opposite approach—he kept his distance, left no written instructions, and his appearances were relatively infrequent.

When he appeared, his athletes paid rapt attention. They listened carefully to what he had to say and watched him like a hawk—how he dressed, how he carried himself, how he approached challenges, big or small, in effect, how he lived his life. All these years later, his presence continues to be carried in the hearts and minds of his athletes. One could conclude that his lack of physical presence amplified his influence while creating the conditions that demanded individual responsibility and reliance on fellow team members. This commitment to team defined the essence of the Villanova track experience. The lesson to coaches is this: more presence does not necessarily lead to better outcomes. Apply your time and manage your presence carefully.

One bright Saturday morning in late April, always the feature and final day of Penn Relays Week in Philadelphia, a gathering took place. It was none other than the 1968 Villanova Track Team assembling on campus to celebrate the 50th Anniversary of the team that had won five Championship Relays of America at Penn Relays for the very first time—a feat that had never been done before.

The Five-Peat[4] has been done a total of four times—each time by a Villanova team. David Patrick, the leader, both as former captain but more importantly by his example and spirit, greeted everyone. He held nothing back as he displayed his delight in seeing all his former teammates as they celebrated their achievements and their coming together. Once again, the Patrick-Messenger comradery arose in full display as they joked and jostled amicably with each other and amongst their former teammates.

At the ensuing breakfast, Dave addressed the group, leading off with four words: "Touching Greatness, Forever Together." No four words could better capture that historic achievement back in 1968. And no words could better describe the era from 1966 to 1981—16 consecutive DMR wins at the Penn Relays. In retrospect, no one other than Dave Patrick—the athlete who began it all, the man who is respected as the Villanova Track Team Captain regardless of the year, or the era—is better suited to speak these words.

After his final race and his 10th Penn Relays victory, the words of Mark Belger echo clearly, "...you think of your big-name people that have run for Villanova in the past....after the (Penn) Relays are over, it's like the Dave Patricks never left..."[5]

Indeed, the spirit of Dave Patrick lingers on. And while many years have passed and rationalizations to explain continue, the "mysterious experience" remains.

Front Row: Dave Patrick, Paul Denis, Jim Sansevero, Billy McLaughlin, Charlie Messenger, Kevin Leonard, Glen Bogue

Second Row: Larry James, Ed Takacs, Warren Clark, Jim Weir, Jerry Bouma, Brian McElroy, Marty Patwell, Phil Kane, Eamonn Coghlan, John Burns, Karl Kinscherf, George MacKay, Marty Liquori, Mike McDonnell III, Ken Schappert, Steve Dorsey.

Statue of Jumbo Elliott: Overlooking the Track

Epilogue: Return to Alma Mater

Saturday, April 24, 2010. My former teammate and dear friend Ed Takacs and I traveled east on Lancaster Avenue. Silent and with anticipation. Both lost in our thoughts.

And then we were there. Coming up the last stretch of the avenue (or The Pike, as we called it) that we had run so many times—the last mile of the old and welcoming Radnor Five. Everything looked familiar. Oh, so familiar. And while some new buildings had emerged, the campus spread sublime as we crossed Route 320. It was all the same as it had been before.

We knew exactly where to go. We parked. And before our car even rolled to a stop, we were overcome with an even deeper silence. Or perhaps overwhelmed with the almost excruciating familiarity and specialness of this place.

Instantly, we were thrust between the world of past and present. But effectively more past than present. All our adult worries, pains, and memories melted away—we were suddenly hurled back to our late teens when all things were possible, being the fastest, the best, part of the most heralded middle distance running program of any school in the country.

And in one brief moment, the full impact of what could have been, what might have been, the victories, the numbing workouts, the hopes, the disappointments, the dreams, the moments of despair, the friendships now deeper and more meaningful than we could possibly have imagined, when we were in this very place all those years ago—life's hopes and failures—flashed before us. It was if we had re-entered the womb of our early adulthood—nothing had changed. The Chapel stood with veneration and strength; the massive oaks guarded the paths and walkways with their omnipresent dignity. Austin Hall—the only place to live for us self-absorbed jocks—seemed to nod a quiet hello as we walked by, just like the all too familiar neighbour that never says much but is always there.

Reflecting on Jumbo, Ed Takacs and Jerry Bouma, 2018

Without thought or comment, we naturally moved toward Kennedy Mall—the place which embodied the culmination of our abiding bond and shared experience. The chains still hung in their lazy parabolic state—where years ago we sat and "hung" against the curb. This was the place where we found true meaning and purpose. Oh yes—the track was our workplace—the anvil where body and soul were tempered and shaped like fine steel. But right here was the place where we bantered, busted, relaxed, commiserated, and participated in non-stop interaction.

Our memories returned to those warm spring days—after lunch, after workouts, after dinner, between classes. This is where the characters were formed, stories created, and reputations enhanced. This is where we analyzed the workout yet to take place or the one just behind us. Or the races ahead. The races past—we talked about the miles, dreams, possibilities, time trials, repeats, hills, loops, the even bigger hills. This is where we admired the growing flock of lovely co-eds—and dared to dream of the rendezvous that usually remained in the realm of our own juvenile imaginations.

Ed and I barely spoke—but we both knew we were lost on a sea of emotion—both on our respective vessels, pitching on the waves of memory. Trying to stay upright and not betray the veil of control each of us had mastered to perfection.

Perhaps it was better not to speak. What we were feeling had to be felt—not verbalized. Now, with years of experience and weathered by the victories and vagaries of life, we both realized how absolutely special this place really was to us—how we would not be the people we are today without having been shaped and formed here first. Yet there was a sense of sadness and loss knowing full-well that we never again experienced what we did on these grounds. The ensuing events were never as memorable, the lessons never as acute, the friendships never as deep, and the shared purpose never as clear, as they had been here. Simply, we did not really know what we truly had until all those years later.

Villanova University and the opportunity to be part of the much heralded and historic Track and Field Team had given us wealth that only few would ever experience. Could we have done more? Could we have run faster? Could we have made a bigger contribution to this incredible team history? Could Villanova have won a 17th or perhaps an 18th consecutive DMR? Of course, the answer to these questions is yes or at least a maybe. But then there is not an athlete or a team anywhere at any time or place that would not provide the same answer. But one thing was clear, the Jumbo era was over and would never again return.

Nothing could have replaced what we experienced here. This place, this heritage, these team members, and these coaches, Jumbo Elliott and Jack Pyrah, had enriched us and impacted each of us in ways we could never have imagined. With the wins, the hard work, the times together, the memories and most of all, the deep lifelong friendships, our lives would never be the same. Indeed, there we stood knowing that we had "touched greatness and are forever together."

Endnotes

Note to Reader: This book contains numerous quotations. There are two types: (1) those sourced directly from newspaper and magazine articles cited by source listed below; and 2) those based on direct communications between the author and the person being interviewed. These are not cited per se and are considered as "personal communications."

Prologue

1. Jim Denison has written several books including *Bannister and Beyond: The Mystique of the Four Minute Mile;* and *The Greatest: The Haile Gebrselassie Story.*

2. The Place

1. Wikipedia s.v. "Philadelphia Main Line," (last modified August 28, 2021), https://en.wikipedia.org/wiki/Philadelphia_Main_Line.
2. The name Pennsylvania was coined on the suggestion from Charles II when he granted William Penn the land tract in the 1600s, as a way of paying tribute to William's father, who had loaned the king money. The word was formed by joining the surname Penn with the Latin *sylvania,* meaning woods, to mean "Penn's Woods." Online Etymology Dictionary s.v. "Pennsylvania," https://www.etymonline.com/word/pennsylvania.
3. Named after the famed Gregor Mendel (1822–1884), the Augustinian prelate, botanist, and plant breeder, who is considered the "father" of modern genetics.
4. A "repeat" is a method of training for races that requires the athlete to run quickly over a set distance, then recover, and run the same set distance again, and again, for a set number of times. This approach is also called interval training or "intervals."
5. The cinder track was upgraded to all-weather tartan surface in 1980.
6. Skip Myslenski, "A Monkey Rides the Easy Rider," *Sports Illustrated,* (March 2, 1970): 30–52.
7. According to findwords.info, "minga" is "An impolite Sicilian slang term used to denote frustration or as a derogatory descriptive term for a person."

3. Jumbo Elliott—A Character with Many "Colors"

1. Winston Churchill, "The Russian Enigma," Broadcast, October 1, 1939, London: The Churchill Society, http://churchill-society-london.org.uk/RusnEnig.html.
2. Rick Telander, "Nobody is Bigger Than Jumbo," *Sports Illustrated,* (March 10, 1980): 64–77, http://villanovarunning.blogspot.com/2012/01/march-1980-si-profile-of-jumbo-elliott.html.
3. Jumbo had a slight stutter that would become accentuated when he was excited or angry.
4. Also referred to as the IC4A's—Intercollegiate Association of Amateur Athletes of America. Established in 1875, the association was the preeminent collegiate track and field organization prior to the establishment of the NCAA in 1906.
5. Telander, "Nobody is Bigger."
6. Jerry Bouma, John Burns, Noel Carrol, Tom Donnelly, Fred Dwyer, Mike England, Tom Gregan, Ken Lucks, Charlie Messenger, Brian McElroy, Kevin McCarey, Tom Sullivan, and Ed Takacs.
7. These quotes are word for word what was said, but the actual authors of those voices are kept in confidence.
8. James Francis Jumbo Elliott and Theodore J. Berry, *Jumbo Elliott: Maker of Milers, Maker of Men,* New York: St Martins Press, 1982.

4. Villanova's DMR Streak Begins: The Patrick-Messenger Era

1. The Villanova Track Team continues to sit in this area of Franklin Field to this very day.
2. Villanova University became a co-ed school in 1968 when women arrived on campus to the newly-opened School of Nursing.
3. Frank Dolson, "Sophs Hold Key to Villanova Hopes in Penn Relays," *Philadelphia Inquirer,* (April 29, 1966): 30.
4. Tom Cushman, "Villanova Wheezes to D-M Crown," *Philadelphia Daily News,* (April 29, 1967): 31.
5. Cushman, "Villanova Wheezes," 31.

6. Cushman, "Villanova Wheezes," 31.
7. Gordon Forbes, "Patrick Collapses, Villanova Loses 2-Mile," *Philadelphia Inquirer,* (April 30, 1967): 1-Section 3.
8. The boycott itself was a success. Entire sections of Madison Square Garden, usually filled for this event, remained empty. The protest resulted in many of the top athletes in the world standing either outside on the sidewalk, or far away from the arena, resulting in few noteworthy events during the meet. The press declared the contest was essentially empty without black competitors, and black athletes left the event energized and ready for further action.
9. Staff Writer, "Villanova Wins Track—Tennessee Wins Field," by, *Knoxville News Sentinel,* (April 7, 1968): 1.
10. Greg Swatek, "Denied His Olympic Dream 50 Years Ago, Dave Patrick Still on the Move," Pressbox online, (October 15, 2018), https://pressboxonline.com/2018/10/15/denied-his-olympic-dream-50-years-ago-dave-patrick-still-on-the-move/

5. The Streak Continues: The Liquori-Mason Era

1. Skip Myslenski, "An Exhilarating Nip of Liquori," *Sports Illustrated,* (March 24, 1969): 24–25.
2. West Philadelphia was at that time a very tough neighborhood and the location of the infamous "race riots" in 1966 and 1967. Many of the storefronts and row houses were boarded up. Those that were occupied had iron grates placed in front of doors and windows to prevent break-ins. Many of the buildings were covered in graffiti while the streets were often covered with garbage and debris. It could not be more opposite to the Main Line.
3. Tom Cushman, "Watching Jumbo Get Even Half the Fun of Penn Relays," Philadelphia Daily News, (April 25, 1969): 70.
4. Tom Donnelly was a man of few words but a clear leader. He would often be seen quietly giving advice or encouraging the team when it was most needed. After graduating, Tom became the head track coach at Haverford College. On the side he coached both Sidney Maree and Marcus O'Sullivan to become world-leading 1500-meter runners during the 1980s.

5. Dick Buerkle arrived at Villanova in September 1966 with very modest track credentials. He was determined to improve and by the end of his sophomore year, he became the best two-miler on the team. That earned him a full scholarship and by his senior year, Dick was a leading three-miler, finishing third in the 1970 NCAA Outdoor Championships. Eight years later, after making two Olympic Teams (1972, 1976). Dick shocked the track world by breaking the world indoor record for the mile in 3:54.9 on January 13, 1978, at the CYO Invitational, Cole Field House in College Park, Maryland.
6. Gordon Forbes, "Villanova Retains 5 Titles in Penn Relays," *Philadelphia Inquirer,* (April 27, 1969): 1-Section 3.
7. Frank Dolson, "The Mouth Roars at Penn Relays," *Philadelphia Inquirer,* (April 24, 1970): 29.
8. Tom Cushman, "Cats Hurricane in Penn Relays," *Philadelphia Daily News,* (April 25, 1970):34.
9. Gordon Forbes, "Villanova Scores 3rd Relay Sweep," *Philadelphia Inquirer,* (April 26, 1970): 1- Section 3.
10. "Redshirt" is a term used in the United States to describe college transfers or injuries. When an athlete transfers from one university to another, that athlete must sit out for a year before he or she is again eligible to compete. In the case of an extended or serious injury, a decision may be made to withhold the athlete's eligibility for a year thereby extending that athlete's college career for a fifth year.
11. Tom Cushman, "Challengers to Villanova Reign Limp to Starting Line," *Philadelphia Daily News* (April 23, 197): 49.

6. Hartnett-Schappert: A New Generation Takes the Lead

1. Merion. But not easily distinguishable to the unfamiliar ear.
2. Frank Dolson, "For a Change, the Penn Relays Didn't Belong to Jumbo's Cats," *Philadelphia Inquirer,* (April 30,1972): 1- Section D.
3. Bob Kennedy, "Villanova, Quakers on Spot in 78th Penn Relays," Courier Post, (April 27, 1972):46.
4. Frank Dolson, "For a Change, the Penn Relays Didn't Belong to Jumbo's Cats," *Philadelphia Inquirer,* (April 30,1972): 1-Section D.

5. Allen Lewis, "Villanova Is Victor in Distance Relay at Penn's Carnival, *Philadelphia Inquirer,* (April 29,1972):19.
6. Joe Greenday, "Twas a Ripe Time for Cats to Unveil Latest Imports," Philadelphia Daily News, (April 29, 1972):32.
7. "Troubles" was the term commonly used by the Irish to describe the tensions and conflicts in Northern Ireland.
8. Frank Dolson, "For a Change, ,": 14.
9. Dave Wottle was the first runner to wear a baseball cap when competing.
10. Tom Cushman, "Wildcats Dry Off, Hope to Add 2nd and 3rd Titles Today," *Philadelphia Daily News,* (April 28, 1973):27.
11. Cushman, "Wildcats Dry Off," 27.
12. Cushman, "Wildcats Dry Off," 27.
13. Frank Dolson, "Jumbo's as Cool As His Runners, After the Race," *Philadelphia Inquirer,* (April 29, 1973):10–Section D.
14. Allen Lewis, "Villanova Wins Two More Titles," *Philadelphia Inquirer,* (April 29, 1973):1–Section D.
15. Allen Lewis, "Villanova Sets Distance Mark," *Philadelphia Inquirer,* (April 27, 1974):1–Section C.
16. Tom Cushman, "Villanova Zings a Medley on Catguts," *Philadelphia Bulletin,* (April 27, 1974):29.

7. A Day in the Life

1. Reserve Officers Training Corps or ROTC was a program instituted by the US Navy. A ROTC recruit would receive financial support and in turn commit to four years of training upon graduation.
2. Sargent Shriver was George McGovern's running mate. McGovern was the Democratic candidate for President and a brother-in-law of Ted Kennedy.

8. Coghlan Continues

1. Eamonn was appointed to the Irish Seanad (Senate) in 2011, serving until 2016.
2. Russ Ebbets is the author of Supernova, a quasi-fictional version of the characters and activities of a group of Villanova track athletes from 1972 to 1974.
3. Gene Courtney, "Villanova Dominates Relays Again," *Philadelphia Inquirer,* (April 27, 1975):1–Section D.
4. Ron Reid, "A Record Goes Bust," *Sports Illustrated,* (May 26, 1975):21–23.
5. Matt Bonesteel, "Rio Police Arrest Irish IOC Member Pat Hickey Over Ties to Alleged Ticket-Scalping Scheme," *Washington Post,* August 17, 2016, https://www.washingtonpost.com/news/early-lead/wp/2016/08/17/irish-ioc-member-arrested-over-ticket-selling-scheme/.

9. New York's Finest: The Belger-Paige Era

1. Gordon Forbes, "It's No Longer Villanova's Party," *Philadelphia Inquirer,* (April 24, 1977):13–Section E
2. Forbes, "It's No Longer," 13- Section E.
3. The first Canadian being myself.
4. Mike Holdridge, "Sports of all Sorts," *The Post Standard* (Syracuse), (June 7, 1975):13.
5. Rodney Lee, "Paige, 7-Foot Jump Intersectional Gems," *Press and Sun Bulletin* (Binghamton), (June 8, 1975):4-Section B.
6. Gordon Forbes, "Villanova Wins With Fast ¾ Leg," *Philadelphia Inquirer,* (April 30, 1977):1–Section B.
7. Forbes, "Villanova Wins With Fast ¾," 1–Section B.
8. Gordon Forbes, "Villanova Wins a 13th Relay in a Row," *Philadelphia Inquirer,* (April 29,1978):5-Section C.
9. Frank Dolson, "Villanova Gets 5 for 5 Sweep," *Philadelphia Inquirer,* (April 30, 1978):1–Section F.

10. Frank Dolson, "Tradition: Villanova the Northeast Fans," *Philadelphia Inquirer,* (April 30, 1978): 1-Section F.

11. Gordon Forbes, "Villanova Wins a 13th," 5- Section C.

12. Gordon Forbes, "Villanova Wins Distance Medley in 9.29.2" *Philadelphia Inquirer,* (April 28,1979):1-Section C.

13. Gordon Forbes, "Wildcats Win Distance Medley Relay" *Philadelphia Inquirer,* (April 28,1979):4-Section C.

14. BC, "These Five Things: Mark Belger," *Villanova Running* (blog), (April 29, 2013), http://villanovarunning.blogspot.com/2013/04/these-five-things-mark-belger.html

15. Joe Marshall, "Fine Times Were Had...By Almost All," *Sports Illustrated,* (February 19, 1979):13.

16. BC, "These Five Things: Mark Belger,"

17. Gordon Forbes, "Villanova Runners 5-for-5in Greatest Day at Relays" *Philadelphia Inquirer,* (April 30,1978):14-Secton - F.

10. Never Faster: The Sydney Maree Era

1. Laager is an encirclement. In this case, the Boers used "covered wagons" and bound them together with chains, thorn bushes, and any other obstacle they could gather in this remote region.

2. Gary Smith, "He Ran but Knew Not Why," *Sports Illustrated,* (July 18, 1983):64–90.

3. Smith, "He Ran but Knew Not Why," 64–90.

4. Smith, "He Ran but Knew Not Why," 64–90.

5. Smith, "He Ran but Knew Not Why," 74.

6. Smith, "He Ran but Knew Not Why," 76.

7. Smith, "He Ran but Knew Not Why." 77.

8. *Springboks* is the name of the South African rugby team.

9. Frank Dolson, "Penn Relays Brings Sanity to Sports World Gone Mad," *Philadelphia Inquirer,* (April 25, 1980): 1-Section C.
10. Gordon Forbes, "Another Clinic of Relays, Villanova Wins 3 More," *Philadelphia Inquirer,* (April 27, 1980): 12–Section F.
11. Forbes, "Another Clinic of Relays," 12-Section F.
12. Gail Shister, "Cripple Controls Drama of Jumbo's Race," *Philadelphia Inquirer,* (April 25, 1981):4–Section C.
13. Shister, "Cripple Controls" 4-Section C.
14. Shister, "Cripple Controls," 4-Section C.
15. Shister, "Cripple Controls," 4-Section C.
16. Shister, "Cripple Controls," 4-Section C
17. Lewis Freedman, "Villanova, Tennessee win at Relays," *Philadelphia Inquirer,* (April 26, 1981):1-Section D.
18. Gary Smith, "He Ran but Knew Not Why," (July 18, 1983):80.
19. Smith, "He Ran but Knew Not Why," 80.

11. The Streak Ends

1. Dick Weiss, "It's Like Coming Home For Jenkins," *Philadelphia Daily News,* (April 23, 1982):136.
2. Frank Litsky, "Georgetown Ends Villanova's Streak," *New York Times,* (April 1982):55.
3. Gordon Forbes, "Georgetown Snaps Villanova's Streak," *Philadelphia Inquirer,* (April 25, 1982):1–C.
4. Forbes, "Georgetown Snaps Villanova's Streak," 3-C
5. Forbes, "Georgetown Snaps Villanova's Streak," 3–C.
6. Lewis Freedman, "For 'Cats' Donoghue There Was No Sunny Side," *Philadelphia Inquirer,* (April 25, 1982):13–E.

7. Steve Scott leads this distinctive achievement having run 136 sub, four-minute miles, followed by John Walker with 135 sub,four-minute miles.

12. Coach Jack "Mother" Pyrah

1. Jack Heath, "Remembering Jack Pyrah," CNB News online, (September 14, 2007), https://gloucestercitynews.typepad.com/clearysnotebook/2007/09/remembering-jac.html
2. Jack Heath, "Remembering Jack Pyrah"
3. Jack Heath, "Remembering Jack Pyrah" l
4. Owen Sound, Ontario, Canada is my hometown, where I was born and went to high school.
5. *Villanova Alma Mater Anthem,* lyrics by Al Dubin and music by Joe Burke. Copyright owned by Villanova University.

13. Can It Happen Again?

1. The Villanova Track Alumni, particularly the 1970s group, gather each year for a weekend of comradery at Penn Relays.
2. Syracuse, Georgetown, Princeton, Michigan, Wisconsin, Arkansas, Northern Arizona, Washington State, Stanford, and Oregon, to name some.
3. Title IX—an Act of the US Congress requiring that educational institutions apply the same resources to both male and female athletic programs. Implementation began in the late 1970s.
4. Winning Five Championship Relays of America races in one Penn Relays meet achieved by Villanova in 1968, 1969, 1970, and 1978.
5. Frank Dolson, "Tradition: Villanova the Northeast Fans," Philadelphia Inquirer, (April 30, 1978): 1-Section F.

Appendix

List of Winning Villanova Distance Medley Relay Teams at Penn Relays 1966–1981

1966:	Alan McCafferty	1:53.3
	Bill Heidelberger	48.2
	Ian Hamilton	3:00.3
	Dave Patrick	4:04.6
	Time:	9:46.4
1967:	Frank Murphy	1:50.3
	Bill Heidelberger	48.3
	Charlie Messenger	2:56.2
	Dave Patrick	4:04.8
	Time:	9:39.6
1968:	Ian Hamilton	1:50.9
	Bob Whitehead	48.9
	Frank Murphy	2:53.0
	Dave Patrick	4:05.3
	Time:	9:37.9
1969:	Chris Mason	1:50.9
	Lamotte Hyman	47.3
	Frank Murphy	2:57.1
	Marty Liquori	4:02.9
	Time:	9.38.2
1970:	Wilson Smith	1:51.5
	Greg Govan	47.0
	Chris Mason	2:56.1
	Marty Liquori	4:03.9
	Time:	9:38.5
1971:	Wilson Smith	1:55.4
	Greg Govan	48.4
	Chris Mason	2:56.2
	Marty Liquori	4:04.1
	Time:	9:44.1
1972:	Ken Schappert	1:51.2
	Greg Govan	47.4
	Tom Gregan	2:55.5
	John Hartnett	4:03.4
	Time:	9:37.5
1973:	Brian McElroy	1:50.9
	Jack Garniewski	48.6
	Ken Schappert	2:58.4
	John Hartnett	4:05.7
	Time:	9:43.6

1974:	Brian McElroy	1:50.9
	Greg Eckman	47.9
	Eamonn Coghlan	2:55.8
	John Hartnett	4:02.2
	Time:	9:36.8

1975:	Ken Schappert	1:49.6
	Greg Eckman	46.7
	Tom Gregan	2:55.6
	Eamonn Coghlan	3:56.4
	Time (World Record):	9:28.2

1976[1]:	Mark Belger	1:48.4
	Greg Eckman	47.4
	Phil Kane	3:14.2
	Eamonn Coghlan	3:38.3
	Time:	9:28.8

1977:	Ed Takacs	1:52.9
	Glen Bogue	45.8
	Mark Belger	2:50.1
	Phil Kane	3:59.7
	Time:	9:28.5

1978:	Anthony Tufariello	1:51.5
	Glen Bogue	46.7
	Mark Belger	2:57.3
	Don Paige	4:02.3
	Time:	9:37.8

1979:	Mike England	1:50.7
	Al Graves	47.4
	Don Paige	2:52.5
	Sydney Maree	3:59.3
	Time:	9:29.9

1980:	Don Paige	2:51.6
	Anthony Tufariello	46.8
	Mike England	1:48.4
	Sydney Maree	3:57.4
	Time:	9:24.2

1981:	John Hunter	2:54.5
	Carlton Young	46.5
	Marcus O'Sullivan	1:51.1
	Sydney Maree	4:04.7
	Time:	9:36.78

1976[1] was the first year the DMR was run using metric distances: 800 meters; 400 meters; 1300 meters and 1500 meters. The latter two distances were changed in 1977 to 1200 meters and 1600 meters.

Index to the Players and Personalities

Index to Races, Places, and Institutions

About the Author

Jerry Bouma grew up on a family dairy farm outside Owen Sound, Ontario, Canada. As a boy, he took a great interest in such sports as hockey and baseball, however his daily duties on the farm precluded involvement in team sports. At the age of 14, he took up running, a sport he could pursue on his own schedule and on the roads near the farm.

Self-coached and by the time he was 17 years of age, Jerry set several under-18 age class Canadian records including the indoor 1500 meters in 3:56.9; outdoor 1500 meters in 3:53.3; and the one mile with a time of 4:09.2. He was also the Canadian Junior Outdoor 800 meter champion (1.54.1). In 1970, he became the first Canadian high schooler to secure an athletic scholarship to Villanova University. As a freshman, he led off the winning Four Mile Relay Team at the Penn Relays. Bone spurs in his ankle requiring surgery derailed his sophomore and junior years. Jerry regained form in his senior year, ran 4.05.0 for the mile and anchored the Sprint Medley at the Penn Relays in 1974, serving as Co-Captain of the Villanova Track Team with John Hartnett.

Jerry completed a BSc of Mathematics at Villanova. After graduation he built on his interests in economics and agriculture by completing a MSc of Agricultural Economics, at the University of Guelph. In 1975, while at Guelph, Jerry ran a 2.24.6 – 1000 meters indoors and was ranked number one in the country for that distance. In 1976, he ran a 3.44.8 – 1500 meters finishing sixth in the Canadian Olympic Trials. One year later, Jerry finished third in the Canadian Indoor Championships (1500 meters) and subsequently represented Canada in the Tri-Country Indoor Meet, which included the United States, the USSR, and Canada.

Jerry Bouma

In 2001, Jerry co-chaired the Legends of Gold Gala—a feature event that brought together 25 of the greatest names in the sport of track and field and part of the IAAF World Championships hosted by the City of Edmonton, Alberta. More recently, Jerry chaired the Local Organizing Committee for the hosting of the Pan-American Junior Championships (2015) and the Canadian Athletics Olympic Trials in 2016.

Jerry has spent his entire professional career as a management consultant in the agriculture and food industry. He has written hundreds of reports and proposals, and produced thousands of documents over the past 40 years. Jerry has also published three books of poetry: *Beyond the Woodshed* (2019), *Yearnings—More Reflections on Life, Love, and Loss* (2020), and *Beyond Yearnings* (2021).

The Villanova Track Story 1966–1981 is Jerry Bouma's first non-fiction book.

Jerry has been serving as the Honorary Consul of the Kingdom of the Netherlands, Alberta North Region, since 2019.

Twice as Hard, Half as Fast

There was a time
When four-minute mile pace
Was embedded deep in our flesh and bones.
Every 200; every quarter mile
The occasional half mile repeats.
And the critical ¾ mile time trials.

We approached every repeat
With bounce and lift
And sometimes, we even floated
In pursuit of dreams
And glories yet to come
Enduring those two-minute quarter mile jogs
 in between
That seemed slow.

Now, all these years later
Those two-minute quarter mile jogs
Are deeply embedded in our flesh and bones
Though our wills and memories
Move at twice the speed
As our all too temporal bodies
Are fixed at speeds that are
Twice as hard and half as fast.

So, we are gripped
With our new realities and realizations
That the precise measures of time
And the focus of faster, better, more…
No longer hold sway
On our fading physical forms.
But are replaced by the bonds of brotherhood
Built on seared memories
Of shared goals and experiences
That supersede the markers
Of what was once so important
Including position, balance sheets,
Or public adoration.

We grow in thought and full realization
That emblems of times and records,
The days of youthful DNA,
And superior muscle memory
Now pale in comparison
To those glory days.
And though the run today
Is twice as hard and half as fast
The bonds between us
Are now twice as strong
Than in the past
Elevating our slowing pace
To be a celebration
Of our shared experience.

Jerry Bouma, 2019
Note: Inspired by a run (and a conversation)
with Dave Patrick in 2008.

Three
Rascals
Press

Books available by contacting:
boumaj@telusplanet.net OR
Purchase through Amazon.ca / Amazon.com

Manufactured by Amazon.ca
Bolton, ON

31251511R00133